Ordained Local Ministry in the Church of England

Andrew Bowden, Leslie J. Francis,
Elizabeth Jordan and Oliver Simon

continuum

Continuum International Publishing Group

The Tower Building	80 Maiden Lane
11 York Road	Suite 704
London SE1 7NX	New York NY 10038

www.continuumbooks.com

ISBN 978-1-4411-5955-7

British Library Cataloguing-in-Publication Data
A catalogue record for this book is available from the British Library.

Typeset by Newgen Imaging Systems Pvt, Ltd, Chennai, India
Printed and bound in India

CONTENTS

Foreword

How do churches get from where they are to where their current context requires them to be? Experience suggests that change in the church is almost always incremental. Seldom does significant reformation happen in one bound – it happens step by step.

One major trajectory of change across the Anglican Communion in recent years has been the move from an almost exclusive dependence on a paid priest in every community to largely local, lay and voluntary resourcing and responsibility for ministry and mission. Along with Non-Stipendiary Ministry, Local Non-Stipendiary Ministry, Distinctive Diaconate and the expansion of Reader Ministry, authorized lay ministries and Communion by Extension, we can identify Ordained Local Ministry as a key landmark on this journey. As this important symposium indicates, Ordained Local Ministry has never been seen as an end in itself but always as part of a bigger picture. It is part of a major programme to recover the ministry of the People of God as a whole, which many believe to have been normative in the Apostolic Church, but sadly lost in subsequent centuries.

The development of Ordained Local Ministry has not been without its critics. How can ordination be geographically limited? Aren't we just clericalizing the laity to keep the sacramental show on the road? Isn't there a degree of dumbing down going on here with the currency of ministerial priesthood being progressively devalued? By no means least, the spectre of lay presidency at the bottom of this particular slippery slope has loomed large in the ecclesiological imagination. Oh, and isn't it really about getting ministry on the cheap in a church strapped for cash?

Of course, it is not difficult to counter these concerns. After all, it is not ordained status which is localized but the exercise of ordained ministry. No change there as ministry has typically been subject to local licensing arrangements. Furthermore, if the trajectory has been towards empowering the ministry of the whole people of God, then lay gifting is not so much being clericalized as being liberated. As for dumbing down, there is reliable evidence to show that the rigour and effectiveness of training provision for local ministry, and the contextuality of this formation, has enriched the church in all sorts of ways. Finally, it may well be true that Anglicans only do what is right when they can no longer afford to do what is wrong, in which case, any economic drivers behind Ordained Local Ministry may be positively providential!

But if Ordained Local Ministry is a staging-post on a journey, then that raises questions about whether and when it might have run its course; or, if it does have a permanent place in our vocational repertoire, how might it evolve in the future?

These are questions deserving to be taken seriously by those experienced in the field who have the theological, pastoral and sociological skills to tell the story of Ordained Local Ministry and weigh its implications. The following chapters offer an informed and timely assessment as a contribution towards ongoing debates about future patterns of ministry – and as a tribute to those pioneers who, by God's grace, captured a vision and had the courage and commitment to pursue it wherever it might lead.

John Saxbee

Contributors

Andrew Bowden was an ACORA Commissioner and is the author of *Ministry in the Countryside* (Mowbray), and, with Canon Michael West, of *Dynamic Local Ministry* (Continuum). He helped to set up and run the Local Ministry Scheme in the Diocese of Gloucester; he has studied LM experiments in New Zealand, and was a member of the working party which produced the report *Stranger in the Wings*.

David Bowers read Theology at Manchester University and trained for ministry at Wycliffe Hall, Oxford. He was ordained in 1984 and has worked in the Manchester and Gloucester Dioceses. From 1998 to 2008, he was Associate Diocesan Director of Ordinands for the Gloucester Diocese and worked closely with the development of OLM there. He is currently vicar of the Churnside Benefice, near Cirencester.

Leslie J. Francis is Professor of Religions and Education at the University of Warwick and Canon Theologian at Bangor Cathedral. He also holds visiting professorships at York St John's University and Glyndŵr University, and research associateships at Boston University (USA) and Pretoria University (South Africa). His recent books include *Faith and Psychology* (2005), *British Methodism Today* (2006), *Gone for Good?* (2007), *Preaching with All Our Soul* (2008), and *The Mind of the Anglican Clergy* (2009).

Graham James has been Bishop of Norwich since 1999, and Chair of the Ministry Division of the Church of England since January 2006. In his earlier career, he was Senior Selection Secretary of ACCM (Advisory Council for the Church's Ministry) in the 1980s, a Diocesan Director of Ordinands in the 1990s, as well as a bishop seeking to nurture the vocations of OLMs.

Elizabeth Jordan until recently ran the Local Ministry Department in Lichfield Diocese. Her published research on 'The Place of OLM in the Church of England' identified this indigenous ministry as essential for the churches' mission. Her doctoral work is on the changes to lay perception of priesthood occasioned by OLM. Elizabeth is now the Lay Education and Training Adviser in the Chelmsford Diocese.

Kathy Lawrence is the Senior Local Ministry Officer for Gloucester Diocese and has been heavily involved in the training and formation of OLMs for several years. Her doctoral research seeks to explore the vocational formation and identity of lay members of Anglican congregations.

Tim Morris retired in 2008 after serving in the Scottish Episcopal Church in a range of stipendiary posts and as Dean of the Diocese of Edinburgh. He coordinated the introduction of Local Ministry in Scotland and convened the SEC Local Collaborative Ministry Committee. From 2008 to 2010, he was Ministry Developer in Pembina Hills in the Diocese of Rupert's Land in Canada. He now lives in Berwickshire in Scotland.

John Saxbee, born in Bristol, read Theology there before training for the ordained ministry at Durham and being awarded a PhD for a thesis on Kierkegaard. He held parochial posts in the Diocese of Exeter, and was then appointed as Director of Training for that Diocese just at the time when new patterns of ministry, including NSM and OLM, were being explored and developed. He became Bishop and Archdeacon of Ludlow in the Hereford Diocese and then Bishop of Lincoln – both dioceses noted for their adventurous approach to ministerial provision, especially in rural communities. He retired in 2011.

Oliver Simon was until recently the OLM Adviser in the Diocese of Coventry and OLM Pathway Tutor at the Queen's Foundation, Birmingham. His doctoral thesis examined Ordained Local Ministry from a grounded empirical perspective. Following a spell as Director of Studies in the Diocese of Mauritius, he is now Bishop of Antsiranana in northern Madagascar in the Anglican Province of the Indian Ocean.

Introduction

All mainstream churches have come to recognize that a new context needs new forms of ministry. Ordained ministry in the Church of England is rapidly changing. Soon, the majority of clergy are likely to be self-supporting and, especially in rural areas, female. This book examines the theology and practice of Ordained Local Ministers (OLMs): clergy specifically called out by their local congregation and ordained to minister in collaboration with the people of God in that locality. But what issues of theology and ecclesiology does Ordained Local Ministry raise?

In England, OLMs are ordained within the context of a formal Local Ministry Scheme approved by the House of Bishops. They are members of a Local Ministry Team that is also called out by the local congregation. OLMs are part of the rediscovery of the theology of 'All Member Ministry' or 'Collaborative Ministry' not just in England but throughout the Anglican Communion.[1]

Half the dioceses in England, and in many other provinces in the Anglican Communion, including Australasia, Scotland and North America, have established formal schemes to help this sort of ministry function at the grass-roots level. Some dioceses believe that the process has helped revitalize parishes and has raised the spiritual temperature of congregations. Other dioceses have called for a halt because they believe their schemes have somehow gone wrong or have not 'delivered'.

The time has come for a calm assessment of available evidence on this experiment into which the Church of England has poured considerable time, effort and money. Does it have ongoing value, or is it just one more bright idea that has flourished for a season and has now had its day?

This collection of essays from different authors will result in a variety of perspectives. The contributors themselves have had diverse experiences: diocesan officers, parish priests, a professional researcher and two bishops. One might, indeed, have expected a measure of disagreement among these stakeholders as more than twenty years of activity and reflection is collated, but the commonality of experience and conviction that we find is, from our perspective, encouraging.

It is to be expected that readers of this book will find that some parts match their interests more closely than others. The first three chapters locate Ordained Local Ministry within ecclesiological, historical and theological frameworks, responding to the need for rigorous thinking about the ideological basis of Ordained Local Ministry. In Chapter 1, Oliver Simon sets it within the context of Anglican ecclesiology; in Chapter 2, Andrew Bowden explores the theology of the Local Ministry movement, out of which Ordained Local Ministry has emerged; and in Chapter 3, Oliver Simon charts its genealogy.

Chapters 4 and 5 are stories of Ordained Local Ministry in Scotland and Northern Michigan, by Tim Morris and David Bowers respectively, which are very different in their historical background and present structure. Yet both narratives reveal comparable themes of experiment, retrenchment and rebirth. Neither story is as yet finished nor are the approaches that they take necessarily applicable to the situation in England: they offer perspectives which further illuminate the context in which Ordained Local Ministry operates here.

Following Chapter 5, a series of stories are presented, which intersperse Chapters 6–10. These stories are culled from local collaborative ministries in Scotland and from OLMs in the Gloucester diocese with an introduction and reflection from Kathy Lawrence, the senior Local Ministry officer in the diocese.

Chapters 6–9 are reflections on research and experience. In Chapter 6, Leslie Francis reviews empirical research on Ordained Local Ministry and describes a new comparative study between dioceses which have and have not adopted Ordained Local Ministry. In Chapter 7, Leslie Francis identifies interesting differences in the psychological profiles of OLMs and stipendiary priests, which seem to corroborate the work of Elizabeth Jordan (2008). In Chapter 8, Elizabeth Jordan uses her empirical research to investigate the character of ministerial formation in OLMs, which is found to be related to their congregations. The second part of this chapter enquires whether it is possible to encourage ordained ministry in such a way as to complement lay ministry and discipleship, rather than threaten them. Looking to the future, in Chapter 9, Elizabeth Jordan surveys some of the recent changes in theological education and ministerial development and asks what their impact will be on Ordained Local Ministry and OLMs.

In Chapter 10, Andrew Bowden tells the story of Ordained Local Ministry in one diocese, Gloucester. This chapter brings together many of the themes which have emerged in this book: theology and practice, experiment and inertia, the significant influence of the diocesan bishop. Graham James, as a diocesan bishop and chair of the Church of England's Ministry Division, offers us a personal episcopal perspective in Chapter 11, informed by his involvement in the development of the national church's thinking on Ordained Local Ministry over the period which this book reviews. The final chapter draws out (in a way that is intended to be prophetic) some of the wisdom which emerges from this study.

The editors, themselves contributors, are grateful to those who have shared in and supported this project. Andrew Bowden brought it into being; Leslie Francis contributed his considerable experience in nurturing publications; Elizabeth Jordan and Oliver Simon were the foot soldiers. Bishop John Saxbee enthusiastically contributed the Preface. Caroline Chartres commissioned our work and Nicola Rusk has guided it into print. To our contributors and publisher grateful thanks. Our role has been to try to tell a story which we have observed closely but of which we are not the subject; it is to the several hundred women and men who are that this book is dedicated, to OLMs everywhere, with appreciation.

Note

1 Terminology varies: 'mutual ministry', 'total ministry', 'local collaborative ministry'; for a survey, see Greenwood and Pascoe (2006).

1

The ecclesiological foundations of OLM

Oliver Simon

Introduction

Even when it is claimed that Anglican ecclesiology should be 'special to itself' (Sykes 1995: xii), there is nothing exclusive about it. The discussion that follows reflects the breadth of the influences which contribute to an understanding of Anglican ecclesiology, sources which privilege its sense of continuity but which recognize a continuous engagement with contemporary cultural realities. Fredrica Thompsett comments,

> starting with an understanding of the Church as a people called into relationship with God and each other, Anglican ecclesiology presents a Church that is grounded in society, provisional, inclusive and responsive. (Thompsett 1988: 253)

This chapter investigates three significant features of such a grounded Anglican ecclesiology which inform an explication of Ordained Local Ministry: first, its sense that the church is, above all, relational; second, that it is local; third, that ministry is no longer a clerical prerogative – that a 'seismic' shift (Collins 2006) has taken place in the perception of ministry in the past half century.

The biblical metaphors which have frequently been co-opted in Anglican writing to model this ecclesiology are, 'The Body of Christ' and 'The People of God'. The former expresses mutuality and collaboration; the latter, with roots in the Old Testament, speaks of journeying together. Neither prescribes organization or addresses in executive terms the relationship between the church's contingent and ontological natures. But they help to fashion a theoretical account of ecclesial reality which, in England, has become more relaxed and more participative. So a former Bishop of Durham, Michael Turnbull, writes,

> We are a people called to reflect God's nature in the world. And his nature is not hierarchical and distant but relational and inclusive. That becomes a model of being the Church. (Turnbull 2001: 214)

Relational ecclesiology

While Vatican II came to relational ecclesiology in the 1960s through consideration of the nature of the church as communion (Doyle 2000), Anglicans have tended to appropriate it mystically. A recovered sensibility of the work of the Holy Spirit, liturgically, through the charismatic movement and in theological writing, has clearly been a significant driver. According to one Anglican statement, the ministries of the people of God have a mutuality which

> *animate*[s] [my emphasis] each other, each focusing the activity of God – the work of the Holy Spirit – in each other; each therefore 'brings the other to be' in the way in which God's mission in the world requires. (cited in Heywood 2011: 185)

St Paul anticipated such an ecclesiology: 'my friends, you have died to the law through the body of Christ, so that you may belong[1] to another, to him that has been raised from the dead in order that we may bear fruit for God' (Rom. 7.4). 'For as often as you eat this bread and drink this cup you proclaim the Lord's death until he comes' (1 Cor. 11.26). Fellowship (*koinonia*) is linked to proclamation, God's mission (*missio dei*), and are inseparable.

An understanding of church premised on the experience of divine spirit-mediated love, on the reality of relationships and on formative liturgical acts privileges an anticipatory experience of the fullness of God, the realization in the present of what is anticipated eschatologically. This is the basis of Robin Greenwood's argument (Greenwood 1994) that Anglican ecclesiology is trinitarian, that the community of the mutual indwelling of the persons of the Trinity is, in Colin Gunton's phrase, 'echoed' in the life of the church (Gunton 1997).

> The Church called into existence by the triune God, however faintly, may be said to have the potential in Christ and through the Spirit, to model or

be a sign of that *communion* which is the being of Godself and the shape of his desire for the ultimate ordering of the entire Creation. (Greenwood 1994: 87)

This is most potent when the people of God assemble as The Body of Christ in worship to remember and to be 're-membered'.

Re-membering

Re-membering in the Pauline sense of proclamation is a way of speaking of the formative, regenerative character of relational ecclesial life. Re-membering is a process of reconstruction which has its fundamental basis in the liturgy, in what the people of God do together. The church exists both to remember and be re-membered through the death and resurrection of Jesus who enjoined his disciples: 'do this in remembrance of me' (Lk. 22.19, cf. 1 Cor. 11.24–5). The Eucharist therefore plays a paradigmatic if not exclusive role in the development of Anglican relational ecclesiology.

William Cavanaugh, a Roman Catholic, writes that the Eucharist is 'the imagination of the church'. In the Eucharist, we are united sacrificially 'to God in holy fellowship by reference to our eternal end' (Cavanaugh 1998: 229). Echoing St Augustine, 'One of the peculiarities of the Eucharist feast is that we become the body of Christ by consuming it'[2] and in consequence, Cavanaugh goes on, 'we then become food for the world, to be broken, given away, and consumed' (Cavanaugh 1998: 231, 232). Accordingly, the church finds its identity within the re-membering; its *raison d'être* being to be present, as Christ, to the world, 'ransomed, healed, restored, forgiven', in the words of a well-known nineteenth-century Anglican hymn.[3] For this reason, if for no other, the Anglican Church is irreducibly realized in the coming together for worship of the people of God in any one place at any one time.

The hyphen in re-membering is significant in drawing attention to the dynamic character of this ecclesiology. *An-amnesis*, the technical liturgical term for re-membering, might be translated as 'recovering consciousness and a sense of vocation'. John Paul Lederach writes:

Social amnesia may be useful for political pragmatism, but it is a recipe for weak communities incapable of true identity and correspondingly genuine relationships. The land of forgetfulness creates communities without vocation. The challenge of linking memory and vision lies primarily with the vocation of the moral imagination which can only be exercised in the place that lies between the local and the public, between personal biography and the shaping of responsive social structures. (Lederach 2005: 62)

The notion of the liturgy as an event which links both memory and vision, an 'event . . . moving you from one condition to another. . . . of its essence a transition' (Williams R. 2009), is a powerful engine for ecclesiogenesis. The ordering of the liturgy and its ministry is thus a significant theme in the development of Anglican ecclesiology. First we need to stay with the notion of church as realized wherever bread is broken and wine is shared. Locality, in an ecclesial sense, is the place of epiphany, where humanity meets divinity and where moral imagination is nourished.

Locality

Locality, in its substantive form as territory or 'turf', is far from straightforward. Timothy Jenkins says:

> There are local ways of doing things and of thinking, ways of organising continuity and coping with misfortune which, while they are not unique to any particular locality, are tied in the actors' perceptions to the experience of that locality. In this way 'local particularity' is irreducible, because these ways of life create a sense of identity which relates to a particular place: certain aspects of life are mapped out on the ground and cannot be separated from it. (Jenkins 1999: 77)

Social mobility and immediate global communication have diminished the status of locality. But limits on economic growth and issues of sustainability are factors in the re-evaluation of local as a significant sociological category, a process which has been translated in political discourse in the United Kingdom as 'localism'.

Locality in Anglican ecclesiology

'Local' is a key word in the history of Anglican ecclesiology. Even before the Church *of* England was established in the sixteenth century, *ecclesia Anglicana* – the church *in* England – bore witness to christianity embedded within a geographically framed cultural and historical milieu. The Church of England's website declares that the church has 'a Christian presence in every community'. 'Its network of parishes cover the country, bringing a vital Christian dimension to the nation.'[4] Notwithstanding evident strains on the parish system, it has been consistently reaffirmed. At the heart of this way of configuring Christian presence, and indeed partly responsible for the particular configuration of parish boundaries historically, has been the presence of a 'parson', a representative figure who embodies both the immanent and the divine. The conjunction of parson (with the wherewithal to support him and his household) and parish has been a feature of Anglican ecclesiology since the early middle ages and is culturally deeply resilient.[5]

Notwithstanding such cultural resilience, there has for some time been concern about the viability of the parish system. According to Michael Turnbull, it is collapsing because of low morale, ageing, declining congregations and the alienation of young people; and because such congregations are not financially viable. Turnbull called for an emphasis on 'the value of *locality* but recognize[d] that for most people this is not the *parish* as we have known it'; and that we should 'look to establishing locality ministries', by which he meant clergy and lay teams. Turnbull carefully did not wish to abandon the geographical features of ecclesial organization but rather to change 'present perceptions of what a parish is' (Turnbull 2001: 213).

Others have set the parish system, and hence Anglican ecclesiology, more explicitly within a broader cultural canvas of late modernity or postmodernism. Mission has become the key ecclesial strategy (Heywood 2011). The shift in institutional thinking from a pastoral conception of the church in which territory had a central role to a missionary understanding in which locality is regarded more ambivalently has been bench marked by the report *Mission-Shaped Church* (M-SC), published in 2004, which has greatly influenced the Anglican ecclesial debate. M-SC called for 'a new inculturation of the gospel within our society' (AC 2004: xii). It argued for 'fresh expressions of church' that are culturally sensitive.

M-SC serves to illustrate the persistence of locality within Anglican ecclesiology albeit in a less prescriptive way. It does not undermine whatever is understood by 'parish' but rather speaks of a 'mixed economy'. Indeed, it has become clear that the parish 'is still able to connect with a large proportion of the population' (Croft 2006: 76). This would also be the position taken by some of those who have offered critiques of M-SC (Davison and Milbank (2010), for example). Left to itself, the Church of England might well be compelled for material reasons to withdraw from its commitment to being 'a Christian presence in every community' were it not for the significance of a wider resilient 'tribal' constituency[6] which is supportive of a Christian (Anglican) presence in buildings and worship. So we can still say that locality in the sense of a visible presence is a key principle of Anglican ecclesiology, maintained by a coalition of interests.

Representational ministry

Ordained ministerial agency is an integral part of Anglican ecclesiology. However, in this section, we address the shift in understanding about the nature of the church's ministry, which has taken place since the middle of the twentieth century, the 'revolution in traditional thinking' as John Tiller termed it (Tiller 1983: 65).

The ministry of the people of God

The ecumenical 4th World Conference on Faith and Order in 1963 noticed the change since its last discussion in 1937. The new consensus was summed up in the assertion that, 'All baptized Christians are called to respond to, and participate in the ministry of Christ directed towards the world' (WCC 1964: 67). This formulation owed much to the work of Ernst Käsemann who had argued in an essay, 'Ministry and Community in the New Testament' in 1948, that the gifts of the Spirit, of which St Paul writes in 1 Corinthians 12–14, were appropriated in the early second century by the emergence of office holders, *episkopoi*, *presbyteroi* and *diakonoi*. Such leadership offered stability by assuming authority but emasculated ministerial potential for the church as a whole. Käsemann pointed however to the subversive influence of those who, added to the church through baptism, brought new and varied spiritual gifts, *charismata*. This lead him to propose that 'all the baptized are "officebearers" ' (Käsemann 1964: 78, 80).

Vatican II took a more restrained position, devoting a chapter of *Lumen Gentium* to the lay apostolate, which, without using the word 'ministry', it too linked to baptism.

> Through their baptism and confirmation, all are commissioned to that apostolate by the Lord Himself. Moreover, through the sacraments, especially the Holy Eucharist, there is communicated and nourished that charity towards God and man which is the soul of the entire apostolate. Now, the laity are called in a special way to make the Church present and operative in those places and circumstances where only through them can she become the salt of the earth. Thus every layman, by virtue of the very gifts bestowed upon him, is at the same time a witness and a living instrument of the mission of the Church herself, 'according to the measure of Christ's bestowal'. (Eph. 4.7) (*LG* IV.33)

The ecumenical Lima Report, *Baptism, Eucharist and Ministry* (*BEM*) in 1982, said,

> The word *ministry* in its broadest sense denotes the service to which the whole people of God is called, whether as individuals, as a local community, or as the universal Church. Ministry or ministries can denote the particular institutional forms which this service may take. (WCC 1982: 21)

So confident had some people become about the conjunction of baptism with ministry that an Anglican report in 1993 could speak of the responsibility of each Christian 'to work prayerfully to fulfil their ministry, obedient to the leading of the Holy Spirit' as an 'imperative' (ABM 1993: 4). But by then, the consensus about the relationship between baptism and ministry was already being questioned. Thomas O'Meara offers a helpful summary:

> Not all human activity is ministry, but all baptized men and women are called at times to some precise ministry for the reign of God. That call comes with baptism, but it comes too from the Spirit throughout life. (O'Meara 1983: 4)

Ordained ministry as representational

> . . . a prime task for the Church is to live as a sign to the world of the truth about life. In particular, its vocation is to be a sign of the true meaning of community, of the complex harmony of people of great variety living and working in creative tension. Similarly the ordained ministry has this kind of relationship to the Church as a whole. Bishops, priests and deacons do not merely perform certain functions; they also exist as living signs of the episcopal, priestly and diaconal vocation of every Christian. It follows that a corporate Church needs the signs of a corporate ministry. (GS 660 1985: 16–17)

This comment from a Church of England report systematizes the historic place of ordained ministry within its ecclesiology, functionally and ontologically. The three-fold orders, it declares, are representational of the people of God as a whole, of the universal church. The 1968 Lambeth Conference report on the Renewal of the Church in Ministry said,

> [The] understanding of the ministry of the whole people of God (the *laos*) means that the special function of the priest is all the more emphasized. He is the representative of the whole Church, ordained by the Bishop to preside at the Eucharist and to pronounce in the name of the Church the reconciling and renewing forgiveness of God. Because of his theological insight he has a special task in building up the laity for their task of relating the gospel to the world. He has to stand for God to the people of God who are going out to serve God and find God in the world. A clearer understanding of the ministry of the laity demands a corresponding clarity about the ministry of the priest and the bishop. (Lambeth Conference 1968: 99–100)

A more recent ecumenical statement says,

> The chief responsibility of the ordained ministry is to assemble and build up the Body of Christ by proclaiming and teaching the Word of God, by celebrating baptism and the Eucharist and by guiding the life of the community in its worship, its mission and its service. Essential to its

testimony are not merely its words, but the love of its members for one another, the quality of their service to those in need, a just and disciplined life and a fair exercise of power and authority. (WCC 2005: 51)

Other texts are more cautious. They prefer the notion of a complementary ministry of ordination. A commentary on *BEM* acknowledged that 'the ordained ministry and the community are inextricably related' but that 'the ordained ministry fulfils these functions in a representative way, providing the focus for the unity of the life and witness of the community' (WCC 1982: 22).

On the ordained ministry, *BEM* declared,

In order to fulfil its mission, the Church needs persons who are publicly and continually responsible for pointing to its fundamental dependence on Jesus Christ, and thereby provide, within a multiplicity of gifts, a focus for its unity. The ministry of such persons, who since very early times have been ordained, is constitutive for the life and witness of the Church. (WCC 1982: 21 – IIA.8)

Ordained ministry should however be exercised in collegial and communal ways:

the intimate relationship between the ordained ministry and the community should find expression in a communal dimension where the exercise of the ordained ministry is rooted in the life of the community and requires the community's effective participation in the discovery of God's will and the guidance of the Spirit. (WCC 1982: 26–IIIB.26)

The ecumenical consensus now is that a commitment to ministry is anticipated rather than realized at baptism. It belongs rather to the whole people of God than to a professional, clericalized elite. The place for ordained ministry is, through its relationship to the general ministry of the whole church, representative, particularly, if not exclusively, when the church gathers to re-member.

Among other contributions which have helped inform Anglican thinking on the nature of its ministry, Edward Schillebeeckx O. P. encouraged the view that ordained ministry has been locally accountable since earliest times. St Cyprian, martyred in 258 CE, wrote that 'the choice of the minister by the people is a divine right' (*Ep.* 67.4). 'The community calls; this is the "priestly vocation" ' (Schillebeeckx 1980: 58). Such a right had been endorsed by the Council of Chalcedon in 451 CE in terms that stressed that *ordinatio* was pastoral ministry at the behest of the local church. Chalcedon endorsed the understanding that, as Schillebeeckx puts it, 'ministry comes from below, but this is experienced as a gift of the Spirit and therefore from above', charismatically, not institutionally. Significantly, Schillebeeckx observed, 'the actual structures of official ministry [in the early Church] consisted of leaders within a specialized team' (Schillebeeckx 1980: 63–4). Subsequently, with the rise of feudalism, the relationship of the priest to the local church was subverted as the church became enthralled to powerful secular lords. Local churches no longer enjoyed influence in determining their priestly oversight. Ordination became an inalienable right[7] unrelated to any particular context.

> This opened up the way to practices like private masses, which would have been unthinkable for the early church. Formerly it was the body of Christ, the local community, that the minister had been ordained to preside over; now ordination was endowment with special power in connection with another body, the mystical body of Christ in the eucharist. (Bowden 1983: 84)

Schillebeeckx's work draws attention to the influence of early practice on our thinking about the church and its ministry, which is consonant with Anglican self-definition.[8] It helps us to articulate important elements in the debate: about the continuing dialectic between charism (grace) and institution (law); about the constitution of the church as profoundly 'lay'; about the balance of power between the local church and the universal church; about questions of 'fitness' to exercise representative ministries, issues which the advent of OLM calls us to revisit.

Ministry in Anglican ecclesiology

The Church of England understands itself to be both 'catholic' and 'reformed' in its tradition and practice, and it is therefore unremarkable that these dimensions of its self-identity have informed its thinking and practice. The inclusiveness of the vocation to which *All are Called* resides in the claim that,

> Because all human beings are made in the image of God, they are called to become the People of God, the Church, servants and ministers and citizens of the Kingdom, a new humanity in Jesus Christ. (GSBE 1985: 3)

A comment attached to the 2007 Ordinal says,

> There have been significant changes in the Church and in the world since the ASB Ordinal was produced in 1977–8 . . . the need for the ordained to work in closer collaboration with one another and with lay people is more strongly emphasised now, not simply as a practical advantage but as a theologically necessary way of expressing the unity of the Church's ministry. (AC 2007c: 123)

Helen Oppenheimer's observation however that ministry is a 'greedy concept' and, 'Unless ministry can be distinguished from something else which is not ministry it hardly seems worth talking about' (Oppenheimer 1979: 12), has been noted by Paul Avis who has explored the link with baptism. Avis repositions ministry as essentially intra-ecclesiological (Avis 2005: 44). Ministry, he argues,

> is not whatever an individual feels moved to do for the Lord or to offer to the Church, whether it is needed or not. That way of looking at the matter seems to have things the wrong way round. Ministry is something public and representative, rather than private and individual. (Avis 2005: 47)

The constitutive ecclesial activities which are essential to the life of the church follow from the Great Commission (Mt. 28.19), to teach, baptize and make disciples, Avis argues. 'All ministry', he proposes, 'must be related to these three interrelated activities', 'the performance of word, sacrament and pastoral care'. 'Any activity that cannot be ultimately referenced in this way should not properly be called ministry' (Avis 2005: 49). This leads Avis to endorse language which speaks of ordained ministries as 'special ministries'. He invites us to understand that baptism initiates us into *discipleship*, a commitment to follow Jesus, rather than into public, representative ministries, and that much of what, rather loosely, has been inflated as ministry is really the ethical and moral application of being part of a community which, in re-membering, gets involved in the *missio dei*. He offers a provisional differentiation.

> Christian actions are acknowledged by us to be expressions of ministry if they are recognized, expected or mandated by the Church, if they have a public dimension and if they are subject to some kind of accountability and oversight. But if they lack these elements they are not examples of ministry but of everyday Christian discipleship. (Avis 2005:46)

Such a clarification is helpful and has been taken into wider Anglican discussions (AC 2007a: 25, 61) although not yet fully integrated into Anglican thinking.

Having disposed of a rather generalized understanding of ministry and replaced it with something more particular, Avis' account of *representation* is an important next step in helping to frame what ordained ministry is all about. The Anglican Consultative Council had considered this in 1976 and concluded, [The minister] 'is therefore a vital agent in the working of the whole Body' (ACC 1976: 39f). A more recent House of Bishops paper puts it this way

> The ministry of Christ in his body is channelled through every member, graced with the gifts of the Spirit (1 Cor 12:4–12). For all who have

passed from darkness to light through baptism, with its Trinitarian confession of faith, are incorporated into Christ's messianic, Spirit-bearing body (1 Cor 12: 3) and are anointed as a prophetic, royal priesthood (1 Peter 2: 5–9). Within this universal royal priesthood of the baptized there is a divine economy at work: special representative ministries are given authority and grace to speak and act in a public way on behalf of Christ and the Church, as they preach and teach the word, celebrate the sacraments and provide pastoral oversight. (AC 2000: 52 – cf 14–18)

and Avis writes,

The principle of representativeness properly understood and safeguarded, is vital because it insists that the risen Christ works through unworthy human instruments to minister his grace and presence for the salvation of the world. With the authority that comes from Christ in his body, these appointed ministries of word, sacrament and pastoral oversight represent Christ in ways he has ordained within the economy of the one *missio dei*. The diversity of callings that is distributed in a pattern of holy order is part of God's purpose for the Church. (Avis 2005: 100)

This way of describing the representative character of ordained ministry sounds absolute rather than contingent. It has to be linked in Avis' argument with the belief that ordination is inalienable. It is not necessary to interpret, as Avis does, 1 Corinthians 14.40 – 'all things should be done decently and in order' – as an apostolic imperative which might proscribe ecclesial and ministerial innovation (Avis 2005: 88f). Rather, an inductive account asks the question, 'Who is fit for the exercise of representational public ministry in the Church?' An answer to which focuses attention on process as well as doctrine.

Discernment is clearly necessary for the exercise of public ministry. But the process question is, 'whose discernment?' Anglican ordination discernment involves '360 degree' review – drawing insights from a range of people competent to write about the candidate's suitability. A sense of vocation to ordination, whether personal or encouraged by others,[9] is recognized by the bishop usually in concert with a nationally organized advisory panel based on a standard set of criteria issued by the House of Bishops. The discernment process for OLM is exceptional in calling for additional confirmation by a resolution from the candidate's Parochial Church Council (PCC). It is evident however that the discernment process privileges the wider church, rather than any single Christian community or parish. The Ordinal contains a question asked of the congregation, 'Is it now your will that they should be ordained?' (AC/CW 2007b: 17, 39) which acknowledges the consensual character of ordination, albeit in a generalized sense. But there isn't a sense of parity between the interests of the local and the universal churches at the time when vocations are being discerned. Robin Greenwood, writing as a practitioner, comments, 'I believe in the Church of England we do not allow the local congregation sufficient involvement in the selection of clergy. It looks very much like the ruling class perpetuating itself by appointing its own successors' (Greenwood 1988: 69). The church is yet to recover the commitment articulated by St Cyprian and endorsed at Chalcedon that ministry is at the behest of the people of God.

Local Ministry

Local Ministry is an account of the way in which ministry is exercised by the people of God, the *laos*. It reflects and represents a grounded approach informed by Vatican II and *BEM* (Greenwood and Pascoe 2006: 3) as well as the more distant influence of pioneers such as Roland Allen.[10] Local Ministry is capacious, cargoeing some key presumptions: for example, that there is collaboration and team work involving both lay and ordained people; it is representational; it is accountable both within the constituency in which it is exercised and more widely in the church (diocese) and community and is therefore subject to review. Local Ministry (*contra* ordained ministry) is not inalienable; it is taken up and laid down. The phrase itself became popular in the 1990s in Anglican writing but existed in the mid-nineteenth century.[11] A report in January 1991 understood this mutuality:

> Group and Team Ministries are saying something about the essential nature of the church, not simply for those in formalised ministries but for all people in ministry, which of course means the whole church, laity and clergy alike. Good practice will be reflected in a ministry that is fully shared.

Further,

> The real message implicit in Groups and Teams however is that the parish belongs to all of us and therefore we all have a responsibility for what happens; a responsibility not simply to make it happen but to decide what should happen. Good practice will be reflected in corporate decision-making where clergy and laity are genuine partners. (ACCM 1991: 7)

The implication of the 'radical change in attitudes and approach' brought about by the development of groups and teams is that the existing lay representation through the PCC was wanting. PCCs had been established in 1919 to give the laity a share in parochial administration but their function is primarily conciliar rather than ministerial. Nevertheless, the extent to which the work of the PCC requires supplementing does not seem to have been something that has received a great deal of attention in Anglican writing.[12]

Reviewing Local Ministry, Daniel Hardy offers a broad ecclesial systematic: being church by *definition* and being church by *action* (Hardy 2006: 142). The former is characterized by universal values and practice – 'the Church is predefined for the whole world'; the latter aspires to church through 'the consistency of the action of the Church in its diversity of ministry and mission' (Hardy 2006: 142). Defined churches tend to be formed by precedent; active ones evolve. Churches of the defined type are characteristically highly organized with 'standardized notions of ministry'; typically, they espouse the practice of larger churches, whatever their actual size. Churches of the active type, being numerically weaker, employ more fluid strategies which relate both to the resources available and the needs of the context, in which people are 'up close and personal'. Generally, Hardy argued, Local Ministry is a feature of the active type though it is capable of transforming a defined ecclesiology into an active one (Hardy 2006: 145).

Local Ministry articulates a grounded relational ecclesiology. It understands the local church to embody the universal church; it affirms that discipleship and ministry flow from a mature understanding of baptism and holds that the church is essentially a lay movement in which ordained ministries are facilitatory, and that questions of representation are not foreclosed. However, the radical edge of Local Ministry has encountered resistance. The ecclesial (defined) mindset, which can be lay as well as clerical, is wary of reframing ordination in a way that redistributes the authority, power and dependency, which have traditionally been focused on the clergy in general and on stipendiary clergy in particular.

In 1992, Hugh Melinsky, formerly a Chief Secretary of ACCM, commented, 'If the Church of England is unclear about non-stipendiary ministry, it is even less clear about "local ministry" ' (Melinsky 1992: 237). But discussion has coalesced around a series of questions and anxieties about the nature of ordained ministry and who is a fit representative, while the proposition that the church's ministry is in principle jointly held by lay and ordained people has been widely accepted (ABM 1992).

Ordained Local Ministry

Ordained Local Ministry was first named in a report, *Stranger in the Wings* (ABM 1998). Guidelines first issued by the House of Bishops in 1987 aligned what was then called Local Non-Stipendiary Ministry (LNSM) to a calling from the local church within a formally stated commitment to 'shared ministry' (ACCM 1987). A review four years later went further.

It is recognised increasingly by a variety of dioceses with LNSM schemes that this ministry must be the fruit of a commitment by the local church to the ministry of the whole congregation. This means seeking evidence that congregation and PCC are attempting to share the work of the local church and responsibility for it, and that the incumbent works in a collaborative way. It could also mean a commissioning service for the whole congregation, committing all its members to collaborate in the work of ministry, whilst encouraging some members to act as encouragers of such ministry and to train for it. (ABM 1992: 10–11)

This recapitulates the practice in the early church that the 'priestly vocation' is called out and held within the local church. However, it is the Church of England as a whole (sometimes called the 'national' church) that sets out the parameters of ordained ministry, and the House of Bishops has defended its authority in this respect over the years. All that needs to be noted here is the relationship in principle between local/shared ministry and the emergence of OLM and that this has been held, since 1987, to be one of its distinctive characteristics (ACCM 1987: 3, 4).

Conclusion

This chapter has explored a grounded relational–sacramental understanding of Anglican ecclesiology and the place of ordained people as special or public representative ministers within it. Such an ecclesiology is concrete and hence local. The nature of representative ministries is to facilitate re-membering, the constitutive and integrative task of the people of God. But these representative ministries only make sense when their contingency with the ministry of others through baptism and discipleship is understood. Ordained Local Ministry helps to articulate that interdependence.

Notes

1 Greek *genesthai* with the sense of regeneration, 'entering a new condition' (Arndt and Gingrich 1957: 158).
2 'Estote quod videtis et accipite quod estis': 'Be (through the process of consuming) what you see and receive what you are', St Augustine, Sermon 272.
3 Praise my soul the King of Heaven, Henry F. Lyte, 1834.
4 http://www.churchofengland.org/about-us/facts-stats.aspx, *accessed 9 May 2011*. A report in 1993 put it more emphatically. 'Throughout the country every acre is included within parish boundaries, confirming that the Church accepts a care for all that takes place within the land' (ABM 1993: 2).
5 'In origin [the parish] was an area large enough in population and resources to support a church and its priest, and yet small enough for its parishioners to gather at its focal church' (Pounds 1999: 3).
6 Evidenced for example in the language of the Astronomer Royal, Sir Martin Rees: 'I'm a tribal Christian, says scientist in prize row', Oliver Kamm, *The Times*, Saturday, 9 April 2011.

7 Something which the Church of England maintains (Canon C1.2). 'At ordination a minister (*sic*) is set in a distinctive relationship to the Church as a whole, and this is a permanent relationship, signified by the use of the traditional term *character*' (HOB 1997: 31).

8 Something which the Anglican Canons emphasize: the preface to the *Declaration of Assent* reads, 'The Church of England is part of the One, Holy, Catholic and Apostolic Church worshipping the one true God, Father, Son and Holy Spirit. It professes the faith uniquely revealed the Holy Scriptures and set forth in the catholic creeds' (Canon C15).

9 Selection Criterion A says that candidates should be able to speak of 'the extent to which others have confirmed' their sense of vocation to ordination (Church of England Ministry Division criteria summary leaflet, 2005).

10 Roland Allen (1868–1947) is now widely credited as the person whose writings have inspired local self-supporting ministry.

11 The earliest reference in the British Library is J. H. Carr's *The Local Ministry*, which discusses Wesleyan Methodist lay ministry (Carr 1851).

12 Stanley Ott notes that 'committees are almost always task-driven, and only rarely do they facilitate personal relationships among their members and intentionally develop their discipleship as well as accomplish their mission. Ministry teams perform all three functions' (Ott 2004: x).

2

Laity and clergy – a theological odyssey

Andrew Bowden

Since 1900, theologians and practitioners have redeveloped – if not rediscovered – a robust theology of the laity. In doing so, they have made it imperative for us to re-evaluate both our theology of the ordained ministry and our understanding of the church – our ecclesiology. Undoubtedly, schemes for Local Ministry Teams and Ordained Local Ministry have illuminated and helped to point up the discussion.

This chapter surveys this development. We first examine how a theology of the laity began to emerge because the old order was breaking down; it was driven by necessity. We see how the pioneers of new forms of ministry from Roland Allen on returned to their roots in the Bible and discovered there what they perceived as a collaborative all-member-ministry church that seemed to them to be very different from the hierarchical clergy-dominated church they saw around them. We see how this emboldened them to ask awkward questions about what God wanted the church to be and to do; what the ordained ministry was for; and what was the role of the laity. We see how theologians have developed their ideas, and conclude that a recognizable role for the laity has now been outlined with a robust theology to back it up. What has not yet been resolved is where the ordained ministry fits into the new picture. Work is still in progress to develop an ecclesiology that shows how the laity and the ordained can be truly 'members one of another' (Rom. 12.5).

Local Ministry – driven by necessity

The impetus for Local Ministry was largely practical. In England, the number of stipendiary clergy has fallen dramatically, and though these are now paid and housed adequately and trained efficiently, the cost of doing this is becoming beyond the reasonable pocket of dwindling congregations. All the traditional churches had been organized on the assumption that a 'proper' congregation should be served by a full-time stipendiary minister. The fact that this is no longer possible has proved inescapably unsettling both for those who make decisions about the deployment of clergy and for the clergy themselves.

Return to biblical roots

The pioneers of new forms of ministry felt that if they were to find a way out of the impasse, they needed to return to the roots of Christianity. The way in which religion can develop as people ponder on their history is well illustrated by an article by Walter Brueggemann. He suggests that the exiled Israelites managed to refocus their understanding of what God wanted them to do when they set about re-editing their sacred texts and thus inaugurated a 'communing with their past'. For the exiles, the landmarks had been destroyed, and they inevitably asked – 'How can we sing the Lord's song in a strange land?' Are they to go along the path of syncretism, either with the great religions of Mesopotamia or with the local religions of Canaan? Are they to turn in on themselves and root out from their midst the Canaanite women and secure their future by a total exclusivity close to tribalism? Or are they to wait on the Lord, less certain than before, less conceited than before, less voluble than before, so that the Lord may make of them a truly Holy People whom He can use for His purposes? It was, says Brueggemann, in communing with their past that they began to perceive their destiny (Brueggemann and Miller 1994: 263f).

What inspired the pioneers of Local Ministry was reading again about the church in the New Testament, particularly the tantalizingly incomplete snapshots of small, compassionate, whingeing, spirit-filled, cantankerous, hospitable, factional, above all believably human, congregations in the Epistles.

Granted that it is impossible to be dogmatic because the evidence is so fragmentary, granted that the congregations were apparently inventing structures as they went along and were therefore different from each other, what these pioneers believed that they saw in the Epistles were congregations which were essentially local.[1] It was a Christ-centred, Spirit-filled, do-it-yourself church. Although the congregations were so small, they seemed to be extraordinarily committed. Everyone was there because they wanted to be there. Everyone had been touched by the Spirit and it was assumed that they had something to offer, either as a contribution to worship – tongues, singing, healing, prophesy, wisdom – or by way of a gift that helped to build community life and to bind up wounds. 'Behold how these Christians love one another,' said Pliny. Love, compassion as God has compassion, was reckoned to be the supreme gift of the Spirit (1 Cor. 12.27–13 end). And it was a church open to everyone: outsiders were welcome, even to the Eucharist.[2]

These early Christians also seemed to be brim full of expectation – expectation of the coming in of the Kingdom of God. It must have been exhilarating to be a member of that sort of church, and the pioneers of Local Ministry nineteen centuries later caught something of that excitement. A number of theological themes with practical implications for ecclesiology seemed to emerge from the documents of the early church.

Theological theme 1 – Baptism

First, the sacrament of baptism with the laying of hands was of supreme importance. It was regarded as an astonishing privilege and carried with it the awesome responsibility of being a member of the Body of Christ. What was at issue was not when in a person's life baptism should take place, but what the sacrament implied. Some of the most striking passages in Paul's letters recall his readers to the significance of their baptism (Rom. 6.3f; 1 Cor. 12.13; Gal. 3.27f). The teaching is consistent – because of your baptism you have become a new creation, and this has implications for how you live and what you do. By baptism, you are commissioned for ministry within the congregation and for mission in the world.

Whether or not 1 Peter was based on a sermon to baptism candidates, it certainly assumed that every member of the congregation would be called to live an exemplary life, to support other Christians physically and spiritually and to suffer for the faith 'as Christ suffered for you'. The writer assumed that his readers/hearers were all deeply committed and practically involved in the life of a 'priestly community'.

Theological theme 2 – a community of priests

Two metaphors were frequently used to illustrate how everyone was expected to take his or her part both in building up the church and in preaching the Gospel. The first metaphor was that of the body, given its classic statement in 1 Cor. 12–13. It was a metaphor also used in Romans 12, a passage which suggested that the profoundest of the enumerated ministries was simply to lead a holy life – verse 21, 'be not overcome of evil but overcome evil with good'.

The other metaphor was that of the building. 1 Corinthians ch. 3.10–17 speaks of the Corinthian congregation as 'God's Temple', founded by Paul but built up by others. It was a picture echoed in the letter to the Ephesians ch. 2.19–20.

The metaphor was given another twist by the writer of the first letter of Peter – ch. 2.4–5,9. Not only does the community together form the 'building', they have also been called to be a community of priests. And this idea linked in with a theme developed by the writer of the letter to the Hebrews, who described with majestic metaphor the priesthood of Christ and seemed to presuppose a church in which all are priests and where all have the right without further mediation to pass through the curtain into the Holy of Holies (Heb. 10.20f).

Theological theme 3 – the Eucharist as an activity of the whole congregation

The practice of the early church showed that the corporate priesthood of all believers was no empty theological vision but was expressed liturgically in weekly worship. For what emerges from the Epistles is an assumption that the Eucharist is different from the sacrifices at the Jerusalem temple in that it is an action of the whole local congregation. This is well expressed in the House of Bishops of the General Synod of the Church of England report 'Eucharistic Presidency'.

> It would seem that the event of worship for the early Christian communities was typically an experience of the immediacy of God's presence to the whole Christian community through the power of the eschatological Spirit in their midst. Active participation in worship by every member of the congregation appears to have been understood as the norm. (1 Cor. 12 and 14) (HoB 1997: §4.16, 17)

The report goes on to quote with approval the conclusion of the International Anglican Liturgical Consultation: 'In, through and with Christ, the Assembly is the celebrant of the Eucharist.'

A further implication of brief glimpses of practice in the New Testament is that the president(s) at the Eucharist were people who were either local people themselves or who knew local people intimately. Presidency at the Eucharist carried with it a presumption of pastoral oversight. An International Anglican Liturgical Consultation statement observes,

> It would seem then that in the early church each congregation expected to have among their own number those who could celebrate the mysteries, and that these people were in a close pastoral relationship with those who they represented at the altar . . . The liturgical functions of the ordained arise out of pastoral responsibility. Separating liturgical function and

pastoral oversight tends to reduce liturgical presidency to an isolated ritual function. (Holeton 1996: 7)

Furthermore, the statement implies that since the Church is a Eucharistic community, every Christian community has a 'right' to the celebration of the Eucharist; and that in the early days this right took precedence over any insistence that the Eucharist should only be celebrated by highly trained – let alone only celibate – ministers.

Theological theme 4 – leadership in the early church

When the pioneers of new forms of ministry examined the nature of leadership in the New Testament Church, they recognized that they were looking at a developing situation. On the one hand, there is a strong emphasis in Acts on the authority of the Apostles to define what is orthodox and this is also reflected in parts of the letters to the Corinthians, in the list of 'gifts' in the Ephesians and in the Pastorals (1 Cor. 11.23; 2 Cor. 11.1–15; Eph. 4.11–12; 1 Tim. 6.2–5). But even this is tempered by the evident importance of the 'council' of the whole church in Jerusalem.[3] The Apostles do not act as an inner executive committee in isolation from the rest of the community.

When it comes to what happens when no Apostle is present, leadership seems to be exercised in different ways in different congregations depending on the local situation.[4] What is quite clear is that wherever it can be identified, leadership in the early church is corporate. Nowhere was there anyone who might be described in modern parlance as the 'the minister' of a local church.

Theological theme 5 – the importance of the Holy Spirit

Perhaps, most important of all, those who were seeking to find new ways of 'being church' in the twentieth century perceived that the New Testament Church believed itself to be living and working in the power of the Holy Spirit. Paul assumes that those who are baptized in water will also be baptized in the Spirit (Mk 1.8; Acts 2 passim; 8.15–16; 19.1–7; 1 Cor. 12.13). In a famous phrase in Acts, the Council of the Church writes to the Church in Antioch 'it seemed good to the Holy Spirit and to us'. In words attributed to Jesus by John, the Holy Spirit is seen as the one who will guide the Church of Jesus Christ into all truth (Jn 16.7–14). The church is to be a developing reality. Under the lordship of the Holy Spirit, it is an ongoing process, an ongoing revelation – and that is what God the Holy Trinity means it to be. 'Provisionality' is a gift of God to his church.

Free to act

Many writers and practitioners over the last hundred years have had this sort of 'conversation with the past' and have found the experience liberating. Their exploration has convinced them that our inherited understanding of the church is significantly different from that of our New Testament ancestors: and that the model of ministry to which we have become accustomed is only one of many. 'Provisionality' is a gift of the Holy Spirit to us, just as it was in the early church; and they have set about developing new patterns of ministry based on a reformed ecclesiology.

Towards a collaborative theology – the 'problem'

What drives the current debate about ecclesiology is the desire to discern a theological framework in which clergy and laity can work fruitfully together. The job of hammering out a reworked ecclesiology for a re-formed church is not an easy one. The root problem is that for most of the church's history, the theology of 'ministry' has meant in practice the theology of the ministry of the clergy. The rediscovery of a theology of the ministry of the laity has developed in parallel with the theology of clerical ministry, but so far, the two have never been satisfactorily integrated. Indeed, they have become sparring partners, pitched against each other in competition. The theology used to undergird 'all-member-ministry' has often seemed to be an attack on the authority of the clergy, while the theology of the priesthood often seems to be used as an excuse for undervaluing if not emasculating the vocation and gifts of laypeople.

Neglected theological insight 1 – Baptism and the Eucharist

The revived theology of all-member-ministry is rooted in a renewed appreciation of the significance of baptism. It is by baptism that we are incorporated into the body of Christ and as such we become part of a royal priesthood that shares the authority and responsibility of being 'ministers of the Gospel'. Using a language that resonates with an ecologically aware generation, William Countryman writes of the innate human call to a 'fundamental priesthood' which Christians 'understand' but which everyone is born with – 'a life encounter on the borderlands between God and the world' (Countryman 1999: 137–8). The orthodox theologian John Zizioulas goes further and suggests that baptism, which involves for the Orthodox both baptism and confirmation with laying on of hands, is essentially an ordination. In baptism, a person becomes a member of a particular 'ordo' in the Eucharistic community (Zizioulas 1985).

If baptism is then seen as the fundamental rite of ordination to all ministries, it means that there can and should be no subordination of one ministry to another. The report 'Eucharistic Presidency' puts it this way:

> Just as there is no subordination of being within God – Father, Son and Spirit are co-equally God – so in the communion of the Church, by virtue of our baptism into Christ and thus into the Trinity, there is no difference of value or worth of persons before God (Gal. 3.28). (HoB 1997: §2, 17)

As we saw above, the ritual expression of the common priesthood of the whole 'laos' is the Eucharist. In a splendid introduction to his paper 'The Thanksgiving of Eastern Christendom', Maximos Lavriotes writes,

> Liturgy means the dutiful ministry or *service of subjects* to their Ruler, King or God; literally it is the sacrificial/priestly action taken by the people at large, of all people capable and willing to 'serve the Lord with fear' (Ps. 2.11) and contribute to a universal act of gratitude towards the Master and Creator of all.[5] It is a public act which encompasses all mere mortals and as such, cannot be undertaken individually, nor be a matter of privacy, like prayer (Mat. 6.6) . . . It is intended for the human species in its entirety, all races and languages, even all kinds of angelic hosts. In modern parlance, it might be described as a 'Creation Service' in which all creatures endowed with reason should normally be represented in the offertory and thus become a *'rational, yet bloodless self-oblation'*. (Lavriotes 2010: 5)

Neglected theological insight 2 – the Holy Spirit in the church

Alongside the revived understanding of baptism has come a revived recognition of the work of the Holy Spirit both as Lord of the church and as the giver of 'charisms' to all the baptized. As we have seen, Paul assumes that those who are baptized are baptized in the Spirit and that the Spirit confers on each person a variety of charisms that are given for the building up of the whole body of the church. Leadership is certainly one charism, but by no means the supreme one, which is love.

Neglected theological insight 3 – mission and eschatology

As we saw, the New Testament Church was an organization in the making, variable from place to place and ready to adapt to new situations. It was a 'provisional' church, still working out its theology of mission and expecting the imminent transformation of the world at the coming of the Lord. Anthony Hanson draws on his experience in the Church of South India to emphasize the need for the European churches to recover these insights and to move from maintenance to mission,

> The missionary and ecumenical environment of the Church of South India was very different to the settled and assured Church of England soil. Apostolic dynamism rather than stasis was the critical difference . . . The Church was an ongoing creative activity of an apostolic gospel rooted in Christ and the *missio dei*. (cited in Pickard 2009: 81)

Hanson is only one of the many theologians who have helped to revive the sense that this world needs to be changed into His Kingdom on earth as it is in heaven. God's justice needs to prevail, and the time is short. The Holy Trinity longs for the transfiguration of society and for the gathering in of the harvest. We are called to be both a revolutionary and a missionary church operating, as the New Testament Church did 'with a sense that He is coming soon' (Rev. 22.20). As Stephen Pickard puts it,

> The missionary and eschatological context is the new reality within which and from which the question of the Church's ministries are considered. (Pickard 2009: 87)

What is the church for?

There is now an ecumenical consensus that the laity have an essential part to play in the ministry of the whole 'laos of God' (WCC 1982). Everyone now pays lip service to all-member-ministry. But there is as yet no firm agreement about whether all-member-ministry should evolve into collaborative ministry or about what 'collaborative' means. If we are to come to grips with this issue, we must ask the prior question – what is the church for?

The Cyprus Agreed Statement of the International Commission for Anglican Orthodox Theological Dialogue, *The Church of the Triune God* suggests that if we are to speak about the church, we must first speak about the Holy Trinity (A-OD 2006). It is perhaps presumptuous of us to speak of how God in Trinity 'operates', but what we perceive as we contemplate the 'mysterion' that has been revealed to us, as we gaze on what we do know, we recognize that there within the Godhead is loving, collaborative, sacrificial, healing, relationship, and it is that same loving collaborative, sacrificial, healing relationship that Christ wills for his church and through his church for the whole of creation. As C. S. Lewis pictured it in *Perelandra*, God the Holy Trinity draws the church and the creation into 'the divine cosmic dance'. That is the relationship the Creator wills for the creation, and his strategy for its achievement is the drawing together of a community, first through Moses and then through Christ. It is a community that, sharing in the divine relationship and nourished by the Eucharist, draws the creation into the 'transfiguration' that He wills as our destiny.

> By the indwelling grace of the Holy Spirit, the Church is created to be an image of the life in communion of the Triune God: and she lives in this world in anticipation of the day when the whole creation will be renewed, and God will be all in all. (A-OD 2006: §1.9, §1.21)

Or, as Daniel Hardy puts it, 'As God is, so God acts in Christ, and – by the Holy Spirit – in the Church where the Church acts in its mission to the world in accordance with God's activity' (Hardy 2006: 137).

How should the church operate?

The doctrine of the Holy Trinity as it developed over the first four centuries offers us a model for the church's ministry. It is essentially a collaborative model. Robin Greenwood, in his seminal book *Transforming Priesthood*, describes it as a 'relational theology' (Greenwood 1994). The report of the Roman Catholic Bishops on collaborative ministry, *The Sign We Give* (1995: 20), says that it is in relationships, in our communion with each other, rather than in isolation from others that we find fulfilment, and that this is the basis of the mission we share through baptism and confirmation. It is this insight, echoed in much modern writing about society, that has come to underpin the theology of collaborative ministry. It is difficult to overemphasize the excitement Greenwood's work generated among those trying to work out a new theology of ministry: but though it was helpful, it has become evident that a simple Trinitarian–relational theology of 'community' runs the risk of cosiness. Inspired to 'love one another', congregations drift into becoming communities of the like-minded – as one can witness any Sunday morning over coffee after a service, when friends talk to friends while newcomers and the 'difficult' are ignored. Collaborative ministry modelled by the Holy Trinity is not intended to be about cosy community, but about the meshing together of different people of different cultures with different gifts struggling to work together to fulfil the mission and eschatological longings of God for His world. The Holy Trinity indeed models collaborative ministry – but also knows the cost of collaborative ministry.

A provisional or an ordered church

As we saw, the New Testament Church was 'provisional'. At every turn, it had to face unexpected challenges and come to fundamental theological decisions about new issues. The Acts of the Apostles might be read as an account of how the church came to recognize that it was not just called to be a Jewish sect, but an eschatological community with a Gospel for the world. So a return to the New Testament has led to a recognition that provisionality is very important for us today; and this insight goes hand in hand with secular thinking about the provisionality of culture, and even of truth itself.

At the same time, the New Testament Epistles show how difficult it was for the early church to cope with theological provisionality. There was an evident need to defend the truth against perversions of the truth. These pressures led to the belief that the life and ministry of the church should be fundamentally the same wherever it existed – though sensitive to differences of language and custom. This 'universal order' was enforced by Councils of the Church, by Bishops and by an ordained ministry, in obedience to the post–New Testament development of the Apostolic tradition.

So there are now two ecclesiological paradigms: the church is universal, timeless and ordered; and it is provisional and should adapt flexibly to the local context. It is obvious that collaborative ministry fits most comfortably into a church that is provisional.

The place of the clergy in a layperson's church

The church needs a convincing theology of the whole *laos* of God – as a corporate priesthood – characterized by fellowship (*koinonia*) that is realistic. As the previous pages have shown, we have come a good way towards achieving this. What is not so clear is the role of the clergy in a 'Layman's Church'.

The church as we glimpse it in the New Testament is characterized by a vibrant all-member-ministry. In the Epistles, no division is made between laity and clergy. In fact, the first use of the term 'laity' in a divisive sense is by Clement of Rome around 95 CE. He was concerned about divisions in the Corinthian Church, and he suggested the need for a distinction between the 'laikos' and their officers. He draws an analogy with the different ranks in the Roman army and – perhaps unfortunately – references the different ranks within the Levitical priesthood. The development of 'order' within the church was perhaps inevitable but it did clearly move the church away from its collaborative roots.[6]

The theology of ministry that went with the development of 'order' came to separate the 'ordained' from the 'corporate' priesthood. The traditional understanding of clerical ministry assumes that the ordained and corporate priesthoods of all believers are separate aspects of Christ's priesthood, corresponding, according to the Jesuit theologian Rosato, to Christ's divine and human nature (Rosato 1987: 68/1–2: 215–66). It is an idea that appears in the 'Clarifications' to the final report of the first Anglican Roman Catholic International Commission.

> The priesthood of the people of God and the ordained ministry are two distinct realities which relate, each in its own way, to the high priesthood of Christ . . . which is their source and model. (ARCIC 1994: 41)

Stephen Pickard shows how Anglican theologians, from Moberly via Ramsey to Hanson, in moving away from this idea of 'two realities' have rather come to see the ordained person as sharing the corporate priesthood of all believers, though displaying in themselves the 'concentrated meaning – the intensification – the focus' of that priesthood. They are seen, not as 'separate from' but 'along with', with the special function of 'representing' the whole church both to those outside and to those within – above all in the Eucharist. Pickard draws attention to the writings of William Countryman and Kenneth Mason who have pushed the representational idea even further, suggesting that the priest is ordained to be a 'sacrament of humankind' in relation, not only to other humans, but to the whole of creation (Pickard 2009: 85–95). He further argues that the evidence of the epistles suggests that 'order' does not precede the church but rather is part of the DNA of the church that is 'activated' for the benefit of the community of faith when the need arises. 'The ordering of ministries is an ecclesial activity' (Pickard 2009: 36). Or, as the report 'Eucharistic Presidency' puts it:

> Just as there is no more 'real' God 'behind' Father, Son and Spirit in communion, so the Church is not primarily an institution, existing 'behind' or above its members, but is first and foremost a community of persons-in-relation. (HoB 1997: §2, 19)

In short, these theologians see a clear role for the priest in the future as a sort of 'bishop in little', to quote Christopher Donaldson (1992: 55); one who, as in the past, has the responsibility of keeping the church theologically anchored; one who focuses the church's mission and who represents the church; one who helps to identify and nurture vocations (charisms) of laypeople to a whole variety of ministries and who is also called to exercise a ministry of holiness, teaching and enabling so that all may minister.

Ordained and lay collaboration – some current insights

Certainly, these accounts give the priest a role, but they still do not resolve the relationship of the priest's ministry with the ministry of the laity. For even if the priest is 'along with' rather than 'separated out', it remains a very one-sided arrangement. For while in this scenario, it is clear what the priest gives to the laity, it is not clear what the laity give to the priest, and collaboration needs to be mutual. If we are to avoid tension between lay and clerical ministries, it is necessary to show how one 'feeds' the other. To arrive at a truly 'collaborative' theology of ministry, we need to understand how the two modes of ministry can so work that both are fulfilled in their vocation.

As a contribution to this debate, Greenwood, in a fascinating chapter in *Transforming Church,* argues that Christians can learn more about the nature and complexity of collaborative ministry by listening to what scientists and others can tell us about ourselves and about the creation as it truly is. He suggests ways in which a number of 'sciences' join in showing that the whole of life is a mass of complex interrelatedness and that nothing is truly a simple matter of linear cause and effect. He concludes,

> I believe that these insights from physics and the social sciences add weight to the cumulative argument that no thing or person truly exists or can be interpreted as alone, but only as part of a web of negotiations and interplay of personalities, obligations and interplay of mutual interpretations of what is taking place here and now. (Greenwood 2002: 62)

In other words, life is complex, and there is no such thing as a 'simple' organization or hierarchical structure. Collaboration is likely to be difficult, but it is there in the 'given' of creation.

In a closely argued chapter in his seminal book *Theological Foundations for Collaborative Ministry*, Stephen Pickard draws on the insights of evolutionary biologists to show how the creation actually 'works'. Biologists

> reveal living organisms as a dynamically ordered set of relations in which parts and whole contribute to the constituting of the entity and its functioning . . . and instability appears to be the pre-condition of the emergence of a new order.

If this is so, he argues, it illuminates for us how the Holy Trinity works in creation.

Belief in God as creator involves the recognition that this is the character of the processes whereby God actually creates new forms, new entities, structures and processes that emerge with new capabilities. (Pickard 2009: 134–5)

If we apply this to the 'order' of the church, it offers us a new dynamic way of understanding the relationship between the corporate and the ordained ministries. Looking at the church through a biological lens, we can see how a congregation in which the baptized exercise a variety of charisms gives birth to the need for more complex forms of 'order', and these forms of ministry may be novel, indeed unpredictable. Without the 'simpler' ministries, there would be no need for the more complex ministries, but in their turn the more complex ministries enable the simpler ministries to develop – often in unexpected ways. Or, as often happens, truly collaborative clergy coming to work with active Local Ministry Teams help the congregation to 'blossom' and often recognize in the process that at last they are doing the job for which they were trained.

These insights ring true to life as we experience it in the family, the community – and in the Local Ministry Team – and they do suggest a realistic way to understand and 'manage' collaborative ministry.

Ordained Local Ministry

Traditionally, the church has recognized three orders of ordained ministry, each with its own special role. Stephen Croft suggests that, in practice, all clergy operate on a number of different levels on a continuum line along Diakonia, through Presbyterate, to Episcope (Croft 1999). So it should come as no surprise if priests feel called to exercise different ministries within the church at different times. What Pickard and others have delineated is a theologically grounded, important and rewarding role for the stipendiary priest. But there is another equally important role for those called to Ordained Local Ministry. The arrival of Ordained Local Ministry underlines a number of theological truths about all ordained ministry.

First, all vocation to the ordained priesthood needs to derive from and be tested by a local congregation. This was the norm in the early church and is still so in the Orthodox tradition where all priests are seen as 'local' priests (the representative to one particular congregation), and they can neither celebrate the liturgy nor preach for any congregation except their own without the express permission of the bishop. Vocation to the priesthood may come initially through the call of God to an individual, but it has to be confirmed by the call of a congregation. The fact that many priests are effectively 'pressed into service' is reflected in many Orthodox ordination rites. First, the part played by the congregation in signifying that they believe the ordinand to be worthy is an essential part of the sacrament. Second, the ordinand approaches the bishop supported on either side by a priest – in case he may be tempted to try to run away!

The Preface to the 1550 Church of England Ordinal stipulates that ordinations should be 'upon a Sunday or holy day, in the face of the church', but Anglican priests have never been 'local' in the Orthodox sense. Nevertheless, in practice, many clergy returned to minister in the parish in which they were born. For instance, members of the Leir family were rectors of Ditcheat in Somerset – father and son for two hundred and fifty-six years. For most of Christian history therefore, and for most of English history too, there has been a close link between the local settlement, the local congregation and the local priest. 'Local' priesthood is not a new invention, but in Ordained Local Ministry, it can be seen as a recovery of healthy rootedness.

Second, Ordained Local Ministry symbolizes the 'theological authenticity' of the local congregation. The Cyprus Agreement argues that just as God is a communion of persons, so is the church a communion in Christ of many local churches: it is both a local and a universal reality. Catholicity is a quality of each local church in communion with the other local churches, 'just as each Person of the Holy Trinity is a hypostasis of the whole of the divine substance by being in communion with the other two persons' (A-OD 2006: §1.23–4).

Anglicans have always valued the local place and the local congregation, and the fact that this is a central feature of their tradition is still very much evident today – much to the irritation of reorganizing bishops! (Davies et al. 1991: 26).

Third, since Ordained Local Ministers (OLMs) have (officially) to be members of a team which includes laypeople, they symbolize the perception that all priests are called to work collaboratively so that 'though many we should be one body in Christ and individually members one of another' (Rom. 12.1–8).

Perhaps, most important of all, OLM challenges most of our inherited assumptions about ministry. It is good for our creakingly traditional church to be reminded that it is still clergy dominated. OLMs are a symbol that all-member-ministry involves taking laypeople and local knowledge seriously.

To sum up

A theology of the ministry of the laity – the people of God – has now crept into the bloodstream of all the major churches. Many churches have also come to accept that the role of the priest has to change too. Their role is not so much to control the activities of the laity as to walk beside those who are exercising ministries to which they too have been called by the Holy Spirit.

Their role will be to enable and guide a 'provisional' church as well as to see that the church is anchored to the Apostolic Gospel.

Perhaps, the insights of the biological sciences can, as Greenwood and Pickard suggest, help us to understand how and why the lay and the ordained are absolutely necessary for each other: how one can feed the other without condescension. Certainly, these sciences show us why truly collaborative mutual ministry is so difficult to achieve[7]; but they also show us that complex interrelatedness is an essential element in the process of creative evolution. The Holy Trinity is indeed the right and essential model for a ministry of the church that is creative. Collaborative ministry may be difficult, but 'living creatively in relationship' is, in the wisdom of the Holy Trinity, mediated through Jesus Christ and his Holy Spirit, the only way we can come to experience 'life in all its fullness' (Jn 10.10).

Notes

1 Col. 4.16 and Philemon passim. Paul writes separate letters to the Colossians and to the Laodiceans, and tells them to swap their mail when they have read it (Col. 4.16). The congregations are small enough for Paul to know many of them by name; the letter to Philemon gives an enchanting insight into the human scale of the early church.

2 M. Lavriotes points out that 1 Cor. 14.22–5 shows that the presence of unbelievers at the Eucharist was a routine procedure. 'Initially the sole requirement for taking part in the Eucharist was nothing more than being human' (Lavriotes 2010: 10).

3 The first mission of Paul and Barnabas offers an interesting example. The leadership at Antioch (Acts 13.1) consisted of a group of 'prophets and teachers'. From these, two are commissioned to go on a missionary expedition. Never one to operate alone, Paul sets off with the support of a team. The outcome of their tour is a theological bombshell – their conviction that God intends that Jews and Gentiles should be one in the Body of Christ. Such a radical suggestion is held to be too much for the local church to handle; so the matter is referred to a 'Council of the Whole Church' in Jerusalem.

4 In one of his earliest letters to the church in Thessaloniki, Paul refers to 'workers who lead and guide the church' (1 Thess. 5.12). In Phil. 1.1, he refers to overseers and servers. In Acts 20.17–28, the leaders of the local congregations are invited to meet Paul at Ephesus, and they are described, first as presbyters and, 10 verses later, as overseers.

5 Philo – De Vita Mosis II 224–5 and De Specialibus Legibus II 145.

6 The significant role of those who came to be called the laity did not evaporate overnight. Faivre (1990) lists among their functions, participation in the selection of clergy and especially bishops, consultation by the theologically able in matters requiring theological discernment, the apostolate of the godparent through pre-baptismal catechesis – besides their wider apostolate in the world. The Apostolic Constitutions (ca. 660 CE) lists a whole range of orders apart

from the three-fold order of bishops, priests and deacons. See also Bulley (2000) and Patzia (2001).

7 S. Pickard (2010). An expanded form of this article emphasizes the difficulty of collaborative ministry and underlines the critical importance of the concept of 'friendship' if we are to make it work. See also Thew Forrester (2003) and Kujawa-Holbrook and Thompsett (2010).

3

OLM in context – a genealogy

Oliver Simon

Introduction

An understanding of Anglican ecclesiology as relational, the task of the church as re-membering and ordained ministry as representational, underpins the debates and experimentation from which Ordained Local Ministry emerges. Ordained Local Ministry is a response to a search for representational ministry which valorizes the local church. It inverts the powerful and abiding 'clerical default' (Cundy 2006), the clergyperson as a singular ecclesial estate upon whom alone the responsibility of the kingdom subsists. Ordained Local Ministry starts from a very different set of assumptions; it holds that representational ordained ministry can be found from among those who inhabit apparently unpropitious 'Nazareth' contexts. It is a *voluntary, indigenous* ministry. Ordained Local Ministry is thus one answer to the rhetorical question posed by F. R. Barry in 1930, 'Who are fit persons' to exercise public representative ministry?

In the early 1980s, the Partners in Mission Consultation in England (PIM) and the influential Lima document, *Baptism, Eucharist and Ministry (BEM)*, triggered some serious reflection on shared ministry within the Church of England (Tiller 1983). Missionary practice in other parts of the world has been very important in framing the debate in England about Ordained Local Ministers (OLMs). Equally a small project in the east end of London in the late 1960s and early 1970s proved iconic. More generally, the genesis of OLM was assisted by a recovery of interest in the practices of the early church, particularly St Paul's church-planting strategy. The genealogy of Ordained Local Ministry is thus an interweaving of insight, conviction and practice which the Church of England subsequently regulated. These strands are interlinked and they are explored in this chapter as facets of the one phenomenon. Facet 1 is an account of a local initiative which modestly blazed a trail; Facet 2 locates that initiative within a discussion of 'voluntary', now 'self-supporting', ordained ministry; and Facet 3 explores the tentative ways in which this has been received by the church as a whole.

Facet 1: an experiment in indigeneity

Ted Roberts became vicar of the parishes of St James the Less, Bethnal Green, and St Mark, Victoria Park, in 1961. Although Roberts writes inclusively, it is clear that he initiated a project to train parishioners for what he called 'supplementary' ministry with the active support of his area bishop, Trevor Huddleston. In 1969, Roberts invited seven men,[1] six of whom accepted, to begin training, though two subsequently withdrew. Of the four in training, two were locally born, one came from India and all had lived in the area for most of their lives.[2]

Roberts, an 'imported minister' (Roberts 1972: 74), based his argument for indigenous clergy on 'the wider issue, the alienation of the working class from the church' (Roberts 1972: 67, cf. 21–7).[3] He was clear about the limited impact of the strenuous work of 'heroic' clergy and laity in the past. A more locally representative ordained ministry would, he argued, be the antidote to a church, which had simply 'not taken root and thrived in East London' (Roberts 1972: 12). He summarized the characteristics of the Bethnal Green Scheme for Supplementary Ministry under six heads:

1. 'A team rather than solitary ministers': team work radically challenges the power structure of clericalism.

2. 'Call by the local church rather than an outside appointment': Roberts rejected a congregational model of the church but argued for the recovery of 'an ancient and important principle', the role of the local church in sharing in the appointment of ministers.

3. 'Settled rather than itinerant ministry': here Roberts privileged the experience of those who were born and bred in the area. He coupled this with an account of his own relearning in context. Being rooted, being a settled inhabitant, reframed the clerical–lay relationship although Roberts recognized that ordination could desocialize existing relationships.

4. 'Training – local and practical': Jesus had trained his disciples as apprentices.

5. 'A specific term of service rather than open ended commitment':
   while Roberts acknowledged the argument for 'the indelibility of
   orders' (about which he was personally ambivalent), he saw in
   this temporal provision the opportunity for clergy to review their
   commitment and to be free to withdraw, 'if God so guided, without
   a sense of failure' (Roberts 1972: 43). His thinking anticipated
   subsequent decisions about tenure in team ministries as well as the
   importance of ministerial review.

6. 'Voluntary rather than paid': for Roberts, the voluntary principle,
   which he took from Roland Allen, helped to address the superior–
   inferior relationship which resulted from paternalistic clericalism in
   the East End of London and elsewhere. He suggested that unpaid
   supplementary clergy were less likely to be the focus of dependency
   because of their established relationship with their community
   but he recognized that there was no certainty that this would not
   happen.

These criteria were arrived at empirically, Roberts claimed, yet they reflect
the sensitivity to insights about the incarnational nature of the church
which were coming to the fore in postwar Britain and have been widely
endorsed subsequently. The language of inclusion and alienation was still
controversial however.

Facet 2: indigenous convictions

The representational concerns with which the Bethnal Green experiment
engaged had long featured in the discourse of Anglican overseas mission
agencies. Henry Venn, the Clerical Organising Secretary of the Church
Missionary Society (CMS; 1842–71) put forward a philosophy of ecclesial
self-development which attempted to excise the paternalism of much
contemporary missionary activity.

Churches, he said, should be helped to be 'native' (i.e. indigenous), 'self-
governing, self-supporting, and self-propagating', 'the three-self' principle
which he developed with the American Congregationalist, Rufus Anderson.
Venn used the rather forbidding metaphor of 'euthanasia' to describe how
missionary activity should be self-limiting, even though this was difficult to
achieve in practice partly because the CMS was committed to its 'voluntary',
that is its independent status, and was therefore financially dependent on
its supporters. So, for pragmatic as well as principled reasons, Venn argued
for some specialization, that the missionary should exist outside the daily
organization of the local church (by which he understood a national entity)
with its indigenous leadership. In his 'Second Paper on the Native Church'
in 1861, Venn proposed that evangelism was the task of the missionary

while that of the local, indigenous church leader was to pastor. This distinction, between missionary (apostolic) and local ministries, had roots in the missionary practice of St Paul.

Half a century later, Roland Allen (1868–1947) arrived at similar conclusions, again from the experience of Christian mission outside Europe.[4] Allen's convictions about how God 'spontaneously' establishes and grows the Church were influenced by his time as a Society for the Propagation of the Gospel (*SPG*) missionary in northern China from 1895 to 1903. His ecclesial roots were Tractarian. However, he came to hold a high doctrine of the Holy Spirit, which made him sceptical of institutional or organizational strategies. Allen developed a critique of Western ecclesiology in *Missionary Methods. St Paul's or Ours?* (1912). Later he published *The Spontaneous Expansion of the Church and the Causes which Hinder It* (1927) but the 1920s saw him focusing on a specific and, as he saw it, crucial element in the expansion of the Gospel, the necessity of self-supporting clergy. His little book, *Voluntary Clergy*, was published in 1923, followed in 1928 by *Voluntary Clergy Overseas*, both of which were combined in *The Case for Voluntary Clergy* (1930). Allen held that stipendiary ministry was 'only suitable for some settled churches at some periods' (Paton 1960: 137), but he was perfectly happy to entertain the coexistence of stipendiary and voluntary clergy. During 'expansion' (church planting), however, stipendiary ministry 'is the greatest possible hindrance. It binds the church in chains and has compelled us to adopt practices which contradict the very idea of the Church' (Paton 1960: 137). For Allen, particularly in such emergent contexts, ministry was to be found locally from within the Christian community,

> we must think first and foremost of the group as the church in that place, and of the ministers as naturally and normally members of that group, attached to it by every tie, spiritual and social. (Paton 1960: 146)

St Paul had evidently trusted the competence of local communities of Christians to call out their own ministerial leadership in the early church, so why not now? Among a number of advantages, he cited that of identification

> the church sorely needs clergy in close touch with the ordinary life of the laity [. . .] sharing their difficulties and understanding their trials by close personal experience. Stipendiary clergy cut off by training and life from that common experience are constantly struggling to get close to the laity by wearing lay clothing, sharing in lay amusements, and organizing lay clubs; but they never quite succeed. (Paton 1960: 150)

Allen held that there was something innate in certain people which others instinctively appreciated as priestly. Such people do not require 'training', he said. Their charisms were already evident. Working within a catholic ecclesiology, Allen dismissed the suggestion that this was 'pure congregationalism'.

> The presence and action of the bishop makes all the difference. . . . if they went to the place and told the congregation the plain truth: 'You know quite well you cannot have a stipendiary minister; I have not the men and you have not the money' – if they asked them, 'Have you not two or three men fit to serve who between them could lead the church and minister the sacraments: men whose ministration you will accept?' often they would be answered: 'Yes, we have'. And if the bishops then solemnly and openly put it to those men: 'It is your duty to do this service: in the name of Christ and in the name of the church I demand that you shall serve', not many men would refuse. (Paton 1960: 144–5)

Allen's ecclesiology might best be described as mystical. His passion was to allow the sufficiency of 'the gift-bearing missionary Spirit' (Paton 1968: 29) to make the necessary provision for the people of God. 'In a deeply ironic way Allen was the restless soul of a post-Christian West and the inaudible voice of post-western Christianity' (Sanneh 2008: 218).[5]

In *The Spontaneous Expansion*, Allen drew on two articles by Fr Herbert Kelly (1860–1950), the founder of the Society of the Sacred Mission. Kelly argued that it was the church which was the primary agent of mission and that its priesthood and episcopacy were essential in fulfilling that goal. 'In the early days, "to found a Church" does not mean to preach the Gospel, but to provide a bishop' (Kelly 1916: 183). However, bishops had become increasingly distant as statesmen and politicians. 'Our home dioceses', Kelly wrote from Japan, 'were once a unity and they retain a somewhat dubious unity of heart still, but formally they are federation of parishes' (Kelly 1916: 192).

The parish, Kelly argued, had become a self-serving system in which the priest's role of maintenance was reciprocated by the necessity of the people to maintain him. Local Ministry would be self-supporting (or locally supported). Kelly did not oppose what he called professional (i.e. diocesan) clergy, but this category was not fundamental. 'It grew up where it was wanted, and the business which called it into being provided the means for its support' (Kelly 1916: 432). 'The professional clergy belong to the diocese and are maintained out of the single diocesan fund and can be used anywhere within the diocese.' By contrast, local pastors, drawn from among the people, 'belong in the first instance to their flock and are not normally removable' (Kelly 1916: 439). Nailing his colours to the mast, he wrote, 'the young college-trained man and the old "local" priest represent two sides of life, of which the simple minded Christianity is the more essential and fundamental, just as existence is more fundamental than growth' (Kelly 1916: 438).

F. R. Barry (1890–1976), a liberal theologian and ecclesiastic, reviewed Allen's *The Case* when it was published in 1930. He held that, 'in its essentials', it 'is unanswerable'. Noting the institutional resistance to self-supporting clergy, he was one of those advocates who, when he became a bishop, continued to argue for reform and against clericalism. But there were detractors. Rev Dr W. F. France, who was Overseas Secretary of SPG, had 'grave objections' to the ideas of 'enthusiasts like Mr Roland Allen' (France 1929: 334).[6]

It was to be another three decades before David Paton's edition of Allen's writings reintroduced him to an audience that found his ideas resonated with the contemporary debate on self-supporting ministry. Forty years on, an inter-diocesan working party jointly convened by the bishops of Stepney and Woolwich picked up the earlier arguments for indigenous ministry. Like Ted Roberts (who was a member), the working party was concerned about 'the long-standing alienation of the working classes from the Church'. Their report, titled *Local Ministry in Urban and Industrial Areas* (possibly the first time 'local ministry' was formally used in Anglican ecclesiology) advocated 'local ordained ministry' (Huddleston and Shepherd 1972: 8f). 'It is the thesis of this working party that there is indigenous leadership with intelligence and ability which cannot be easily measured by academic yardsticks' (Huddleston and Shepherd 1972: 7). Endorsing a *laos*-centred ecclesiology, the report said, 'All ordained ministry should be seen as supporting and caring for the lay presence in the world' (Huddleston and Shepherd 1972: 12). And such ministry should not be the sole responsibility of the clergy person. The report spoke of 'diaconal' groups which 'will need ordained laymen [*sic*] to initiate [. . .] and preside over them'. Thus, 'the ordination of a group of men in any one locality ought to be seen as part of the diversification of the life of the Church' (Huddleston and Shepherd 1972: 12). Put side by side however, these statements implied different outcomes; either the emergence of Local Ministry Teams, 'diaconal groups' of ordained and lay people or a clericalization of lay ministry, 'the ordination of a group of men', as was happening in Bethnal Green.

The 1980s were particularly fruitful in the development of thinking about Local Ministry. PIM and *BEM* have already been noted. The Archbishop of Canterbury's Commission on Urban Priority Areas (ACUPA) *Faith in the City* had some significant things to say. *ACUPA* gave voice to what Huddleston and Shepherd had been saying.

[I]n theological terms: the Church must be aware that its locality is the first place in which God is to be both encountered and served. Such a stance demands attentiveness to the individual and social realities of local life and a readiness to share in and interpret them in the light of the Gospel. (ACUPA 1985: 76)

A universal church crosses boundaries among ethnic groups, classes and cultures. At the same time, an authentic mark of the presence of the church in any particular place is that it should be rooted in the culture and character of that locality (ACUPA 1985: 107).

The Commission called for 'A Participating Church' with a strong presumption in favour of clerical and lay collaboration. It devoted a chapter to 'Developing the People of God'. Opting for indigeneity as the key representational category, it said, 'Only those who are in, and of a local area can say how God is speaking there. They can tell each other and the wider Church' (ACUPA 1985: 106). Following Roberts, it recognized 'the historical domination of leadership [in UPAs] by those of other cultures' alongside 'a concentration on words and books and equating intelligence and vocation with academic ability, a dependence on professionals, and a degree of conservatism among the laity' (ACUPA 1985: 106).

Faith in the City acknowledged Roland Allen's influence on Anglican ecclesiological thinking and again drew from the world church in framing its proposals for UPAs in England. It commended the development of a Church Leadership programme which affirmed the characteristics of collaborative team working involving both lay and ordained people. The report noted 'widespread support' for the idea of local priests. The main arguments against such ministry were noted – that it promoted a congregational rather than a catholic ecclesiology, that it was 'second class' and that it reinforced clericalism. Leaving aside questions about the actual universality of the existing ordained ministry, the Commission argued that the authentication of vocations by the wider church and ordination by the bishop was the way to preserve catholic order.

At the same time, the Anglican Consultative Council was also looking at Allen's writings. The report of its meeting in 1985 commended indigenization, shared ministry and what it termed 'local priests' (ACC 1985: 62f). As in Allen's and Kelly's writings, this was done descriptively.

After the bishop has explained to the parish or the congregation the meaning and purpose of this ministry, the congregation is asked over a period of time to select someone to be nominated to the bishop for training and ordination. The candidate must be seen as someone who is respected and clearly identified with the people, as witnessed by his sharing in their common life. The training of the candidates does not seem to be either structured or intense. The period of training is shorter (e.g. one year before being made deacon and a further six months before being ordained to the priesthood). In some parts of the Communion, the training of this kind of priest is shared with the congregation (especially content and process) so as to define expectations for ministry. The bishop and his staff give continuing support and supervision after ordination. The local priest, unlike the non-stipendiary priest, serves continually in one place from which he was chosen (ACC 1985: 67).

Responding to the 1981 *PIM* consultation, the Standing Committee of the General Synod asked the Chief Secretary of its ministry department, Canon John Tiller, 'to make "shared ministry" an important dimension' of a reflective report. Several considerations contributed to this focus: a sense of alienation from indigenous populations in urban areas, the disappearance of the resident parson in rural areas and the influence of the charismatic movement associated with growing churches. Tiller said at the outset, 'The vision to which I have been led is controversial' (Tiller 1983: 4). His *Strategy* for mission-focused ministry was based on 'two essential ideas' which have a strong, though not acknowledged, likeness to what Fr Herbert Kelly had been saying nearly sixty years before.

- The local church, as the Body of Christ in a particular place, should be responsible for undertaking the ministry of the Gospel in its own area.
- The bishop, as chief pastor in the diocese, should be responsible for ensuring that each local Church has, from within its own resources or from those of the diocese, the ministry which it needs.

The *Strategy* was progressive rather than radical. Tiller regarded the priestly ministry of the people of God as something which is shared. It is not 'a way of rallying to the aid of the clergy', he said, but 'a response to the calling of all who are baptised into Christ to act as his Body in the world' (Tiller 1983: 81). So while Tiller recognized diversity in patterns of leadership within the local church and was very careful not to undermine the role of the Parochial Church Council, he leaned towards an eldership model of ecclesial governance and argued that *every* (his emphasis) local church has responsibility for its ministry including calling out 'local priests' who would be voluntary.[7] His *Strategy* envisaged local voluntary clergy who were embedded within the local church and diocesan clergy whose ministry was facilitatory – both of the life of the local church and of the bishop's ministry and missiological strategies.

Although Tiller did not say that stipendiary clergy would vacate their benefices under his *Strategy*, there was a good deal of anxiety about the assumed disassociation which the report evoked. Amidst a great deal of debate, the assumption that stipendiary clergy would increasingly be a problem-solving, 'fire fighting' elite, distanced from the laity was read into the *Strategy*. Some argued against the suggestion that leadership could be shared as opposed to being delegated. Essentially, it was too neat a proposal. The Church of England was not ready to entertain a perceived retreat on the part of stipendiary clergy from traditional pastoral ministries and equally not ready in general to embrace and validate such a significant role as Tiller proposed for 'local' priests. More than three-quarters of a century after Herbert Kelly's articles, Tiller concluded that pastoral reorganization was more likely to be premised on the principle of maintaining a stipendiary pastoral presence than on any other principle but that this inhibited mission and constricted the flourishing of the people of God.[8]

Facet 3: ecclesial reception

The theme of this genealogical account is that as the church ruminates on local initiative and reflections from the margins, it develops regulative frameworks which generalize and order innovation. This process of reception can be traced through the medium of the reports of working parties.

The unpublished *Report of a Working Party on Supplementary Ministries* in 1961 challenged the perception that ministry was exclusively a priestly office and that priests were always parochial (ACCM 1968: 9). During the 1960s, schemes had been set up in the dioceses of Southwark and in Gloucester to train clergy on a part-time basis – some for stipendiary and some for 'part-time' ministry. So in 1966, a working party, chaired by Canon Paul Welsby, was asked to review what was going on. Their report, *A Supporting Ministry* (1968), started by taking supplementary ministries as given. It endorsed them and also encouraged the work of team ministries. It argued against those who held that priesthood was not compatible with secular employment and, as Roland Allen had already done, rejected completely the misnomer of 'part-time' priesthood. The report also dismissed 'the idea that auxiliary priests should be regarded as "second best" ' and emphasized 'that standards of selection and training should be as careful as for full-time ministry' (ACCM 1968: 17).

This was undoubtedly a significant and affirmative report which has been described as 'the foundation charter for non-stipendiary ministry in the Church of England' (Vaughan 1983: 18). It led to regulations from the House of Bishops for the selection and training of candidates for what was called 'auxiliary pastoral ministry' (APM) in 1970. The regulations acknowledged that APM was a collective phrase – 'several forms of auxiliary ordained ministry are being discussed or explored at the present time' – all of which were 'self-supporting' ministries (SSM).[9]

Four years later, however, another Advisory Council for the Church's Ministry (ACCM) working party took a decidedly more conservative position in their report, *The Place of Auxiliary Pastoral Ministry, Ordained and Lay*. Their remit had been to look at both lay and ordained ministries and the title of the report implied that APM embraced both. The working party analysed the Bethnal Green experiment and the Huddleston–Sheppard *Local Ministry* report. The burden of their condemnation was that these represented a retreat from Anglican catholicity towards congregationalism.

They were suspicious of the underlying sociological analysis. Their anxiety is conveyed by a sentence such as, 'The concept of an indigenous church owes more to political expediency than to catholicity.' Indigenous leadership was intrinsically limited, they said. Huddleston and Shepherd's *Local Ministry* and Roberts' *Partners and Ministers* were socially deterministic. 'We do not favour schemes for local ministry, all of which as presented to us, however much their advocates protest to the contrary, would lower standards in selection and provide less than adequate training' (ACCM 1973: 25). Here are set out many of the arguments against Ordained Local Ministry. However, the report was not sympathetically received. A debate in the General Synod, on a private member's motion, criticized its findings and asked ACCM to do further work. Mr T. L. Dye said,

> An indigenous Church just means that the Church in that area or nation should express the Christian faith in ways that are readily understood by people of that culture, and that that Church should be the cutting edge in that culture on the moral and social ills of that culture. (GS 1974: 583)

In 1987, the House of Bishops issued further 'regulations' for Non-Stipendiary Ministry (NSM) and 'guidelines' for Local Non-Stipendiary Ministry (LNSM) in order to assist those 'setting up experiments', evaluating them and looking to see how they fitted into the work of the diocese. The distinction between 'regulations' and 'guidelines' reflected 'divided views about Local Non-Stipendiary Ministry and as yet the Church has not come to a common mind' (ACCM 1987b: 2). The guidelines acknowledged that LNSM 'rouses heated debate' and went on to summarize its 'commonly understood' distinctive features

- The call of God to this ministry comes to the candidate, in the first place, through the local congregation of which the individual is a member. To this call, the individual responds and, following selection, is prepared in an appropriate way. Ordination is the church's validation of this call, to which the individual has responded.
- A Local Non-Stipendiary Minister exercises this ministry as part of a team of people, ordained and lay, working together in the same parish or locality.
- This team may include lay people, with whom the Local Non-Stipendiary Minister has trained or shared the same training course.
- The training of a Local Non-Stipendiary Minister does pay attention to and have full regard for the local situation, where that ministry will be exercised, and to the development of the necessary theological insights and ministry skills that may be required.
- The ministry is local, in that it is confined by licence.

These guidelines bench mark the church's understanding of LNSM and have not changed significantly since. LNSM would emerge locally and in that sense it was 'indigenous'; it was embedded within a lay team which trained with the LNSM. The LNSM's ministerial context was proscribed by licence.

The emphasis on this proscription, which has contributed to a negative perception of Ordained Local Ministry, seems to have arisen from the designation, 'local', even though, as a later report noted, there is

> . . . the general and historic recognition of the distinction between holy orders which are for life, and the licence to exercise those orders in a diocese for a specified time in a particular place: confinement of the Local Non-Stipendiary Ministers to a particular area by licence conforms with the usual practice of the church. (ABM 1991: 10)

A working party report, *Local NSM*, in 1991 was to become the base line for future documents and therefore marks a significant stage in the genealogy of reception. The report began by defining 'Local Ministry' – for the first time in an official document – as a generic term which included 'Local Ordained Ministry'[10] as well as 'recognised lay ministries where these form part of a local ministerial team' (ABM 1991: 5). Based on the evidence from a survey of dioceses, it identified five features of the emerging understanding of LNSM:

- A renewed appreciation of the significance of the varieties of ministries which God gives in the local church's life.
- The importance of the local church in an age of seemingly remote centralized government and large institutions.
- The wish to encourage indigenous ministries, particularly in situations of urban priority areas, as a contribution to better communication of the Gospel.
- The value of the collaborative nature of ministry, which within the manageable compass of the local community can illustrate how all ministries, including that of the ordained, are Christ's and are his gift shared with us in the church for the sake of all the world.
- A recognition that there may well emerge a shortage of stipendiary clergy, creating a need to complement their work with non-stipendiary ministries. (ABM 1991: 6–7)

Experience showed that LNSM needed to hold these insights together. The report therefore proposed, and the House of Bishops accepted with a minor amendment, a generic statement, that

> Local Non-Stipendiary Ministry is part of the ministry of Christ which he shares with all baptised members of the [local] church. Those called to this

ministry by their local church need to have made the calling their own. For its effective operation, LNSM requires the local church's commitment to shared ministry, including the collaboration of local church leaders, ordained and lay. It is a development in ministry open to parishes and candidates of all social backgrounds.

As in Tiller's *Strategy*, 'local' is nuanced: it is 'a principle source of vocation', 'a principal source of training', 'the location of ministry', 'a geographical area not greater than a parish or group of parishes' (ABM 1991: 8). The report was aware of 'the passionate feelings and advocates' in the debate about the extent to which LNSM was a legitimate expression of Anglican ministry but stepped back from discussing this, remarking that it had already been addressed. Nevertheless, it identified three marks of LNSM which 'appear to be necessary for its effective functioning' (ABM 1991: 8).

The first mark, catholic order, means that an LNSM is an authentic representation of the universal church particularly referenced or orientated to 'the service of the local church and community'. This is expressed through the Bishop's licence. The second mark, the collaborative ministry of the whole local church, followed from the 1987 guidelines. Thirty years after the 1961 report on supplementary ministries and following a number of more recent statements, including *BEM*, it was no longer the case, at least officially, that ministry was understood to refer exclusively to ordination. The third mark, a commitment to work in teams, follows from this.

The Local NSM confirmed and settled the ecclesial and regulative framework for LNSM. But six years later, another working party was convened. *Stranger in the Wings* is a more grounded report than most of its predecessors. For the first time, information was explicitly taken by questionnaire from practitioners and reported verbatim. The title, however, conveys the sense that here is something which is scarcely recognized by the church at large. *Stranger* argued for a higher profile for LNSM and proposed a name change – to *Ordained Local Ministry* – a term which privileged the context of Local Ministry out of which a vocation to ordination has come. This, it was admitted, was more a matter of convenience for the institution than for the recipient. '[W]e recognize that LNSMs locally, are like other clergy called vicar, curate, priest, father, Christian name and so on' (ABM 1998: 26). A number of other issues were addressed: the importance of sympathetic stipendiary appointments to benefices where collaborative ministry was practised was one of them. As with previous reports (ACCM 1987b and ABM 1991), considerable attention was given to the arrangements for training LNSMs and their support in ministry. *Stranger* however ventured into an initial conversation about the pedagogy of the formation, including a section on Method and an appendix on Transformative Learning, which argued in favour of inductive grounded learning.

In 2006, a question about the current situation of Ordained Local Ministry led to a low-key survey among diocesan bishops. The results were sent to the

House of Bishops in a short document titled 'OLM – a ministry in flux' (AC 2007). The findings of the survey suggest a degree of consensus about OLM in the mix of vocational responses to ordination. But there were questions whether Ordained Local Ministry was a maintenance- or a mission-focused ministry and problems of oversight and management.

The survey shows that there are still concerns about the status of Ordained Local Ministry and its title indicates a degree of uncertainty about practice which overlays other anxieties which are not formally documented.

Conclusion

As an institution, the church is slow to respond to demands for change. The debates occasioned by pressure for Local Ministry and Ordained Local Ministry have contributed to the process of being attentive both to God and to the world, theology and sociology. Its genealogy illuminates a persistent debate about the consistent and contingent nature of the ministry of the church. Its development parallels the same processes of eccentric initiation and subsequent reception as, for example, the emergence of religious communities in the nineteenth century or the ordination of women in the twentieth century – the development of orthodoxy from what was initially regarded as heterodoxy. Whether on the basis of Christian teaching about exclusion, or from a sense of injustice, or the antecedent practices of the early church, or pragmatically – as a result of the decline in vocations, retirement of significant numbers of stipendiaries or financial pressures – the due recognition of the charisms of 'ordinary folk', including their potential as ordained representatives of the people of God, reflects a continuing faithfulness to Gospel imperatives, to the coming of the Kingdom of God. This account of the genealogy of Ordained Local Ministry has indicated how its development and reception reflect a grounded engagement with theology and society. Ordained Local Ministry cannot resolve anxieties about the church's competence to engage with a culture which is indifferent to the survival of institutions, but it does provide a means of enlarging capacity by challenging inherited prescriptions about who are fit persons to exercise representative public ministries.

Notes

1 The experiment of course predated the ordination of women in the Church of England.
2 By the end of the 1980s, two of the four that were ordained in 1976 were exercising their ministries in the benefice, one had become a hospital chaplain and one had died (Melinsky 1992: 238).

3   Reflecting thirty years later, Roberts commented, 'My one concern is that the alienation of the working class from the Church does not seem to have been given the priority it deserves' (Roberts 2006: 16).
4   In his introduction to Sidney J. W. Clark's *The Indigenous Church* (1923), Allen commends Venn's 'Three Self Movement' (Sanneh 2008: 233).
5   For a survey of Allen's influence, see Long and Rowthorn (1998: 361–3).
6   Paradoxically, France's article was part of a series on 'The Shortage of Clergy'.
7   Tiller does not recognize Roland Allen's work explicitly either, but others have seen the connection (Williams P, 1984: 55).
8   For a detailed study of Tiller's contribution to Anglican ecclesiology, see Beach (2010).
9   A term preferred by the Lambeth Conference, in 1968.
10 The term which had been used since at least 1980 (GS 442). ABM Ministry Paper No 4 (1992) proposed that LOM should be consistently replaced with LNSM because the phrase, 'local ordained ministry', falsely suggested that this was a form of ministry in which ordination was local rather than catholic (ABM 1992: 4).

4

The relevance of the Northern Michigan experience of Local Ministry to the English context

David Bowers

From 1998 to 2008, I worked in a dual role, partly as incumbent of six rural communities in Gloucestershire and partly as Associate Diocesan Director of Ordinands for the Gloucester Diocese. Part of my particular brief in the sector role was the development of Ordained Local Ministry in the diocese and I worked alongside the Local Ministry officers, as it was from the Local Ministry Teams that Ordained Local Ministers (OLMs) were selected. It was in this context that I first encountered the reputation of the Diocese of Northern Michigan in the Episcopal Church in the United States (ECUSA) and heard of its radical reshaping of ministry and leadership in its local congregations. This process, known as 'Mutual Ministry', had developed a growing reputation throughout the Anglican Communion and was attracting many interested people to their special visitors' weekends, where they could witness it at first hand. There are similar models, for example, in New Zealand, but this one particularly caught my imagination.

In 2004, as part of my preparation for a dissertation for a clergy course at St George's House, Windsor, I had the opportunity to visit Northern Michigan myself and to meet some of the diocesan officers and congregations. Much of this chapter is based on that project. I was interested to hear the story from their perspective and to see how the vision was taking shape in the local congregations and in diocesan life. One of the most impressive aspects of my time was the consistency I saw between the ethos of mutual ministry and the practice.

The move towards mutual ministry in Northern Michigan has been part of a wider movement within the Episcopal Church and two of the key figures in this were two successive bishops in the Nevada Diocese, Wesley Frensdorff and Stewart Zabriskie. Frensdorff was Bishop of Nevada from 1972 and was succeeded by Zabriskie in 1986. Both have had a considerable influence on collaborative models of ministry in the United States and beyond. Frensdorff had been a pioneer of what became known in Nevada Diocese as Total Ministry, using the term, 'the captivity of the sacraments' to describe the problem of the dependency of the local church for its sacramental life on a professionalized ministry system:

> Sacraments are primarily available where a professional, stipendiary priest is available. This clerically centred model of congregational life and mission increasingly limits both ministry delivery and the sacramental life of the Church (Frensdorff 1992: 5).

Total Ministry in Nevada was based on congregations being ministering communities, containing within themselves the necessary gifts and ministries, including those of the so-called local priests. The aim was that seminary trained priests would become enablers, trainers and encouragers. Stewart Zabriskie reflects on the development of this in his influential book, *Total Ministry* (1995) and looks beyond to some of the wider implications for a non-hierarchical model of ministry.

One of the striking aspects of the Northern Michigan story for me was how the situation in which they found themselves in the early 1980s had many parallels with that increasingly faced by the Church of England, especially in rural areas. Although the Northern Michigan approach could not be directly transferable to the Church of England, I felt that the ethos and principles behind their programme provide significant and challenging lessons. I write not as an academic or specialist in ministry, but simply as a priest who has always tried to work collaboratively and who longs to see the ministry of all the baptized as a living reality in our churches and communities.

Mutual ministry in the Diocese of Northern Michigan

In addition to the following, which is based on my own observations in 2004 and updated through continued contact with the diocese, there is an inspirational account of the development of mutual ministry by Bishops Tom Ray and Jim Kelsey in *Local Ministry: Story, Process and Meaning* (Ray and Kelsey 2006). After my visit, Bishop Jim Kelsey tragically died in a road accident in 2007 and has recently been succeeded (2011) by Rayford J. Ray, who has worked in the diocese as a ministry developer. In 2004, the key post of Ministry Development Coordinator was held by Kevin Thew Forrester, who is now rector of St Paul, Marquette, and a ministry developer.

The Diocese of Northern Michigan covers the Upper Peninsula of the state and is surrounded by Lakes Superior, Huron and Michigan, its only land border being with Wisconsin. It is linked to the rest of Michigan by the Mackinac Bridge in the south-east and to Canada at Sault Ste. Marie in the north-east. Despite the road and air communications with the rest of the United States, the area, with a population of just over 300,000, feels remote, partly due to its weather conditions and its geography, with 90 per cent of the 16,538 square miles covered by forest.

The area has traditionally provided employment in mining, timber and fishing, and had in the past attracted immigrants from areas such as Scandinavia and Cornwall. However, it is now in economic decline and has a shrinking population as many young people have to leave to find work. The area has a significant number of people who live there during the spring/summer and a few of the congregations are seasonal, that is, they close during the autumn/winter. During the winter months, the weather can be extreme, with frequent heavy snowfalls.

The diocese is one of the smallest in the ECUSA, with less than 30 congregations scattered throughout the Upper Peninsula. The largest denominations in the area are the Roman Catholics and the Lutherans, with Episcopalians accounting for a small minority of the Christian community.

By the 1980s, the traditional one priest/one church model had largely broken down and many congregations were able to celebrate the Eucharist only occasionally, whenever a priest was able to visit them. The economic factor was significant as many of the churches in the diocese were categorized as 'mission churches', indicating that they were unable to sustain the costs of having their own priest and relied on the financial support of the diocese and the wider church. The growth of mutual ministry in its present form began shortly after the appointment of Tom Ray as Bishop in 1982. From his vision and leadership, and from the discussions within the Commission on Ministry and the Standing Committee, the diocese began a scheme to gather together a number of members of congregations to begin a training programme for Local Ministry which would, it was hoped, produce a number of local priests, who would be ordained under the provisions of Canon 9, a measure which allowed for the ordination of those who were referred to as 'local priests and deacons'. This was short lived, however. It was discovered, when the scheme was evaluated, that the people who had been trained, who had been recognized and respected members of their congregations, were now viewed with some suspicion and they themselves felt somehow as though they had become detached from the local context. The diocese now looks back at this as 'Phase One' in the history of mutual ministry.

A new way was explored. Dan Weingarten, in a history of the diocese written for the centennial celebrations in 1995, writes: 'The diocese realised that the program had to be done locally, that it had to involve a team of people, and that merely placing the job description of a seminary-trained priest onto a locally ordained priest was a recipe for failure.' Instead of taking people away from their communities, the training became locally based and involved a number of people identified and called by the local church for the particular ministries which would be needed. From this discernment and calling, a 'Covenant Group' would be formed and would begin training (or 'formation' as they prefer to call it now). At the Commissioning, which includes the ordination of priests and deacons from within the local church, the Covenant Group would become the Ministry Support Team.

Principles of the scheme

It is impossible to isolate local priesthood from the understanding in Northern Michigan of mutual ministry as a whole. Priests are part of a wider team and there is a deliberate move to emphasize the shared nature of the ministry of all the baptized. As Bishop Jim Kelsey put it: 'Our focus has evolved from training and ordaining local priests to developing the ministry of all the baptised in every community' (Kelsey 2003: 9). 'Mutual ministry', writes Kevin Thew Forrester, 'was not simply a means of survival made possible by the introduction of Canon 9, but a way of awakening us to an entirely different way of being the people of God' (Thew Forrester 2003: 65).

A number of key principles support the scheme:

1. The decision to adopt mutual ministry is that of the local vestry (the Episcopalian equivalent of the Parochial Church Council) and congregation and is taken after consultations with the bishop or a representative.

2. It is held to be good practice for at least two priests and two deacons to be identified as members of the Covenant Group. This reduces the possibility of the local priest/deacon being drawn into an inappropriate role of being the 'minister in charge'. This number can vary. For example, at Iron Mountain, there were at the time of my visit, four local priests in the Ministry Support Team. Other roles in the team could include preacher and worship coordinator. St Paul, Marquette, which was about to embark on mutual ministry during my visit, had a Covenant Group made up of 35 people, which included three priests and three deacons. The ministry roles within a team are grouped together under the headings of 'Diaconal,

Apostolic and Priestly'. Having embarked on the journey in 2004, St Paul, Marquette, completed its second-generation discernment process in 2010.

3. The diocese is careful to try to avoid a 'consumerist' view of ministry, that is, ministry as something that is dispensed to a congregation by either an individual or a team. Thus, it is seen as important that each member of the team is a reminder to the congregation of his or her own ministry.

4. The formation process for Covenant Groups is now based on 'LifeCycles',[1] an educational programme developed in the dioceses of Northern Michigan, Wyoming and Nevada and partly written by Kevin Thew Forrester. According to its information leaflet, it is intended to go beyond initial team formation and to provide lifelong learning and an 'ongoing support system for those engaged in ministry'.

5. Each church is linked to a 'ministry developer', who is seminary trained and acts as a source of advice and guidance to the team. The ministry developer has no power to make decisions for the team or to veto their decisions. They are there as a critical friend and companion. Sometimes, a church will be in a period of transition, where there is a rector who is moving into the role of ministry developer. Although in practice all the missioners are ordained, there is no reason, under the diocesan ethos, why a suitably trained non-ordained person could not take on this role. Originally, they were known as 'missioners', but the title has now changed to reflect more accurately their role and work.

6. Decision-making is seen as a mutual process and there is no identified team leader. Difficult decisions are made by working towards a consensus or, if necessary, a compromise.

7. The Vestry remains the statutory body for policy decisions in a local congregation although, in practice, the Ministry Support Team directs the worship and outreach of the church. The Vestry usually contains some members of the team.

8. The diocesan leadership itself tries to model collaboration, and there have been developments in 'shared episcopacy', in which decisions and issues were shared initially between the bishop and a 'Core Team', which included ministry developers. After Jim Kelsey's death, the Core Team was dissolved and replaced with the 'Episcopal Ministry Support Team' (EMST). This group meets every three weeks for ongoing formation, using 'LifeCycles', and to support execute the episcopal ministry of the diocese. Generally, it is seen as important that the diocesan structures are conducive to collaborative ministry and that there is a willingness to change and adapt where necessary.

My impression from interviews and observations was that there was a widespread grasp and understanding of collaborative ministry and priesthood. While I was alert to notice gaps between the diocesan perspective and the view 'on the ground', there were actually very few. This is partly due to the fact that they have been practising this since the 1980s but it must also be a result of the strong and consistent ethos communicated throughout the diocese.

Northern Michigan continues to attract interest and the Visitors' Weekends are a regular feature of the diocese, designed to gather a number of enquirers about mutual ministry together rather than have smaller groups of visitors throughout the year. The weekends include meetings with members of local congregations and hearing their stories, as well as discussion and worship. There is a concluding debriefing session on the Sunday evening, which is especially geared to encourage participants to apply the lessons of the weekend to their home environment.

The influence of mutual ministry has spread far beyond Northern Michigan and their diocesan website includes a comment from a congregation in Iowa which has embraced this way of church life. This statement is a clear explanation of what mutual ministry means to the life of a local congregation:

> For a long time and in many places, we have allowed ourselves to be communities gathered around a minister rather than being ministering communities. . . . Mutual ministry is a commitment to recognize that we all share in Christ's ministry. It is a process as we listen prayerfully together, as we discern various gifts, and as we become more and more in touch with ministry as a way of life, living out our ministries in the church and in daily life.
>
> One of the ways the process is lived out is through the creation of various ministry support teams that help us discern what God is calling us to do individually and collectively, matching our gifts to our calls. In a mutual ministry congregation, clergy are part of the team, not the directors or sole providers of ministry. Pastoral care, Christian formation, preaching, leading, teaching, and spiritual guidance are shared by all the members. (www.upepsicopal.org)

In many ways, mutual ministry is particularly fitted to the congregational and gathered structure of Episcopal Church life and, in particular, to the more sparsely populated parts of the United States. My visit gave me a sense of the circumstances in which they work, particularly the isolated setting of the Upper Peninsula and the minority status of the Episcopalian Church. My interviews and meetings were carried out in various locations and involved long road journeys, sometimes through heavy snowstorms. These geographical factors have helped to shape their way of doing things and the stark contrast with the Church of England struck me forcibly. Nevertheless, I was constantly able to draw on parallel experiences and problems from my home setting and I felt that the principles behind their programme, rather than the programme itself, could provide some guidance for the Church of England.

Learning from mutual ministry

It has become almost obligatory when speaking of the inherited, and in some quarters prevailing, image of Anglican ordained parochial ministry over the last few hundred years, to name George Herbert, the seventeenth-century priest and poet, as its main exemplar. This is epitomized in the interesting title of Justin Lewis-Anthony's 2009 book: *If You Meet George Herbert on the Road, Kill Him: Radically Re-Thinking Priestly Ministry*. The 'George Herbert' model remains the default understanding of the role of the parish priest in many parts of the Church of England and continues to be reflected in welcoming liturgies for a new incumbent or priest-in-charge. This culture is often seen most clearly when a new incumbent arrives and much of the work which had been successfully done collaboratively during the vacancy is dropped into the lap of the new man or woman.

The example of George Herbert (or at least that attributed to him) is alive but by no means well in the Church of England. The reality is that the pattern of parish ministry inherited from the past is unsustainable due to factors such as economic stringency, social change and decreasing numbers of stipendiary clergy. Many hard-pressed parish priests are attempting to cover the work in a group of parishes which had previously (perhaps even up to the 1980s or even 1990s) been covered by two or three stipendiary clergy. It is clear that, even if the Church of England were inclined to maintain the inherited model, it is encountering considerable difficulty in doing so.

The inherited 'George Herbert' model is both stressful and guilt inducing for the incumbent and deskilling and disempowering for laypeople. This clericalism struck me forcibly several years ago when I facilitated a group from a rural parish which was engaged in an exercise of mapping the history of their church as it looked towards the future. The history related by this group was not so much the history of their church community as the account of the personalities and styles of various incumbents over the last fifty years or so. There was no doubt that many faithful laypeople had shared in the life and work of this parish over many years. However, the really important and significant work was understood to be that carried out by the vicar.

At the same time, there has been an increasing move towards a more collaborative understanding of ministry in the Church of England over the last few decades, expressed in far-reaching explorations such as John Tiller's *A Strategy for the Church's Ministry* (1983). Ordained Local Ministry has been a significant step forward in this direction, though it is debatable whether the expectations generated by the *Stranger in the Wings* report of 1998 have been achieved. The report spoke of a 'continuum', leading in stages from all clerical ministries to that of all members. How far though, has Ordained Local Ministry taken us in this direction, despite it opening the door to ordained ministry for many who would never previously have considered it? Within the inherited clerical model of the Church of England, how far has Ordained Local Ministry been 'new wine in old wineskins'? Often the discussion about Ordained Local Ministry has been more dominated by tired structural questions, such as 'What happens if they move?' or 'Can they take services out of their home parish?' rather than looking at the distinctive, team-based nature of what this ministry is intended to be.

The Church of England carries a weight of tradition, structure and history that would make such a radical restructuring in the style of Northern Michigan difficult if not impossible in the foreseeable future. Yet the traditional model of ministry is both unsustainable, because of economics and numbers, and undesirable, because of its effective denial of the ministry of all God's people. As we reflect on the experience of Ordained Local Ministry and look to where this will take us in the future, there are some principles and signposts provided by mutual ministry. These are highlighted in three main areas.

Taking the local context seriously

Priests in mutual ministry are seen as part of a congregation that is expected to contain within itself the necessary gifts and ministries for being the church locally, with ministry developers providing the perspective and theological insight of the wider church. From a Church of England standpoint, the priests in the Ministry Support Teams in Northern Michigan look very different from OLMs, who in England, go through a very similar selection procedure to other ordination candidates and who train for much of the time away from their local setting. The emphasis in mutual ministry has shifted away from the individual to the community, maintaining the local context throughout for discernment, training and ministry. One of the early lessons learned by the Diocese of Northern Michigan was that training and formation had to be rooted in the local church and the ministry support team. This strengthens the focus on the team rather than the individual priest and helps to break down the sense of the separation of priest and congregation.

One of the lessons for the Church of England is the particular importance of the local context in training, involving the local team and congregation in a closer way, helping priesthood to be truly rooted in a local and collaborative church community. It would involve taking seriously the other gifts that make up the ministering congregation and not setting priesthood on a pedestal as the ultimate expression of Christian service. A local church depends on a whole range of gifts and ministries and the idea of one person being expected to possess them all is alien to the New Testament.

A further question raised by the Northern Michigan experience is whether it is good practice for a congregation to have just one local priest, who may attract pressure to be a 'priest in charge', despite his best intentions. Having more than one local priest dilutes this pressure and strengthens the team ethos. One of the problems that has sometimes arisen in both Ordained Local Ministry and similar schemes in the Church of England is when a local priest has gradually worked free of the team and has effectively become a permanent and immovable one-person ministry. In the Truro Diocese, for example, where the Ordained Local Ministry scheme was discontinued, the diocesan bishop, Bill Ind (who had chaired the group which produced 'Stranger in the Wings'), wrote in a Diocesan publication in 2001 that, while it had produced a number of good local priests, they had not been able '*to change the pattern of clerical dependence. Indeed, through no fault of their own, in a way they have confirmed it*'. He goes on to say, 'all the emphasis was on the training of the priest, and not of equipping the People of God in a particular place, to understand and to themselves be ministers' (Ind 2001: 28–9).

If Ordained Local Ministry is used as a 'sticking plaster' solution to compensate for declining numbers of other clergy, this will do nothing to address deeper issues of clericalism and will leave OLMs in a position in which they are unsupported by the wider diocese and misunderstood within their parish.

Reshaping the structures of the church

In the Church of England, the term 'collaborative ministry' has become an assumed article of belief, and it would be rare to find any church leader now who would verbally disagree with it. Yet, at the parish level, whether it happens or not can still depend on the character or approach of an incumbent. It is still possible, for example, for a new vicar to dismantle a collaborative team that has been built up from the community and has been working well up to that point. Steven Croft, in his book, *Ministry in Three Dimensions* (1999), highlights this problem. He speaks of situations where there has been frustration among lay people that their gifts are not being recognized or used. This is often, he says, 'because their minister or incumbent is still operating in "inherited mode" and has not wanted or been able to learn the different way of working collaboratively, using and supporting the gifts and ministries of others' (Croft 1999:11).

This highlights the problems of working towards a collaborative model of church, which is not sustained by the very structures by which it operates. Here, Northern Michigan provides an example of a situation in which radical decisions have been taken. These include taking seriously the ministerial sufficiency of the local congregation and their ability to make decisions and, if necessary, to learn from their own mistakes. It also includes an attempt to practice collaboration in every part of diocesan life, including the developments in 'shared episcopacy'. Bishops Tom Ray and Jim Kelsey recalled how the Diocese 'recognised and responded to the need to re-shape its own canons' in order to facilitate change (Ray and Kelsey 2006: 52).

One ministry developer I met reflected on his role in an email to an enquirer in 2000, noting that the changes in the structure of ministry locally *'are greatly aided and abetted by the systematic impact of 'mutual ministry' on our whole diocese. It is reflected in every aspect of who we are (canons included), however imperfectly'*. One of the key factors in the growth of mutual ministry has been the willingness of the diocese to change, where necessary, the administrative structures, and to try to model collaboration in decision-making. The idea of shared episcopacy is an example of this, though in practice, this may not be very different from a bishop's staff meeting in England.

The willingness to change sometimes places the diocese on the edge of the ECUSA canons, though there is a faithfulness to the wider Church that prevents it from stepping outside. The active support of Northern Michigan towards the integration of the separate canons for local and other priests and deacons adopted by the ECUSA General Convention in 2003 illustrates the willingness of the diocese to work within the national structures. They have an accountability to the wider church alongside their commitment to press towards the ministry of all the baptized. The diocese is part of a North American network of Mutual (or Total) Ministry dioceses known as 'Living Stones'.[2] Their annual consultation provides a forum for the sharing of issues.

The bishop is also a key person in the working of mutual ministry. Both Tom Ray and James Kelsey helped to set the tone by an informal and approachable style and it was an interesting culture shock during my visit to meet a bishop who, for most of the week, did not wear a clerical collar and who was known throughout the diocese as 'Jim'. Even in such a self-consciously non-hierarchical diocese, however, it is evident that the bishop plays a significant role in putting the ethos into practice.

The understanding of incumbency in a collaborative church

I have already mentioned the tendency to see the history of a parish as that of its incumbents, often symbolically expressed in the rows of photographs of previous clergy on the walls of many vestries. In many ways, this view of parish history is at least partly due to the culture of dependency between a local church and the incumbent, the view that sees a vacancy as a period when nothing too exciting can be done because the laity must wait for their new vicar before they can make significant decisions. This model sees the incumbent as exercising his or her own ministry, supported by the laypeople. A more positive way is to understand that an itinerant incumbent comes alongside the local church in its ongoing journey. This does not mean that a new vicar will not be expected to challenge and help the church to move forward. What it means is that incumbency is seen as a resource and the local Christian community has the primary ownership of ministry and mission.

One of the most exciting parts of the Northern Michigan experience is the role played by the ministry developers in reshaping the role of stipendiary, seminary trained priests. Their developing role in mutual ministry points to a way forward for the Church of England as it looks at a situation in which the traditional understanding of incumbency is, in many areas, either unsustainable or inappropriate. Is it possible that, for example, in multi-parish benefices, stipendiary clergy could begin to work more in the manner of ministry developers and be liberated from the 'nuts and bolts' of running several local churches? How far can local church communities, motivated by ministry teams, be responsible for their own life and mission alongside the companionship of a stipendiary priest?

The relationship between the ministry developer and the local team and congregation seems to be a vital element in the working of mutual ministry. The ministry developer provides not just a theological resource but also a bridge with the wider diocese and church, helping to overcome the divisive aspects of parochialism. He or she also has to find the right level of support, keeping in touch with and being available for teams and congregations, but resisting the temptation or pressure to make decisions for them. In the words of the early twentieth-century Anglican writer, Roland Allen, congregations are given 'power to fall' (Allen 1962b: 16). The phrase used by Allen ('Power to fall is power to rise') speaks of what can be a difficult process of allowing people to grow in confidence by stepping back to enable congregations to learn from mistakes as well as from successes.

Seminary-trained priests with appropriate gifts seem to be an essential part of the mutual ministry programme. A great deal of responsibility for congregational development rests on their shoulders, yet their role is far removed from that of a traditional incumbent. There appears to be a sense of fulfilment and satisfaction in their role. One, in a conversation, spoke of being freed from the detail of day-to-day church life and being able at last to use his seminary education in training and facilitating, something not possible to the same degree in a traditional incumbency position.

Of course, there are many imaginative incumbents in the Church of England who are able to encourage and develop the ministry of all God's people and who are gifted and passionate in doing so. There are many examples of how collaborative ministry can thrive in local situations. However, do these exist because of, or in spite of, the structures of the wider church? Should such positive examples be solely due to the approach and personality of the individual incumbent or should they be actively encouraged, resourced and supported? Changing structures cannot create collaboration, but it can affirm and set high expectations.

Conclusion

Like the ministry developers of Northern Michigan, I am aware that I am providing more questions than answers, but the Church of England is on a journey and at a crossroads. The mutual ministry approach in Northern Michigan, which began when its journey was at a similar crossroads, can, I believe, be helpful in shaping the questions and in helping us to think about the future direction of our church.

For the sake of both overstretched and guilt-ridden incumbents and poorly resourced congregations, especially in multi-parish benefices, we need to find a better way. Ordained Local Ministry has helped to reshape our understanding of local and collaborative priesthood, but it has often fitted awkwardly into a system in which clergy are set apart from their communities and ministry is often seen as something which is dispensed by the clergy to the laity.

In the three areas outlined above, we can learn from and be encouraged by a diocese in the Anglican Communion that has taken a bold step towards making the ministry of all the baptized a reality.

Notes

1   Details may be found at http://www.upepiscopal.org/Mutual%20Ministry/lifecycles.html.
2   http://www.livingstonespartnership.org/.

St Ebba's story

Chapter 5, which follows, discusses the experience of Local Collaborative Ministry in the Scottish Episcopal Church. This story, contributed by Tim Morris, with quotations from Jennifer Edie, the parish minister, serves as an introduction.

Eyemouth is located in the south-east corner of the Diocese of Edinburgh, adjacent to the English border. Full stipendiary ministry in this historic fishing town ceased in 1998. Local Collaborative Ministry (LCM) was introduced to St Ebba's with the appointment of a part-time Companion Missioner and with various members engaging in diocesan discussions on future patterns of ministry. It was then that, 'We were beginning to appreciate that LCM was more than just a panic reaction to financial and personnel shortages'.

Visits to other LCM locations moved the church from theoretical thinking to a more concrete understanding of what LCM might mean, and led to a process where core tasks for ministry were identified and prioritized by the whole congregation. A pastoral visiting team was nominated, trained and commissioned by the Bishop and, 'We felt we were at last making a positive move towards a whole-member acceptance of responsibility for the life and mission of St. Ebba's'.

In 2002, the congregation engaged in a province-wide mission appraisal project, enabling it to take a hard look at where it was and where it hoped to go. This provided a valuable introduction to the necessary pattern of small-group learning, formulation of plans and communication and adoption of these by the wider congregation.

Contact with other churches was invaluable in opening paths to progress but they learned that, 'We have to forge our own path in the light of these experiences because no two congregations are identical . . . all contacts have been threaded into the pattern we are weaving for ourselves.'

For some time, laypeople had been reading lessons and leading intercessions, and this was extended to administering the chalice. During interregnums, two Readers led worship with Communion from the Reserved Sacrament; so the congregation was accustomed to a variety of people officiating in diverse ways. In 2004, these Readers were ordained to the priesthood to work alongside the retired stipendiary priest. Three years later, a full ministry team was nominated and after local training, guided by the provincial LCM officers and diocesan-appointed consultants, it was commissioned in 2011.

We are content to move slowly forward in our attempt to serve God in our community. We welcome all that He gives us, especially the people who have supported us so strongly . . . it is an adventure and we are eager to see what is over the next horizon.

5

Local Ministry in Scotland

Tim Morris

Introduction

The story of how the Scottish Episcopal Church (SEC) moved into Local Collaborative Ministry (LCM) with the identification of some of its distinctive features has already been told (Morris 2006). This chapter updates the progress from 2005 to 2011, identifying and analysing some of the strengths and weaknesses of this movement throughout its development. It will also describe innovations in Local Ministry being undertaken by the Church of Scotland and indicate possible future directions for LCM within the evolving policies of the SEC.

Setting the scene

To understand the nature and role of LCM in Scotland, it is important to note that the SEC has under 5% of the national church membership and attendance and is ranked among the smaller Christian traditions. The Presbyterian Church of Scotland and the Roman Catholic Church have a much larger presence. Although often, mistakenly, seen as the Church of England imported into an alien culture, the SEC has deep roots in Scotland reaching back before the Scottish reformation to Celtic origins and is a separate and distinctive province in the Anglican Communion. This history has left it with two practical legacies. The first is a pattern of Sunday worship which, in contrast with the Church of Scotland, is predominantly eucharistic. Most Episcopalians will expect a celebration of the Eucharist or the opportunity to receive Holy Communion through the reserved sacrament. This meant that issues around ordination and priestly ministry were vital and important in the emergence of LCM.

The second feature is the geographical spread of SEC congregations and church buildings across the nation, which includes many small groups in the scattered communities of the highlands and the islands. We have, though, inherited neither parish structures nor buildings inappropriate for today in terms of size and function. While there are some historic and architectural treasures, most of our buildings are located within small towns and cities and were built during the second half of the nineteenth century in areas in Scotland outside the major centres of population. The challenge is to continue effective ministry in these 'rural and remote' places and to respond to new mission opportunities. The SEC faces the same question expressed by Bishop Tom Ray of Northern Michigan: 'How will we set a table in the wilderness?' (Thew Forrester 2003: 59).

Significant factors in the development of LCM

The role of finance

The initial trigger for ministry development in Scotland was often financial.[1] As local congregations in Scotland are directly responsible for the funding of the rector, with augmentation of stipend from provincial funds available to cover shortfalls, it was a constant struggle to maintain the inherited pattern of stipendiary ministry. Joint charges, shared stipendiary clergy and clustering of congregations were actively considered. The experience of the established churches in Scotland and England suggested that such ecclesiastical re-engineering could not, by itself, halt the decline in membership numbers or motivate and mobilize the congregations in mission and renewal. Loss of local church identity, further alienation of local people and communities from the church and burnout for a diminishing number of stipendiary clergy were likely. Such measures were even less applicable to the particular context of the SEC in terms of geography and liturgical requirements.

To those working in ministry development, it seemed that only when all other options had been tried and found wanting was LCM considered as a possible alternative way to sustain congregational life in a particular locale: 'the last chance' for their survival. The essential foundational theology of LCM was rarely part of the conversation between congregation and diocese, except as an explanatory justification after the event.

To acknowledge finance as a significant factor in the way LCM developed should not downplay its theological importance. There are a number of examples within the Bible and the history of the church where the work of God's mission was initiated and directed by financial issues. Some of the later missionary travels of the apostle Paul were prompted by the financial straits of 'poor among the saints in Jerusalem' (Rom. 15.25–9; 2 Cor. 8 and 9).[2]

The role of bishops

Within a small and intimate church, such as the SEC, the particular gifts and personality of the bishop are crucial. Dioceses are small (e.g. the Diocese of Argyll and the Isles has 34 potential congregations with its bishop and six stipendiary clergy[3]); bishops are chosen by diocesan election. There are expectations that bishops are known personally, that they are available both to clergy and individual congregational members and that they know their dioceses. LCM in Scotland benefitted from a number of far-sighted bishops committed to some form of collaborative ministry and often prepared to support imaginative projects and radical individuals. Some were wholeheartedly supportive in encouraging congregations to make use of LCM resources. Others were more neutral in attitude, holding different theological positions while still recognizing the valuable contribution that some form of LCM might make. None presented active opposition to the development of LCM, but dependence on their support proved a two-edged sword. Bishops with little experience or understanding of LCM either in Scotland or elsewhere or whose energies were taken up by other more pressing concerns in their diocese were later elected. Others had different emphases on mission and ministry from their predecessors. LCM congregations had functioned without diocesan guidelines surrounding and safeguarding their status and modus operandi, and all might be changed with a new bishop. Individuals who had invested much time and energy in LCM in their local congregations could be left deeply hurt by the personal rejection implied by such changes.

The role of the Provincial Local Collaborative Ministry Officer

LCM developed in Scotland from a provincial rather than a diocesan base. It appealed to smaller, more geographically dispersed and financially vulnerable congregations offering them a theology and the necessary practical support to be mission-orientated and self-sustaining. Such congregations in Scotland were predominantly located in the two largest but also poorest dioceses, Argyll and the Isles and Moray, Ross and Caithness, which were always going to lean heavily on provincial resources. The appointment of a Provincial Local Collaborative Ministry (PLCM) Officer was a necessary consequence of the ecclesiastical geography of Scotland.

The strategic significance of this appointment by and for the whole province cannot be underestimated. The establishment of the SEC was seen as uniquely investing a large amount of its annual mission and training budget in ordinary, run-of-the-mill congregations. For small church communities, often harbouring memories of years of neglect and isolation from the centre of church life, the impact of being at the cutting edge of developments and being recipients of visits, training and resourcing was enormous.[4] The PLCM was often the first representative of the province ever to visit these small and scattered congregations and affirm them as being essential to God's kingdom work. As these groups met for worship and dispersed in their daily life of mission, they came to recognize themselves as much and as important a part of the SEC as any large city cathedral. The province thus recognized and re-established the primacy of the local congregation in mission and offered real and practical support for it.

In practical terms, the PLCM Officer produced and worked with four tools which were vital for and instrumental in the steady growth of LCM from 1995 to 2008.

The continuum

From the outset, LCM employed the language of journeying to emphasize the need for congregations to shape the project according to their individual local context. A much used leaflet, produced by the Officer, described LCM in terms of a 'Continuum'. Congregations decided where they wished to locate themselves on this continuum and chose if and when they wanted to move further on their LCM journey. It was recognized that such empowerment represented a deep and significant shift away from central diocesan to local congregational control and reflected a theological cornerstone of LCM – that the path of Christian maturity is discovered in the move from dependence to interdependence.

At the General Synod in 2008, the PLCM Officer reported that she was in contact with over 40 congregations. Many of these were in the 'Enquiry' stage on the continuum, investigating 'what baptismal ministry-for-mission is all about' (Cameron and Gavine 2008: 7), utilizing the PLCM Officer's gifts in teaching and training through weekend visitations and workshops. Others were moving into a more explicit Exploration stage, developing LCM by the intentional use of educational materials and working with the Officer to establish and resource ministry teams.

A few congregations saw themselves at the 'Covenant' stage (Cameron and Gavine 2008: 64). These had established Ministry (or Leadership) Teams responsible for the support and enabling of the ministry and mission of all members in the congregation. Some of those teams included ordained people, often identified by a calling from the membership and affirmed by due provincial process.

The continuum proved an important tool for congregations in the process of developing LCM but was always designed as a guide to be operated with flexibility rather than a strict policy identifying procedures and timelines. For example, to ensure the continuance of eucharistic worship, ordination of Ordained Local Ministers (OLMs) took place for two churches in the Diocese of Argyll and the Isles prior to the congregations entering into formal covenants as set out in the continuum.

Congregational annual review

Almost from the start of their exploration of LCM, congregations were invited to undertake an annual review of their mission and ministry. Facilitated by the PLCM Officer and in the presence of the bishop, the whole congregation carried out a self-assessment of their life together. Drawing on the liturgical resource of the Baptismal Covenant contained within our Initiation Service, this review was usually completed during or after the Sunday Eucharist and engaged all ages in preparatory work, reflection on the previous year, discussion and planning for the future.

For many congregations, this review proved invaluable, offering a necessary complement to the business reports required at an Annual General Meeting. Its processes of collaboration, self-review and agreed targeted planning removed the fearfulness engendered by external diocesan audits. The presence and participation of the bishop gave real substance and meaning to pastoral oversight.[5]

Congregational competencies

A competency framework for individuals under training for ministry was introduced by the Theological Institute for the Scottish Episcopal Church (TISEC) in 2001. Since collaborative ministry presupposes the sharing of gifts and ministries within a congregation and in any Ministry Support Team which might arise, an individualistic approach was unsuitable for use in LCM congregations where the range of competencies would be expected to be evidenced and developed across the whole gifted congregation. The PLCM Officer reshaped the competency framework for congregational use as a tool for Ministry Support Teams and/or as part of the Annual Review.

LCM workbooks

In response to regular requests from local congregations for information, education and skills training, the PLCM Officer wrote a series of resource workbooks. LCM has a foundational principle that Christian education should be delivered at the local level and available to all the baptized;

so such workbooks were initially designed for use in and by small LCM congregations. Covering basic topics, such as mission, ministry, church life and others, they contained practical learning and skilltraining based on solid theological foundations. Widely praised by those for whom they were designed, these workbooks have been used by churches of all sizes and traditions throughout Scotland and exported to other Anglican provinces and denominations.

2008 – the year of change

By 2008, LCM had an accepted and valued place within the formal structures of the Episcopal Church. It was an integral part of the SEC's mission strategy and found its natural home within the Provincial Home Mission Committee's policy titled 'The Journey of the Baptised' (SEC 2003). The Committee responded to the growth of LCM by establishing an LCM Mentor Scheme. About 15 theological reflectors/facilitators were recruited to work with LCM congregations, providing regular contact, linking with the PLCM Officer and offering the support of a 'critical friend'.

For a number of reasons, the growth in LCM appeared to stall in 2008. First, some of the leaders of the LCM movement in Scotland changed jobs or stepped back from frontline advocacy of and work for LCM and there was a lack of people willing or able to step up to replace them.

Second, one of these who left at the end of her contract in 2008 was the PLCM Officer. Replacement by two (or possibly three) full-time or part-time stipendiary LCM workers across groupings of the seven dioceses was envisaged, but no additional resources were devolved to the dioceses to resource their LCM responsibilities.

Third, the province initiated a review of its strategies for mission and ministry, which placed on hold any developments in LCM. Lacking the input of the PLCM Officer, the newly instituted LCM Mentor Scheme struggled to establish itself, and some newer LCM congregations felt the effects of the withdrawal of support and resources.

Finally, as with any institution in a period of uncertainty, there was the subtle but substantial pressure on bishops and diocesan authorities to revert to the 'safe-mode' of time-tested working practices, and lively and often eccentric LCM congregations, which had often been considered within their dioceses to be 'loose cannons', were required to conform.

The strengths and weaknesses of LCM

In describing the development of LCM in Scotland, certain good and bad features have already been highlighted. It is also important to identify and examine five other areas which play a significant part in its history.

Underlying process

When LCM was introduced, no attempt was made formally to draw up strict regulations about the process of implementation. Rather, there evolved a process of encouragement and support for the development of a variety of local congregational and diocesan initiatives in the name and the spirit of LCM. A thousand seeds were scattered to see which might emerge and grow.

This meant that the interpretation of what constituted LCM was left to individual congregations. This could be regarded as a high-risk strategy. On the one hand, congregations with rotas of laypeople reading lessons and leading intercessions felt that they were already 'doing LCM' and had no further need to explore its wider principles and application. On the other hand, others believed that in not having clear boundaries, LCM contained a hidden and dangerous agenda, perhaps that of 'mass priests' or lay presidency, and so they resisted finding out more.

After a decade of experience of local (Mutual) ministry in six of its seven dioceses, the Anglican Church in New Zealand/Aotearoa drew up its first set of 'Guidelines for Mutual Ministry' in 1995/96. This came out of discussions by congregations and Mutual Ministry officers and brought together the good ideas and practices which seemed common across their parochial experiences. It provided an agreed framework for provincial conversations and a foundation for future development in the dioceses.

It was believed that a similar comprehensive and agreed understanding of LCM in Scotland would emerge leading to a distinctive articulation of the Scottish experience within a set of written guidelines or other policy documents and, in due course, to the introduction of any necessary canonical changes. This approach to process was built on the 'action–reflection' cycle of theological reflection, widely used in LCM congregations; was non-hierarchical in honouring the primacy of local experience and so was fundamentally appropriate to the LCM vision of how God might be known.

Although criticized in the early years of LCM, this methodology proved right. It enabled a multitude of new ideas to take root, grow and be established without being subject to constant unnecessary scrutiny. Some ideas flourished and became widely used in both LCM and traditional congregations (e.g. the principle of congregational calling of people to exercise ministries rather than asking for volunteers); some are still dormant (e.g. true proportionality between ordained and non-ordained in the corridors of diocesan and provincial power) and others have and may never surface (e.g. having truly local bishops).

This process did have a deep and fundamental flaw. LCM took root in local congregations, inspired and resourced by the province. The seven SEC dioceses neither endorsed the whole project nor adopted and sponsored individual LCM congregations. This lack of any real commitment to LCM at diocesan level proved a serious handicap when, in 2008–10, cutbacks in provincial financing led to a reappraisal by some bishops of the nature of the relationship between the province and diocese with calls for a greater focus on diocesan authority and initiative-taking in mission and ministry.

Structural changes

A second intentional policy followed in the introduction and development of LCM was to work within the flexibility offered by the existing canons and structures of the SEC wherever possible. Rather than creating a separate and distinct form of ministry, the existing licensing system was adapted and the provincial processes for selection and recruitment for ordination modified to accommodate LCM contexts (Morris 2006: 41).

Throughout the years of development, LCM found a particular niche within the SEC, and those involved in its advocacy intentionally built wide networks of relationships, official and unofficial. The PLCM Officers met regularly with bishops to advice them on the situation of congregations from their dioceses. Workshops, road shows and conferences were set up to invite all to hear about and discuss the principles of LCM. Every opportunity was seized to spread the message and integrate LCM into the arteries of the church rather than attempting time-consuming and enervating canonical change. But the policy also weakened the movement in that without any specific canons or structures offering protection, LCM congregations are left exposed and vulnerable if and when diocesan or provincial policies change.

Timescales

There is no doubt that substantial time is necessary for any form of ministry development to be implemented and successful. One bishop who is broadly sympathetic to the movement suggested that LCM ran too quickly ahead of itself and created too many antagonisms and false perceptions.

Internationally, the fruits of Mutual/Total/Shared ministry are now being seen in those dioceses, such as Northern Michigan in the United States and Auckland in New Zealand, which have sustained their practice for twenty years or more. It would have been good for all congregations engaged in the Scottish LCM to have had experience over similar timescale to provide the security in which to lay proper foundations and to effect changes in congregational perceptions. St John's Church in Selkirk, for example, speaks of a history of twenty-five years journeying towards Local Ministry, culminating in the appointment in 2007 of a Priest-in-Charge for a four-year term with the stated purpose of leading them into the next step of Collaborative Ministry. Foundations have been laid through participation in study courses, visits, workshops and the liturgy, and people have had time to find their own way into the development that is being explored (Cameron and Gavine 2008: 54).

In reality, it was often a crisis in the provision of eucharistic ministry which motivated a bishop to request the PLCM Officer to make an initial visit to a congregation. LCM sometimes became a fire-fighting measure, without proper consideration of either the context or the longer-term congregational or diocesan needs. In retrospect, it might have been wiser to have resisted some episcopal and diocesan pressures and recognized earlier that crisis intervention sometimes did more harm than good.

Diocesan interventions were sometimes too hasty and ill judged. This was evidenced in two particular ways. First, when problems did arise – power conflicts within a team or occasionally strained relationships with clergy who predated LCM – blame was often focused exclusively on the LCM process, and consequently, the diocese, in panic, tended to change policy, usually reverting to older models of ministry. There was an apparent reluctance to allow LCM congregations the same scope to handle conflict as would have been given to larger congregations.

Second, there were a number of occasions when clergy were appointed to an emerging LCM congregation without apparent reference to its history and context or an appreciation of the gifts and personality required to work effectively within an LCM congregation. Those experienced in LCM were rarely asked to advise about or engage in the interview process for such an appointment.

Theology

There are a number of scholarly theological works and reports from doctrinal commissions which set out the missiology and ecclesiology behind LCM forms of ministry development, and it was assumed that these would be sufficient to stimulate and resource debate within the SEC.[6] Additionally, papers on the diaconate, the nature of 'local', collaborative synodical government and the paradigm shift involved in Local Ministry and ordination were produced and circulated by the LCM Think Tank and Working Party in the period from 1995 to 2007. As requests to the SEC Doctrine Committee for discussion of matters, such as baptism, diaconal and priestly ministry and ordination were ignored, it was concluded that the theology of LCM as set out and interpreted in practice was generally acceptable to the wider church.

History has shown this assumption to be wrong. The strength of resistance to LCM, particularly from some clergy who questioned the whole nature of LCM and its 'radical' theology of ministry and ordination, constantly surprised its advocates and did not abate. On occasions when LCM was discussed formally or informally at synods and clergy conferences, the paramount concerns often raised – especially by younger clergy – were those of careers, professional status and job security. The personal authority of the rector/priest in a congregation seemed to be the biggest issue for traditionally trained non-stipendiary or retired clergy. The fundamental theology of LCM was rarely on the agenda or considered a worthwhile topic for discussion.

Theology was more apparent in the church's liturgy. The SEC's Ordinal[7] has a very clear expression of a theology of ministry arising out of baptism, and LCM takes this as its theological base. This contrasts with other episcopal services, such as liturgies used for the institution of a new rector, which articulate a more conservative theology of ministry. Similarly, despite many requests to the College of Bishops and individuals, the distinctive liturgical ministry of the diaconate that LCM was seeking to establish in congregational contexts was almost entirely neglected in the development of diocesan and episcopal liturgies.

It was a mistake to focus so much attention on the actual practice of implementing LCM in congregations at the expense of communicating what was going on through theological writing.

Training

This failure to communicate the theological basis of LCM was compounded by the lack of real and substantial changes to training being offered to students at the Theological Institute (TISEC). Relationships with this body were never easy, but over time, the provincial LCM Officer was invited to address the students at the annual Summer School, often receiving an enthusiastic response to her Presentation. After 2003, devolution of much of ministerial training to the dioceses gave the opportunity to introduce new ways of training, together with local congregation- or region-based learning on which LCM depends, but this was not taken up, and the underlying ethos of training post-devolution remained untouched.

Although collaboration is one of the competencies required, the implicit message given by the majority of the courses is that the priest-to-be will be a special creature outside of and to some extent above the congregation. Despite the church's parlous financial state since the millennium, this has been evidenced by a cry for more 'professionalism', based on higher educational qualifications, and a nostalgic yearning for a return to residential training.

A further factor was the desire of some bishops to have the priests within their dioceses, stipendiary or not, identifiable as a separate 'college' and so by implication deployable under their personal control. This ran counter to the priority of congregational accountability for OLMs within LCM ecclesiology. With recruitment and selection processes remaining in central control, those called and identified for ordination in an LCM congregation tended to be separated from others equally but differently gifted.

Ultimately, the implications of baptismal theology as empowering the whole people of God in ministry and mission presented both a theological and a practical challenge to existing authority. It was a real mistake not to appreciate how this process of empowerment could – and inevitably would – clash with the deeply enshrined powerbases of the clergy in Synods, TISEC and the College of Bishops.

Ordained Local Ministry within the Church of Scotland

It is ironic that at the same time that the SEC was withdrawing from LCM, the Church of Scotland at its General Assembly in 2011 agreed to initiate a programme of Ordained Local Ministry. The Kirk, the established church in Scotland, maintains a national parish network, with worship led by the ordained, graduate, ministry in every community. The stipendiary Minister of Word and Sacrament is supported by the ordained eldership, Readers, who may preach and offer pastoral care, and an increasingly significant Diaconate. The Auxiliary Ministry, intended to be a locally based, non-stipendiary ministry of Word and Sacrament, had struggled to become widely established, for reasons very similar to those seen in the SEC – largely because of the reluctance of stipendiary ministers to cede power. In 2011, there were only 46 Auxiliary Ministers throughout Scotland as compared with 900 parish ministers (called National Ministry, NM) and 200 chaplaincy ministers.

By 2011, the Church of Scotland acknowledged that the existing ministry pattern was unsustainable. With falls in congregational attendance and giving, the Ministries Council faced a deficit of £4.3 million. At the same time, 658 stipendiary ministers (70% of the workforce) were over fifty years of age and due to retire within fifteen years. The sustenance of the inherited parochial model would require 40 new ministers to be called and trained every year for twenty years. Faced with such a personnel and financial crisis, the Ministries Division drew up a radical policy which envisaged larger parochial units with stipendiary ministers as team leaders facilitating and enabling the gifts of all the membership in ministry and mission.

The aims of this policy were to balance the budget by 2014 by a reduction in the stipendiary numbers from 975 to 870. To achieve this would need greater flexibility and a different style of training for the stipendiary workforce, and the development of a locally based non-stipendiary ministry (Ordained Local Ministry). Auxiliary Ministers would be incorporated into the OLM, and the Readership would have the option to transfer if approved by a discernment and assessment processes. These processes contain local, presbytery and national representatives and are designed to assess all potential OLMs by the same criteria as used for stipendiary ministry.

Whereas the call expressed in ordination is identical, there would be a fundamental difference maintained in the functions of OLM and NM. OLMs would be appointed by a Presbytery (a group of parishes equivalent to a deanery in size but with significantly greater powers) to work either within a particular local parish or within the presbytery itself. They would not be able to apply for a stipendiary post (for which further training in leadership skills would be necessary) nor have an automatic right to work in another presbytery without fresh authorization.

The Church of Scotland has much to do to flesh out these basic proposals but already there is a willingness and enthusiasm to work ecumenically with the SEC and others to share ideas and models of good practice. In past years, ecumenical parishes have been established with a full recognition and interchange of ministry between denominations (e.g. Livingston in West Lothian, Murrayfield in Edinburgh). These have tended to be in centres of large populations, but with the advent of OLM in the established church, there may be a hope for the introduction of ecumenical LCM parishes in more rural and remote areas.

Into the future

By 2010, with fifteen years of experience of LCM in the SEC, the time would have been right to engage in a thorough process of review and assessment to produce a set of policies and guidelines for LCM for the future. There would have been an opportunity to reflect on the continuing enthusiasm for LCM found within the SEC, especially in those congregations which have quietly continued their development without external interferences.

It is now unlikely that such a rigorous and constructive exercise will be undertaken in the rush to produce flagship alternative policies and programmes. If the timescale for the introduction of LCM might have been criticized as being too quick, the fear is that there is likely to be an even quicker flight away from it.[8]

In 2011, a new policy document emerged from the Provincial Mission and Ministry Board and was approved by the General Synod. First, in what is described as a 'Whole-Church' approach, there is a substantial shift from a provincial to diocesan policy and focus for mission. There is a consensus that now, more than ever before, a bishop has to be the leader of mission within the diocese.[9] This role is primarily undertaken in the identification and development of the existing missional energies within their diocese. To assist in this process, Diocesan Mission Officers would be appointed. In consequence, there is a significantly reduced profile for the province, whose future role is limited to

> being a supporter and resourcer for dioceses in their mission, enabling the development of consistent and coherent patterns of mission and ministry across the dioceses and encouraging appropriate inter-diocesan collaboration and co-operation. (SEC GS 2011: 121)

The experience of LCM has demonstrated not only the value of such diocesan ownership but also the necessity for formal provincial structures in a body which is still provincially governed by General Synod, the College of Bishops and canon law.

Second, the new diocesan mission focus is based on congregational missional leadership being exercised by stipendiary clergy. Although it recognizes that 'this is not exclusively the task of clergy' (SEC GS 2011: 124), most of the new policy focuses on the recruitment, ministerial development and deployment of suitable candidates for leadership and uses the term 'vocation' exclusively for the ordained. The policy recognizes that

> Congregations should strive to be world-facing communities, able to make connections with all who seek hospitality, community and a spiritual home. . . . They should be populated by missional disciples who are equipped and encouraged to live as active apostles of Christ in the world, naturally fulfilling the Great Commission in their daily lives and work. (SEC GS 2011: 122)

But there is little suggestion how this is to be brought about in practice. The contrast with the previous mission policy ('The Journey of the Baptised') is marked in style (clerically rather than congregationally led) and language (disciples/apostles rather than baptismal ministry). The experience of LCM has demonstrated the continuing need for trained and (where possible) stipendiary workers to resource congregations in mission but that ordination is not an absolute job requirement. LCM experience found that it is usually from 'missional disciples' or 'active apostles' that the best local leadership of mission is to be found.

Third, where the 'Whole-Church' policy discusses patterns of ministry, it accepts that

> The challenges of ministry in Scotland – particularly in large geographical areas where the population is small – have always been recognized in our church as calling for flexibility and creativity in the provision of ministry. (SEC GS 2011: 123)

and acknowledges that financial viability and stipendiary ministry in every context will never be a possibility. Few of the LCM insights into flexibility, creativity and congregational self-sufficiency appear in the body of the text. Alongside the acknowledgement of the need for substantial local flexibility in new models of ministry, the policy simultaneously argues for coherence in their application across the province, which raises the spectre of a more rigidly defined training framework and greater central control.

Conclusion

Although it is suggested that the effect of the new 'Whole Church' policy will be to mainstream LCM within the life of the SEC, it is difficult to see how that will take place in practice when so many of the structures that supported LCM congregations have been dismantled. The new policy seems rather to be an intentional rolling back of the advances in congregational empowerment that LCM has brought over the last fifteen years with a reversion to older theologies and models. There has always been a healthy discussion in the SEC as to whether LCM can be easily accommodated in our existing church traditions or whether it should be understood as a new way (a 'fresh expression') of being church. Initial attempts to make LCM work within the context of the known and loved SEC were successful but it may be that a different economic, social and ecclesiological context requires a different and perhaps more radical approach.

The next decade should provide some answers to this question. In the interim, many small congregations throughout Scotland will continue to implement LCM in their work of local mission and worship, sometimes without much outside support and resourcing. They have concluded that, whatever province or diocese may do or not do, not only is LCM the only realistic way forward for them, but they have found that it also continues to bring great joy and meaning to their Christian experience.

Notes

1   The development of LCM in St John's, Dumfries, in the Diocese of Glasgow and Galloway is an exception to this general principle. This large congregation (120–150 regular worshippers on an average Sunday) began the exploration of LCM as a result of work undertaken on size transition with a Consultant from the Alban Institute, and the desire to extend their mission. Part of the LCM process titled 'Soaring with the eagle' involved the pledging of £20,000 for five years to a street worker working with homeless children in Colombia.

2   'Christians must ask theological questions: at their simplest, what God is saying and doing, what words of judgement and hope there are for us in a present crisis' (Forrester 2000: 63). For further theological reflection on the role of finance, see Allen 1962a: 49–61.

3   SEC Directory 2010/11.

4   The resident membership of the little congregation of All Saints, Inveraray, on the Mull of Kintyre, is often in single figures but they have an active ministry both in the community and to many visitors who come to the town. They write: '(The) PLCM Officer has been an inspiration, assessing our weakest points, supporting and encouraging when difficulties arise, invaluable in guidance. We could not be the church we are without this kind of Provincial support' (Cameron and Gavine 2008).

5   The Diocese of Glasgow and Galloway now requires all congregations to undertake an Annual Review as part of the 2011 mission policy.

6   Especially, ACCM (1974), WCC (1982), Tiller (1983), Zabriskie (1995), Maybee (2001), Greenwood (2002), Thew Forrester (2003).

7   Scottish Ordinal Edinburgh General Synod of the Scottish Episcopal Church 1984.

8   'A strong current of nostalgia for the days when the Church had a place in stable communities makes for an absence of clear thinking and a tendency to look for fast solutions in addressing the sharp questions that are arising' (Greenwood 2002: 9).

9   'The understanding of episcopal ministry shared by current members of the College of Bishops places a growing value on the role of the bishop as "leader of mission" and the diocese as the primary location for the engendering of missional energy' (SEC GS 2011: 120).

OLM stories

The testimonies which intersperse the following chapters have been collected by Canon Kathy Lawrence, Senior Local Ministry Officer in the diocese of Gloucester. Here she explains the context. Later, following Chapter 10, she summarizes the key insights from this empirical material.

Gloucester Diocese was one of the first to embrace the concept of Local Ministry Teams from which vocations to Ordained Local Ministry were identified. This had far reaching implications which, apart from the visionaries involved in setting up and pioneering the scheme, were not immediately apparent to those who authorized it. As a result, there was a mixed reception and a certain amount of hostility which still persists. In recent years, the changes (discussed in Chapter 10) have seen a major reduction in the investment and commitment to Ordained Local Ministry. OLMs have been re-categorized as Associate Priests, their OLM identity swept away at the stroke of a pen. Several OLMs have been redeployed as non-stipendiaries or 'House for Duty' clergy and now operate away from their team and parish of origin. Some OLMs in large rural multi-parish benefices have felt obliged to take on sole responsibility for a parish and its Parochial Church Council, as their incumbents struggle to cope with the increased responsibility that goes with pastoral reorganization. For some OLMs this has been confusing; it has undermined their vocational identity. Others have found that they were ready to take on extra responsibility, and a few have seen this as a way of being taken more seriously as a priest, even though it has meant compromising their original calling to Ordained Local Ministry, working with and within a Local Ministry Team.

OLM–LM has raised awareness of the breadth of vocations to ministry particularly as expressed by the non-ordained. OLM–LM invites a reconfiguring of institutional perceptions of 'ordinary' Christians; and a new recognition that 'local' does not necessarily mean 'inexpert' but rather can be seen as 'respected' and 'empowered'. In order to understand this better, we need to listen to those who are ministering as Christ's Body locally to appreciate their difficulties and their potential. We need to recognize their enormous self-doubt, their lack of confidence in ministry, their deeply rooted reluctances, their assumptions about dependency and about vocation; and at the same time to know and affirm their strengths, their gifts, memories and aspirations that comprise the collective personality of every congregation. Instead of just listening to the stories of the incumbent, the Area Dean, the Archdeacon, the Diocesan Director of Ordinands, the Director of Ministry or the Bishop, we need to acquire more self-knowledge and understanding by listening to the other stories, those which remain untold, unheard or ignored, of those who comprise the majority of the royal priesthood, the Body of Christ as well as the OLM stories included in this book.

Four OLMs from Gloucester Diocese volunteered to tell their stories. For reasons of anonymity, their names have been changed. They reflect a spectrum of experience and years of service within a breadth of socio-economic contexts. Each conversation begins with the words: 'Tell me about your journey as an OLM.'

6

The empirical evaluation of OLM

Leslie Francis

Introduction

According to the Gospel tradition, when Jesus' followers asked him profound theological questions, he often responded by inviting them to become keen empirically based scientists. When the disciples asked Jesus to talk theologically about the Kingdom of God in Mark 4, Jesus invited them to go and to observe the sower and to note carefully what they observed. There seemed to be a consistent pattern emerging that associated growth with the good soil, rather than with the path, the stony ground or the thorny patch. On another occasion, Jesus invited them to go and to observe the baker in the kitchen and to document the activity of the yeast. Here is the biological scientist at work. On yet another occasion, Jesus invited them to become participant observers at the feast and to document the behaviour of the guests. Here is the social scientist at work. There seems then to be sound dominical authority for the empirical sciences to be brought into play in assessing matters of theological import.

Working within the contemporary tradition of empirical theology, as modelled by the *Journal of Empirical Theology*, the present chapter sets out to examine the range of empirical evidence so far available relevant to assisting our understanding of and our evaluation of Ordained Local Ministry as exercised and expressed within the Church of England. The first part of this chapter provides a relatively succinct overview of six main strands of empirical research relevant to this field. The second part of this chapter provides a more detailed introduction to a new study that sets out to assess whether the introduction of Ordained Local Ministry brought discernable benefits to those dioceses that have introduced this form of ministry, in comparison with those dioceses that have not done so.

Researching Ordained Local Ministry

In spite of the controversial nature of Ordained Local Ministry, and in spite of the significant claims that could be made regarding both the beneficial and detrimental impact of this development, very little empirical research has been undertaken to assess this crucial experiment within the life of the Church of England. While this lack of concern with empirical evidence is not, in any sense, unusual in the life of major churches, it is, nonetheless, possibly unwise. The empirical research so far conducted into various aspects of Ordained Local Ministry can be grouped within six main categories concerned with: listening to the views of stipendiary clergy; listening to the experiences of Ordained Local Ministers (OLMs) themselves; listening to perceptions concerning the training programmes; assessing the impact of training on the development of the candidates; profiling the history and development of Ordained Local Ministry within an individual diocese and listening to the perceptions of diocesan bishops.

One strand of research has examined the views of stipendiary clergy concerning the development of Ordained Local Ministry. Davies et al. (1991: 61) in their book *Church and Religion in Rural England* investigated the view of stipendiary rural clergy on those who were at that time called locally ordained ministers (LOMs). They found that 44 per cent of those surveyed thought LOMs were good, 16 per cent could see problems but thought that these problems could be resolved and 32 per cent thought they were bad. A major problem of orders was found in the survey and the question 'is it possible to be a priest in an Anglican church and not be "acceptable" throughout the Anglican Communion' was raised. On average, 10 per cent of the clergy thought that the idea of Ordained Local Ministry was bad because of the notion of a restricted ministry. Other comments included that they were too close to the people, that prophets were not without honour except in their own country, that such a person may serve for too long a period and that they get all the 'kudos with none of the responsibility'. All in all, at the time when this survey was conducted, the idea of the non-stipendiary priest seemed to take preference over the ordained local priest. The idea of listening to the perceptions of stipendiary clergy on the important development of Ordained Local Ministry perhaps makes enough sense to justify replicating this aspect of Davies' project some twenty-five years on.

A second strand of research has listened to OLMs themselves speak about their post-ordination experience of ministry. A major strength of the report *Strangers in the Wings* (Advisory Board of Ministry 1998) was that it included a questionnaire survey conducted among those ordained to local ministry, providing both quantitative and qualitative data. This survey drew 65 responses from an unspecified number of questionnaires distributed. The data enabled the following issues to be explored: the social profile of the OLMs; a profile of the benefices in which they served; their liturgical role; the role of appraisal within Ordained Local Ministry; the effects of ordination on a minister's personal life; the effects of and on the family; adjustments in work and in community; the acceptance of Local Ministry and relationships with the bishop and the incumbent.

According to chapter four of *Strangers in the Wings*, of the 65 OLMs who responded to the survey, at the time of ordination, 30 were in full-time paid employment, 10 were in part-time paid employment and 20 were retired (leaving 5 unaccounted for). Of the occupations that were classified, 22 were defined as professional occupations and 11 as managerial and administration occupations. The most frequently cited occupational category was the teaching profession (15). The average age of the respondents was fifty-seven years. Most of the respondents lived in the benefice in which they served (47) and a further 17 lived just over the parish boundary in a nearby town. Of the 47 who lived in the benefice, 36 had lived there for more than ten years. The largest group of the respondents described their churchmanship as central (25), followed by open evangelical (15), modern catholic (9), conservative evangelical (8) and traditional catholic (4).

The final conclusion from this survey reads as follows:

> Many respondents felt that they were not accepted as a 'proper' priest by other clergy – indeed, that they were 'second class.' Several examples of this were offered, some in considerable detail. Support from the incumbent was considered central to the LNSM's experience, and in some cases this was not forthcoming. This situation can lead to anxiety, frustration and disillusionment. While LNSMs 'muddle on,' as one respondent says: 'I don't think it an adequate response merely to hope it will go away!' Some respondents thought that other members of the church needed (re) training to work effectively with LNSMs. (Advisory Board of Ministry 1998: 64)

A second study in this tradition was provided by Watkin (2006) in his report 'A survey of ordained local ministry in the Diocese of Lichfield'. Again, this survey generated both quantitative and qualitative data. For example, using quantitative data, he found that all OLMs were engaged in eucharistic presidency, in leading Sunday worship and in preaching. The proportions were lower for conducting baptisms (91%), conducting funerals (91%), leading mid-week worship (82%) and conducting weddings (74%). Using qualitative data, he found a diversity of experience. One OLM said that 'I would describe my ministry as assistant. There are few opportunities for me to initiate a project or design new approaches.' Another OLM gave a very different account, saying that 'My pastoral and church-based ministry is exactly as that of the incumbent and I have a reasonably free hand to take that where I will'. Watkin formulated the following conclusion from his data.

> The survey data confirms the strongly held view that OLMs are well positioned to consolidate and to build relationships and to form local faith communities. They reinforce the identity of the church within the locality, and extend its relevance and its concern for God's people into workplace and other secular contexts, within and often beyond the geographical confines of the parish. They are agents of mission within our church. They constitute a new form of ordained ministry that has been called to 'proclaim afresh' the faith that our church is called to do in each generation.

These two studies reported by the Advisory Board for Ministry (1998) and by Watkin (2006) offer good examples of how a mixture of quantitative and qualitative data generated by questionnaire surveys can be used to examine the perceptions of those actually engaged in Ordained Local Ministry. There would be value in building on this foundation.

A third strand of research has focused specifically on evaluating the training provided for OLMs by listening both to the candidates and to the incumbents with whom they work. Bracegirdle (2005) employed a mixed-method approach including a questionnaire sent to 56 OLMs (80 % response) and to 47 incumbents (60 % response). The five main conclusions drawn from these data were that there were higher levels of dissatisfaction with the course in the early years; there was a feeling from incumbents and OLMs that sufficient post-ordination links with the training scheme were not there; there was recognition of a great variation in candidates' prior learning; there was a strong feeling among OLMs against shared teaching with other groups and most OLMs recognized a continued value in what they were able to learn during training. This research model of listening to the perceptions of the training programme held both by candidates and by incumbents offers really useful developmental feedback for those who provide training.

A fourth strand of research has focused on the way in which the programme of training for Ordained Local Ministry impacts on the self-image of the candidate. Jordan (2008) interviewed what she styles 'an illustrative sample' of OLM ordinands and those recently ordained (the precise number is not disclosed), and compared these responses with theological, psychological and sociological approaches to identity formation. The data revealed a reluctance to change in ways that would threaten relationships with the congregation. Here again is a seminal exercise in research that would be well worth replication and extension.

A fifth strand of research has taken the case study approach. The collection of essays edited by Torry and Heskins (2006) set out to profile the development of Ordained Local Ministry within the Diocese of Southwark and to evaluate its contribution to the life of the diocese. The range of perspectives employed included chapters by Ted Roberts (2006) who pioneered the experiment, by Stephen Lyon (2006) who served as the first principal of the Southwark Ordained Local Ministry Scheme in 1992 and by Nigel Godfrey (2006) who served as principal of the scheme at the time of writing. Alyson Peberdy (2006) profiled the incumbents' views of working alongside OLMs by drawing on her own experience, by interviewing 11 incumbents in depth and by seeking wider written comments. Another two chapters are provided by two clergy serving in Ordained Local Ministry in the diocese, Arthur Obiora (2006) who was ordained in 1995 and Eileen Serbutt (2006) who was ordained in 2001. Jeffrey Heskins (2006) listened to a sample of clergy serving in Ordained Local Ministry in the diocese, representing a mixture of men and women, and of different ethnicities. Heskins commented on his sample as follows.

> Each served a different category of community, of which some were urban, some rural, and some from the suburbs of London. Most had been ordained priest for three or four years, and one was still in deacon's orders. All were well established in the communities they had been called to serve and most had undertaken a variety of different ministries in the local church. (Heskins 2006: 104)

In this collection of essays, the Diocese of Southwark has provided the wider Church of England with a very useful account of a local experiment. This is a model that other dioceses may wish to consider following in order to help to evaluate and to assess their own experiences.

A sixth strand of research has tried to gain an overview of how diocesan bishops within the Church of England view the development of Ordained Local Ministry. In 2006, the Bishop of Norwich, in his capacity as Chair of the Ministry Division of the Church of England, wrote directly to the diocesan bishops. From the pool of 43 dioceses, he received 35 substantive responses. These responses were summarized in a Ministry Division paper given the working title, *OLM: A Ministry in Flux* (AC 2007a). Twelve responses were broadly in favour of OLMs. Six responses indicated that a review of Ordained Local Ministry was taking place in the diocese, four responses indicating that the diocese was looking into the possibility of OLM and a further two responses were either reconsidering Ordained Local Ministry or raising serious questions about it. Fourteen responses indicated that the diocese did not have an OLM Scheme and was not likely to have one. Three responses gave no strong views.

Those with OLM Schemes reflected that there was a value in having OLM Schemes. It was felt that Ordained Local Ministry gave a healthy understanding of vocation, that Ordained Local Ministry had rediscovered the local or contextual dimensions of ministry, that collaborative learning helped to build teams and that there was some flexibility about Ordained Local Ministry and deployment.

There were also objections to Ordained Local Ministry. Some concerns were voiced that it undermines the catholicity of ministry, that Ordained Local Ministry introduces a different status in ministry, that OLMs do in fact move parishes because of the fluid nature of society and that candidates have the same profile as other self-supporting ministers, but have a less demanding training than is offered by the regional courses.

The overview supplied by the report suggests that Ordained Local Ministry is understood by different dioceses in different ways and that the debate surrounding this category of ministry is extremely fluid. However, around this time, the Diocese of Southwark decided to withdraw from Ordained Local Ministry and the scheme in the Diocese of Truro ceased to recruit. Towards the end of the first decade of the twenty-first century, Ordained Local Ministry seemed not only to be a ministry in flux, but a ministry in question. The idea of listening to diocesan bishops through a systematic enquiry may prove, within an episcopal church, a very sensible way in which to assess the direction of strategy on controversial issues like Ordained Local Ministry.

These six strands of empirical research pose a range of different research questions, employ a range of different research methods, and reflect different levels of research rigour. Taken together, however, they demonstrate a serious commitment to the empirical evaluation of an important innovation within the ministry of the Church of England and a selection of empirical evidence against which practice can be assessed.

Assessing the impact of
Ordained Local Ministry

The empirical research so far reviewed in this chapter has listened in a disciplined and systematic way to a range of views on Ordained Local Ministry and to the experiences both of those serving as OLMs and of those working with OLMs. None of these studies, however, has tried to assess the impact of Ordained Local Ministry on the life of the dioceses that have embraced this form of ministry. The study undertaken and reported by Jones et al. (2011) set out to fill this gap.

Jones et al. (2011) started from the assumption that, when dioceses undertake serious experiments in ministry, these experiments are not an end in themselves, but they are undertaken for some purpose. Returning to the parable of the sower, from which this chapter started, it is reasonable to assume that changes made to the sower's activity may result in changes in the patterns of growth. Changes made to the ways in which dioceses overall develop and resource ministry may result in changes in the patterns of growth (or decline) within those dioceses. Such an assumption, nonetheless, is far from easy to investigate with empirical techniques without making further assumptions about how growth in dioceses (or growth in the Kingdom of God) may be assessed. Critics of our standpoint in empirical theology are ready to note that growth in the Kingdom of God may well elude empirical observation.

Our defence against such criticism is twofold. First, we are keen to remain loyal to the dominical command to continue to observe and to note the experience of the sower who sows the seed, of the baker who kneads the yeast and of the master of ceremonies who organizes the feast. Second, we are among the first to admit that our empirical observations and our empirical measures can capture only a part of the tale, but we maintain that this part of the tale is at least worth taking seriously.

Against this background and with these caveats, we noted that in 2001, there were, according to the statistics published centrally by the Church of England, 20 dioceses that had licensed OLMs serving within them and 23 dioceses that had no serving licensed OLMs. Where dioceses had OLMs, the number ranged from 1 in Birmingham to 54 in Manchester, with an average of 20.3 (standard deviation = 16.6). The full picture in 2001 was as follows. The dioceses with OLMs were as follows: Birmingham (1), Blackburn (2), Canterbury (7), Carlisle (7), Gloucester (10), Guildford (29), Hereford (9), Lichfield (32), Lincoln (21), Liverpool (23), Manchester (54), Newcastle (5), Norwich (29), Oxford (42), St Edmundsbury and Ipswich (47), Salisbury (23), Sodor and Man (3), Southwark (43), Truro (13) and Wakefield (6). The dioceses without OLMs at that time were as follows: Bath and Wells, Bradford, Bristol, Chelmsford, Chester, Chichester, Coventry, Derby, Durham, Ely, Exeter, Leicester, London, Peterborough, Portsmouth, Ripon and Leeds, Rochester, St Albans, Sheffield, Southwell, Winchester, Worcester and York.

Given that, by 2001, roughly half of the dioceses of the Church of England had embraced OLMs and roughly half had not, we wondered whether it might be reasonable to employ other statistics published centrally by the Church of England in their series *Church Statistics* and *Statistics of Licensed Ministers* to learn about the correlates of the development of Ordained Local Ministry. On further consideration, we refined our research objective to compare the performances of dioceses with and without OLMs over the period 1991–2003, the period during which this form of ministry became established, and a period embracing the Decade of Evangelism. In particular, we judged it reasonable to ask three specific research questions of the available statistics.

The first research question compares the background characteristics of these two sets of dioceses. Were these two sets of diocese distinctively different? The second research question compares the progress and performance of these two sets of dioceses during the subsequent decade. While, during the key period (1991–2003), the Church of England experienced overall decline across a range of membership indicators, it might be reasonable to hypothesize that effective developments in the area of ministry might help to slow down the rate of decline. Did those dioceses that espoused Ordained Local Ministry experience a lower rate of decline in comparison with those that did not espouse Ordained Local Ministry? The third research question concerns specifically the relationships between Ordained Local Ministry and Reader ministry. Overall, has the development of Ordained Local Ministry released a wholly new pool of vocations to authorized ministry or has this form of ordained ministry provided an alternative route for some who may otherwise exercise the ministry of Reader?

The extent to which we may be able to provide satisfactory answers to these questions is dependent on the usefulness of the indicators we are able to extract from the two series *Church Statistics* and *Statistics of Licensed Ministers*. From these sources, we constructed four kinds of indicators that we styled: baseline diocesan statistics, membership statistics, performance statistics and Reader statistics. We will summarize these four areas in turn, recognizing that fuller information is available in Jones et al. (2011).

Baseline diocesan statistics

Baseline data for diocesan size were taken from 1991 (assuming there was little significant change over the next decade), and comprised figures for population, geographical area (in square miles) and numbers of benefices, parishes and churches. Baseline data for diocesan clergy were taken for 2001 and comprised number of stipendiary clergy, number of non-stipendiary ministers (NSMs) and number of OLMs recorded as a separate category.

Membership statistics

The Church of England collects a range of figures from dioceses that reflect membership and activity related to membership. Those used in this analysis were as follows: numbers on electoral rolls, usual Sunday attendance, Easter communicants, Christmas communicants, infant baptisms (less than one year old), all baptisms, infant baptisms per 100 live births and confirmation candidates. To estimate changes over the decade, average figures for 1991–93 and for 2001–03 were calculated for each diocese. We employed these average figures in order to smooth out some of the more random fluctuations that occur year by year.

Performance statistics

These were derived from the above statistics by calculating the percentage change in membership statistics over the decade. Performance statistics were compared between OLM and non-OLM dioceses using one-way analyses of variance.

Reader statistics

Statistics on Readers were included in order to check whether the presence of Ordained Local Ministry had a significant impact on recruitment and retention within Reader ministry. Since there were no published figures for the number of Readers in 2003, the average of 2001, 2002 and 2004 was used instead.

Assessing statistical evidence

Our first research question wanted to compare the background characteristics of the two sets of dioceses, the 20 dioceses that had developed Ordained Local Ministry and the 23 dioceses that had not developed Ordained Local Ministry. Were these two sets of dioceses distinctively different? This is what we found.

First, we compared the two sets of dioceses in terms of the geographical areas covered, the total population of people living in the diocese and the population density, all as shown by the 1991 figures. There were no significant differences between the two sets of dioceses on any of these three measures. Second, we compared the two sets of dioceses in terms of the numbers of churches, parishes and benefices, again as shown by the 1991 figures. Again, there were no significant differences between the two sets of dioceses on any of these three measures. In other words, there was no evidence to suggest that OLMs had been developed mainly in dioceses with low population density (which might suggest rural rather than urban dioceses) or in dioceses with an above average number of churches to staff. Indeed, there are many cases of dioceses with similar profiles that either did or did not develop Ordained Local Ministry. The decision to adopt OLMs seems to have been made for reasons other than the particular nature of the diocese.

Third, we compared the two sets of dioceses in terms of the numbers of stipendiary clergy and of NSMs in post in 2001. Again, there were no significant differences between the two sets of dioceses on these measures. The data suggested two very similar sets of dioceses staffed by similar numbers of stipendiary and non-stipendiary clergy. Although there was considerable variation between dioceses in terms of stipendiary and non-stipendiary clergy, this variation did not seem to be related to whether or not they supported Ordained Local Ministry. In other words, there was no evidence to suggest that OLMs have been deployed mainly in dioceses where there were fewer stipendiary clergy or fewer non-stipendiary clergy. Moreover, there was no evidence to suggest that the development of Ordained Local Ministry detracted from the recruitment and retention of non-stipendiary clergy. In this sense, the OLMs served as a complete bonus to those dioceses in which they served.

Fourth, we compared the two sets of dioceses in terms of their membership statistics at the beginning of the period under investigation (1991–93). Yet again, there were no significant differences between these two sets of dioceses in terms of the membership data available to us. Overall, dioceses that had adopted Ordained Local Ministry were similar to dioceses that had not adopted Ordained Local Ministry, in terms of electoral roll registrations, usual Sunday attendance, communicants at Easter, communicants at Christmas, infant baptisms, infant baptisms calculated as percentage of live births, all baptisms and confirmations. These data suggest that Ordained Local Ministry was not adopted by dioceses either in the face of low performance or as a consequence of particularly good performances.

Our second research question wanted to compare the progress and performance throughout the period 1991–2003 of the two sets of diocese, the 20 dioceses that had developed Ordained Local Ministry during this period and the 23 dioceses that had not developed Ordained Local Ministry during this period. While recognizing that during this key period of the Decade of Evangelism, the Church of England experienced overall decline across a range of membership indicators, we had argued that it might be reasonable to hypothesize that effective developments in the areas of ministry might help to slow down the rate of decline. Did those dioceses that espoused Ordained Local Ministry experience a lower rate of decline in comparison with those that did not espouse Ordained Local Ministry? This is how we set about answering our second research question and what we found.

It was, in a sense, good news that we found no significant differences in the membership statistics between the two sets of dioceses at the beginning of the period of investigation (1991–93). This meant that the two sets of dioceses began, as it were, on a level playing field. Our task then was to calculate the rate of decline that had taken place between the early 1990s and the early 2000s on each of the nine membership indicators available to us. In order to smooth out chance fluctuations, the figures for the early 1990s were calculated on the average of the figures reported for 1991 and 1993, and the figures for the early 2000s were calculated on the average of the figures reported for 2001 and 2003. The findings from these two sets of dioceses were remarkably similar. Over the decade, electoral roll figures had declined by 14.1 per cent in OLM dioceses and by 13.6 per cent in other dioceses. Usual Sunday attendance had declined by 19.1 per cent in OLM dioceses and by 18.9 per cent in other dioceses. Easter communicants had declined by 20.1 per cent in OLM dioceses and by 18.7 per cent in other dioceses. Christmas communicants had declined by 21.2 per cent in OLM dioceses and by 20.9 per cent in other dioceses. Infant baptisms had declined by 57.3 per cent in OLM dioceses and 56.5 per cent in other dioceses. Infant baptisms as a percentage of live births had declined by 50.3 per cent in OLM dioceses and by 50.5 per cent in other dioceses. All baptisms had declined by 44.7 per cent in OLM dioceses and by 44.0 per cent in other dioceses. Confirmations had declined by 41.3 per cent in OLM dioceses and by 42.4 per cent in other dioceses.

Recognizing that numbers of OLMs varied greatly within the 20 dioceses that had adopted this form of ministry, we took this analysis one step further to test whether the actual number of OLMs predicted differences in the rate of decline. We found that, within OLM dioceses, there were no significant correlations between the percentage change in any of the membership statistics and the number of OLMs serving in the dioceses.

The only conclusion that can be drawn from these data is that, over the period 1991–2003, the adoption of Ordained Local Ministry does not seem to have had any influence on the decline in membership across the dioceses, at least as measured by these indicators. This conclusion is, of course, limited in two important ways. It is limited by the time period over which diocesan performance was assessed, namely the period 1991–2003. From a scientific point of view, this limitation could be addressed by replicating the current analyses for the period 2001–13 as soon as the data become available. It is also limited by the range of indicators over which diocesan performances could be assessed. From a scientific point of view, this limitation could be addressed, at least partially, by expanding the range of indicators available.

While many objections can be (and routinely are) made against assessing developments in the life of the church by means of crude performance indicators related to membership statistics, it may nonetheless be useful to know what can and what cannot be expected to be achieved through the development of Ordained Local Ministry initiatives in terms of the longer-term sustainability of the Church of England.

Our third research question wanted to explore the relationship between Ordained Local Ministry and Reader ministry by comparing the rate of growth (or decline) in Reader ministry within the two sets of dioceses, the 20 dioceses that had developed Ordained Local Ministry during this period and the 23 dioceses that had not developed Ordained Local Ministry during this period. Overall, has the development of Ordained Local Ministry released a wholly new pool of vocations to authorized ministry or has this form of ordained ministry provided an alternative route for some who may otherwise exercise the ministry of Reader? This is what we found.

Overall, throughout the Church of England as a whole, the number of licensed Readers within the 43 dioceses increased between the early 1990s and the early 2000s by about 15 per cent. The 20 OLM dioceses showed a smaller increase (8.8%) compared with the non-OLM dioceses (20.7%). Moreover, the number of OLMs in a diocese in 2001 was inversely correlated with the percentage change in licensed Readers during the previous decade. Of the 20 OLM dioceses, 9 (45%) showed a decline in Readers over the period, compared with only 1 (4%) of the 23 non-OLM dioceses. In order to complete the picture, it is also worth noting that two dioceses showed very high percentage increases in Readers over this period. Portsmouth, a diocese not promoting Ordained Local Ministry, showed a 66 per cent increase in Readers. Lincoln, a diocese promoting Ordained Local Ministry, showed a 96 per cent increase in Readers.

These statistics suggest that OLMs may be replacing licensed Readers in some dioceses. Where Ordained Local Ministry has become an option, individuals who may have tested their vocation for Reader ministry seem perhaps to be testing their vocation for Ordained Local Ministry instead. Since this conclusion is based solely on data for the period 1991–2003, this is an issue that would be worth investigating for the period 2001–13 as soon as the data become available.

Conclusion

This chapter set out to draw together and to assess the empirical studies relevant to an evaluation of Ordained Local Ministry within the Church of England. As is the general case with developments in the life of the Church of England, no central empirical research has been initiated to monitor this radical innovation in Anglican ecclesiology. Yet, a small group of empirical scientists has heeded the dominical command to go and to observe the sower and to record their observations. A range of different empirical methods has been used and a range of different research questions has been asked. Drawn together, these disparate studies begin to provide a useful, if somewhat inconclusive, source of empirical evidence on the experiences of those ordained as OLMs, on the perceptions held of this ministry by stipendiary clergy and by bishops, on the training provided for this ministry and on the impact of this ministry on those dioceses that have embraced it. The main conclusions are that for OLMs themselves, the experience is mixed, good for some and not so good for others; for stipendiary clergy and bishops, the experience is also mixed, with some dioceses ready to explore the development of Ordained Local Ministry afresh and other dioceses ready to withdraw from established programmes; and for the wider church, the experience is overall neutral, neither hastening nor abating the decline in church membership.

Colin's story

Colin was ordained as an OLM three years ago in a large rural market town with a small Local Ministry Team which saw the arrival of a new incumbent about four years ago.

It was suggested that the parish should explore the idea of having a Local Ministry Team and I remember really wanting to be called out to be a part of it. I was elated when my name was put forward through the calling out process. I was elated to think that people thought that I was capable of doing this . . . In the early days the team meetings were wonderful with a dozen of us meeting fortnightly and our incumbent being so supportive and enthusiastic. I remember him praying regularly that someone out of the team would go forward for ordination. Every time he prayed this, I felt a stirring in my tummy. I dismissed this because I thought I couldn't . . . I was divorced, and I was partially sighted so I could not drive.

I was put forward for selection just after the incumbent had left, so the parish was in vacancy.

Being in a team really helped my confidence which grew as we all took it in turns to lead worship, and we all recognized and affirmed gifts in each other and in doing different things.

To be an ordained person within my local area, my parish, was so important because I knew a lot of people and was on any number of committees. I know that many people found church difficult – even just stepping through the church door. I really felt that I could be a link for them but in a much more proactive way as an OLM. They knew me. I had grown up with them – I was trusted and known.

I am proud to be an OLM. Being a priest within my local community is a key role and a privilege to be able to serve the community in that way. I have been known here for some years – as 'the religious one' and it is almost as if the community recognized something in me before I did!'

There are challenges to being an OLM. Always being here in the parish when incumbents come and go. Experience demonstrates that a new incumbent can be appointed who does not understand LM or OLM. This has created difficulties over the past few years. There is also the fact that because I am local, people might prefer me over the incumbent as a 'new comer'. Since being priested three years ago, I haven't done a single funeral!

The language has been changed to associate priest after a curacy of three years as an OLM. So what does this mean for my vocation as an OLM? I have been given the strong impression that as an OLM I am seen as less of a colleague, whereas an Associate Priest is seen and treated as more of a colleague. There is a lot of confusion between status and vocation.

I have always known that my calling was to OLM. On the surface, there is no difference between OLM and Non-Stipendiary Ministry (NSM) etc. It is more a question of how I live and work out my priesthood as a local person.

I did go through a brief period, because no one was recognizing me as an OLM, of wondering whether I should be an NSM. OLM just seems to be treated as the bottom rung of a ladder which it shouldn't be. People do not understand it and keep going on about 'you're not allowed to be a priest out of your own parish.' It is not through lack of trying but priests just don't seem to understand the workings of different experiences of clergy ministries.

As for the future, I will be called an Associate Priest and still be part of a local and clergy team ministry. As a member of a deanery-wide clergy team, I can go to any of the deanery churches. However, being visually disabled and unable to drive is almost safeguarding my OLM identity. Being an OLM member of an LM team is good because I am there to offer support and vice versa. I would hope to carry on being a full member of a healthy LM team, to be involved in discerning and recognizing gifts in others and encouraging and enabling others, and to continue to build on my knowledge and experience of working with others.

7

The psychological profile of OLMs

Leslie Francis

Introduction

Some of the pioneers of Ordained Local Ministry in the Church of England, like Ted Roberts (1972, 2006), have argued that this form of ministry has the potential to recruit a very different kind of priest who is rooted in the local congregation, grounded in the local community and capable of proclaiming and living the Gospel in contexts less accessible to the seminary-trained, stipendiary and mobile professional clergy. The call, discernment and path to priesthood is highly distinctive for Ordained Local Ministers (OLMs). The onus of vocation is placed on a call by the local church from within its local membership. The tasks of theological education and priestly formation are rooted in the local community. The exercise of ordained ministry is limited by licence to the local church and generally within the context of an authorized and recognized ministry team.

If Ordained Local Ministry really is recruiting a very different kind of priest, then it is not unreasonable to try to identify what precisely these differences may be. Questions concerning mapping differences between two groups of people fall within the domain of psychology, and particularly within the field of the psychology of personality and individual differences. The present chapter is located within that field of psychology.

Working within the field of the psychology of personality and individual differences, the argument of the chapter develops in five stages. First, it introduces and discusses the broader context of the individual-differences approach as relevant both to psychology and to theology. Second, it focuses specifically on the model of personality built on the work of Carl Jung and reflected in psychological type theory and psychological temperament theory. Third, it examines the theoretical power of psychological type theory and psychological temperament theory to develop coherent models of individual differences in approaches to Christian ministry. Fourth, it examines the evidence generated by a series of empirical studies concerned with exploring the psychological type profiles and psychological temperament profiles of Church of England congregations, of mobile professional clergy serving in the Church of England and of OLMs serving in the Church of England. Fifth, the implications of these empirical studies are discussed for understanding the particular strengths and weaknesses of OLMs in relation both to congregational dynamics and to the working relationships between resident OLMs and mobile stipendiary clergy. Taken seriously, the psychology of personality and individual differences may have something really interesting to say about the experience of Ordained Local Ministry within the Church of England.

Studying individual differences

The association between personality and religious experience has been a topic of long-standing interest both within psychology and within theology. For theologians, the debate concerning the association between personality and religious experience is classically established by appeal to teaching about the nature of God and by drawing on sources of divine revelation (say scripture) to explore the transforming impact of God on individual lives. On this account, the religious experience becomes the independent variable and human personality becomes the dependent variable. For psychologists, the debate concerning the association between personality and religious experience is classically established by appeal to the psychological understanding of personality (variously conceived) and by drawing on psychological theory regarding ways in which a given variation in personality may influence a range of other individual differences, including religious and spiritual experience. On this account, human personality becomes the independent variable and religious experience becomes the dependent variable.

At this point, an already complex debate becomes more complex by recognition of the variety of ways in which the term 'personality' may be used both by theologians and by psychologists. In much of my own recent writings, I have tried to cut through this complexity by distinguishing between three different constructs which I have wanted to define as character, as personality and as psychological type (see, e.g. Francis 2005). All three constructs are of central importance both to theologians and to psychologists, but I want to argue that it is the notion of psychological type theory that can provide the most efficient and effective starting point for a debate in which both psychologists and (Christian) theologians can engage.

The term 'character' I take to be concerned with qualities that carry a moral valency. We can talk meaningfully about individuals who display a 'good character' and about individuals who display a 'bad character'. Both theologians and psychologists may be properly concerned with distinguishing between such morally laden qualities. Within the Christian tradition, for example, Galatians 5 is often cited as contrasting the moral qualities of the good character (the so-called fruits of the Spirit) with the moral qualities of the bad character (the so-called works of the flesh).

The term 'personality' I take to be concerned with those aspects of the human psyche that psychologists review when they attempt to provide inclusive accounts and measurement of human personality. The problem with such a broad definition is that there is no consensus among personality psychologists regarding what should and what should not be included within such a definition. In fact, the term 'personality' is currently used among personality psychologists to include at least three areas: deep-seated value-free descriptions of normal personality, fundamental descriptions of abnormal personality and psycho-pathologies and more surface and value-laden descriptions of individual differences. It is because of this wide range of usage that I prefer to draw on the notion of psychological type in order to generate dialogue between psychology and theology.

The term 'psychological type' has been defined from a theological perspective, by reference to a doctrine of creation according to which human beings are created to reflect a divine image that embraces and models individual differences. According to Genesis 1.27, both male and female are created in the image of God. By extension, other fundamental human differences, like ethnicity, must reflect the richness and diversity of the divine image. According to this principle, as a theologian, I define psychological type as embracing a small set of key individual differences which are largely immutable and go right to the heart of who an individual is (like sex and ethnicity). Such differences reflect the intention and the diversity of the divine creator and are in effect non-negotiable. From a psychological perspective, psychological type has been defined by reference to the pioneering work of Carl Jung in his classic book *Psychological types* (Jung 1971).

The choice to adopt the Jungian model of psychological type as the platform on which to construct a dialogue between psychology and theology may itself be controversial both among psychologists and among theologians. On the one hand, personality psychologists have been relatively slow to accord the same kind of esteem to the Jungian model of psychological type as accorded, say, to Raymond Cattell's notion of the 16 personality factor model of personality (Cattell et al. 1993), to Hans Eysenck's notion of the three-dimensional model of personality (Eysenck and Eysenck 1991), or to the more recent Big Five factor model of personality (Costa and McCrae 1985). The problem has been, in part, exacerbated by the comparative insularity and distinctive methodological procedures developed by pioneering researchers in the field of psychological type (including perhaps over-reliance on the *Journal of Psychological Type* which concentrates research in this area and keeps it apart from wider debate). In recent years, however, some real attempts have been made to mainstream research in psychological type theory, and such attempts are proving successful. On the other hand, theologians have either ignored or tended to be critical of the way in which psychological type theory has begun to penetrate the Christian community, as evidenced by the collection of essays edited by Kenneth Leech under the title, *Myers-Briggs: Some Critical Reflections* (Leech 1996). In recent years, however, some real attempts have been made to address such criticisms and to clarify some of the misunderstandings on which they have been based (Lloyd 2007).

However, the use of the Jungian model of psychological type has already been well established in church-related circles in Australasia (Dwyer 1995), North America (Baab 2000) and the United Kingdom (Duncan 1993). In particular, in many places, clergy are introduced to this way of thinking in initial ministerial training and in continuing professional development.

Psychological temperament and ministry

The model of psychological type, originally proposed by Jung (1971), has been developed and expanded through a series of psychometric indices, including the Myers–Briggs Type Indicator (MBTI: Myers and McCaulley 1985), the Keirsey Temperament Sorter (KTS: Keirsey and Bates 1978), and the Francis Psychological Type Scales (FPTS: Francis 2005). At its heart, psychological type theory distinguishes between two orientations (extraversion and introversion), two perceiving functions (sensing and intuition), two judging functions (thinking and feeling) and two attitudes towards the outer world (judging and perceiving).

An extension of psychological type theory proposed by Keirsey and Bates (1978), known as psychological temperament theory, has provided a particularly fruitful model in which different approaches to ministry could be located, as illustrated by Oswald and Kroeger (1988) in their book, *Personality Type and Religious Leadership*.

Psychological type data can be reported and interpreted in a number of different ways, drawing on the four dichotomous type preferences (the two orientations, the two perceiving functions, the two judging functions and the two attitudes); on the 16 complete types (like ISTJ or ENFP); on the four dominant types (dominant sensing, dominant intuition, dominant feeling or dominant thinking) or on the eight dominant and auxiliary pairs (like dominant thinking with auxiliary intuition or dominant intuition with auxiliary thinking). Keirsey and Bates (1978) proposed an interpretive framework drawing on and distinguishing between four temperaments characterized as SJ, SP, NT and NF.

In the language shaped by Keirsey and Bates (1978), the Epimethean Temperament characterizes the SJ profile, people who long to be dutiful and exist primarily to be useful to the social units to which they belong. The Dionysian Temperament characterizes the SP profile, people who want to be engaged, involved and doing something new. The Promethean Temperament characterizes the NT profile, people who want to understand, explain, shape and predict realties, and who prize their personal competence. The Apollonian Temperament characterizes the NF profile, people who quest for authenticity and for self-actualization, who are idealistic and who have great capacity for empathic listening. Oswald and Kroeger (1988) built on Keirsey and Bates' (1978) characterization of the four temperaments to create profiles of how these four temperaments shape four very different styles of religious leadership.

The Epimethean Temperament (SJ) is styled 'the conserving, serving pastor'. SJ clergy tend to be the most traditional of all clergy temperaments, bringing stability and continuity in whatever situation they are called to serve. They proclaim a single and straightforward faith, committed to down-to-earth rules for the Christian life. They serve as protectors and conservers of the traditions inherited from the past. If change is to take place, it emerges by evolution, not revolution. They excel at building community, fostering a sense of loyalty and belonging. They bring order and stability to their congregations, creating plans, developing procedures and formulating policies; and they are keen that these procedures should be followed. They can be trusted for their reliability, punctuality and efficiency. They are effective pastors, showing particular concern for the young, the elderly and the weak. They are realists who offer practical and down-to-earth solutions to pastoral problems.

The Dionysian Temperament (SP) is styled 'the action-oriented pastor'. SP clergy tend to be the most fun loving of all clergy temperaments, possessing a compulsive need to be engaged in activity. They have little need for or interest in the abstract, the theoretical and the non-practical aspects of theology and church life. They are flexible and spontaneous people who welcome the unplanned and unpredictable aspects of church life. They can bring the church to life with activities for everyone from cradle to grave. They have a flare for grasping the moment. They are entertainers and performers at heart. They are at their best in a crisis and are good at handling conflict resolution. They are better at starting new initiatives than at seeing things through. SP clergy may be particularly attracted to charismatic worship, responding to the leading of the Holy Spirit, welcoming a free-flowing form that allows for impromptu testimonials, speaking in tongues and spontaneous singing.

The Promethean Temperament (NT) is styled 'the intellectual, competence-seeking pastor'. NT clergy are the most academically and intellectually grounded of all clergy temperaments, motivated by the search for meaning, for truth and for possibilities. They are visionaries who need to excel in all they do, and they tend to push their congregations to excel as well. They enjoy the academic study and analysis of the faith, and may try to run their church as an extension of the seminary. They make great teachers, preachers and advocates for social justice. They look for underlying principles rather than basic applications from their study of scripture. They see the value of opposing views and strive to allow alternative visions to be heard. They are more concerned with finding truth than with engineering harmony and compromise. NT clergy need to be challenged in their ministry and to be able to move from one challenge to the next.

The Apollonian Temperament (NF) is styled 'the authenticity-seeking, relationship-oriented pastor'. NF clergy tend to be the most idealistic and romantic of all clergy temperaments, attracted to helping roles that deal with human suffering. They want to meet the needs of others and to find personal affirmation in so doing. They can be articulate and inspiring communicators, committed to influencing others by touching their hearts. They have good empathic capacity, interpersonal skills and pastoral counselling techniques. They find themselves listening to other people's problems in the most unlikely contexts, and really caring about them. NF clergy tend to be high on inspiration, but lower on the practical down-to-earth aspects of ministry. They are able to draw the best out of people and work well as the catalyst or facilitator in the congregation as long as others are on hand to work with and to implement their vision. They are at their best when leading in people-related projects, such as starting a project for the elderly or for youth. They are most comfortable in unstructured meetings where they are good at facilitating group decision-making processes.

Assessing the evidence

There is now quite a well-established research tradition that has explored the psychological type profile of local church congregations and commented on the way in which congregations tend to attract some types of people rather than other types. Anyone familiar with church congregations will recognize the clearly visible demographic characteristics of churchgoers: they tend to be weighted towards women rather than men and towards older rather than younger individuals. Psychological testing is able to bring some less visible factors into account as well. Overall, church congregations tend to attract feeling types rather than thinking types. The evidence for this is provided by studies conducted in the United States (Gerhardt 1983; Rehak 1998), in Canada (Delis-Bulhoes 1990; Ross 1993, 1995), in Australia (Robbins and Francis 2011) and Wales (Craig et al. 2003; Francis et al. 2007), as well as in England.

The first study of Church of England congregations was reported by Francis et al. (2004), drawing on 116 men and 211 women from five congregations. Compared with the general population, church congregations were weighted towards introverts, feeling types and judging types. In terms of psychological temperament, there was a clear over-representation of the Epimethean Temperament (SJ), accounting for 55 per cent of the women and 56 per cent of the men (see Table 1 in the Appendix to this chapter for a summary of these figures). The problem with this study is that it is based on a relatively small number of churchgoers.

The second study of Church of England congregations, reported by Francis et al. (in press), was much more ambitious, involving 1,169 men and 2,135 women. This larger study confirmed the trends found by the earlier study but also demonstrated even more clearly the over-representation of the Epimethean Temperament (SJ), this time accounting for 73 per cent of the women and 71 per cent of the men. This strong SJ preference helps to explain some of the key characteristics of church congregations and some of the ways in which church congregations seem to function. The SJ worldview, the Epimethean Temperament, is strongly committed to protecting and to preserving things as they are, the tradition as it has been inherited and the established way of doing things. The SJ worldview, the Epimethean Temperament, does not go out of its way to change things, or to welcome change when it is initiated (or imposed) by others.

Alongside the research tradition that has explored the psychological type profile of church congregations, stands an even better-established and more fully documented research tradition that has explored the way in which religious leadership tends to attract some types of people rather than others. Studies show that there are significant differences between clergy working within different denominations (e.g. Roman Catholic or Assemblies of God), between clergy holding different patterns of belief (e.g. liberal or conservative) or between clergy drawing on different spiritual traditions (say mystical or charismatic). In spite of such diversity, there are two ways in which clergymen differ in their personality profile from men in general. They tend to prefer feeling more than men in general. This is a characteristically feminine personality preference and reflects the preferred ethos of church congregations. They also tend to prefer intuition more than men in general. In this respect, clergymen do not reflect the preferred ethos of church congregations. Like clergymen, clergywomen too tend to prefer intuition more than women in general and more than women churchgoers.

The first study of Church of England clergy was reported by Francis et al. (2007), drawing on 626 clergymen and 237 clergywomen. Compared with the general population of men, clergymen were weighted towards intuition (62% compared with 27%), towards feeling (54% compared with 35%) and towards judging (66% compared with 55%). Compared with the general population of women, clergywomen were weighted towards introversion (54% compared with 43%) and towards intuition (65% compared with 21%).

In terms of psychological temperament, there were some startling differences between the profiles of Church of England clergy and Church of England congregations. While, according to Francis et al. (in press),

73 per cent of women churchgoers preferred the Epimethean Temperament (SJ), the proportion fell to 29 per cent among clergywomen. While, according to the same study, 71 per cent of men churchgoers preferred the Epimethean Temperament (SJ), the proportion fell to 31 per cent among clergymen. By way of contrast, the two psychological temperaments most prevalent among clergy were the Apollonian Temperament (NF), accounting for 50 per cent of clergywomen and 35 per cent of clergymen, and the Promethean Temperament (NT), accounting for 15 per cent of clergywomen and 27 per cent of clergymen.

These findings suggest that a number of Epimethean (SJ) congregations find themselves being led by Apollonian (NF) or Promethean (NT) clergy. Both the Apollonian Temperament and the Promethean Temperament are driven by intuition. Intuitive clergy are inspired by future possibilities and by the vision of how things may be changed, developed and improved. It is this fundamental psychological difference between the aspirations of NF and NT clergy and the tendency towards conservation of SJ congregations that may reside at the heart of some of the conflict between established Church of England congregations and newly appointed mobile professional clergy. Apollonian (NF) and Promethean (NT) clergy may be intuitively aware of the benefits to be gained by changing the service time, by changing the form of service and by introducing a new hymn book. Epimethean (SJ) congregations may be perplexed and discomforted by such interference with their established religious world. Some STJ members of the congregation may well stay put to argue their case and to disrupt the process of change. Some SFJ members may quietly withdraw, hurt, baffled and alienated from their spiritual roots.

Although that first study of Church of England clergy was based on a good number of cases (626 clergymen and 237 clergywomen), it remains scientifically unsound to base conclusions on single studies. It is for that reason that two subsequent studies set out to test and to replicate the findings reported by Francis et al. (2007). In a second study, Francis et al. (2010) reported on a survey conducted among 622 clergymen serving in the Church of England. The findings were remarkably similar between this second study and the first study. In the first study, 31 per cent of the clergymen were SJ and so were 27 per cent in the second study. In the first study, 35 per cent of the clergymen were NF and so were 39 per cent in the second study. In the first study, 27 per cent of the clergymen were NT and so were 28 per cent in the second study. In a third study, Francis et al. (2011) reported on a survey conducted among 83 clergywomen serving in the Church of England. Once again, the findings were remarkably similar between this third study and the first study. In the first study, 29 per cent of the clergywomen were SJ and so were 33 per cent in the third study. In the first study, 50 per cent of the clergywomen were NF and so were 49 per cent in the third study. In the first study, 15 per cent of the clergywomen were NT and so were 11 per cent in the third study.

The foregoing studies reported among Church of England congregations and Church of England mobile professional clergy set the context against which the psychological profile of the OLMs may be located. The aspirations of some of the pioneers of Ordained Local Ministry in the Church of England, like Ted Roberts (1972, 2006), with reference to whom this chapter opened, point to two hypotheses that can now be empirically tested. If Ordained Local Ministry does recruit a very different kind of priest from those recruited into mobile professional ministry, then it is reasonable to hypothesize that OLMs will have a significantly different psychological profile from other clergy (hypothesis 1). If Ordained Local Ministry really does reflect the local congregations and the local communities from which such priests are called, then it is reasonable to hypothesize that OLMs will reflect the psychological profile of these congregations more closely than they reflect the psychological profile of other clergy. So far, three studies have set out to test these hypotheses.

In the first study, Francis and Holmes (2011) reported on the findings from a survey conducted among 39 OLMs serving in one mixed urban and rural diocese. The findings were intriguing. According to this study, 56 per cent of OLMs reported the Epimethean Temperament (SJ), which placed them closer to the psychological temperament profiles of the church congregations than to the psychological temperament profile of mobile professional clergy.

In the second study, Francis et al. (in press) reported on the findings from a survey conducted among 144 clergywomen serving in Ordained Local Ministry from across the Church of England. These data were collected as a part of a larger survey sent to all clergywomen serving in the Church of England. These findings confirmed the initial impressions provided by the smaller study reported by Francis and Holmes (in press). According to this second study, 65 per cent of clergywomen serving in Ordained Local Ministry reported the Epimethean Temperament (SJ), compared with 27 per cent of mobile professional clergywomen reported by Francis et al. (2007) and 73 per cent of women attending Church of England congregations.

These first two studies have clear limitations: for the first, the sample is small and for the second, the sample is restricted to clergywomen. In the third study, Francis and Village (in press) reported on the findings from a survey conducted among all 2,190 Anglican clergy ordained deacon between 2004 and 2007 in the United Kingdom. The response rate of 48 per cent generated replies from 79 clergywomen and 56 clergymen ordained as OLMs in England. These findings were very close to the initial impressions provided by Francis and Holmes (in press). According to this study, 54 per cent of the clergywomen and 57 per cent of the clergymen serving in the Ordained Local Ministry reported the Epimethean Temperament (SJ).

As a consequence of the strength of the Epimethean Temperament (SJ) among OLMs, the Apollonian Temperament (NF) and the Promethean Temperament (NT) are less in evidence among OLMs than among mobile professional clergy. The case is well illustrated by comparing the findings of Francis and Village (in press) among OLMs with the findings of Francis et al. (2007) among mobile professional clergy. Among clergywomen, the Apollonian Temperament (NF) falls from 50 per cent to 29 per cent among OLMs, and the Promethean Temperament (NT) falls from 15 per cent to 13 per cent among OLMs. Among clergymen, the Apollonian Temperament (NF) falls from 35 per cent to 29 per cent among OLMs, and the Promethean Temperament (NT) falls from 27 per cent to 9 per cent among OLMs.

Applying the evidence

From a scientific point of view, these studies have tested two hypotheses regarding the psychological profile of men and women recruited into Ordained Local Ministry. The first hypothesis proposed that OLMs will have a significantly different psychological profile from mobile professional clergy. The data supported this first hypothesis. The second hypothesis proposed that, if Ordained Local Ministry really does reflect the local congregation and the local communities from which such priests are called, OLMs will reflect the psychological profile of these congregations more closely than they reflect the psychological profile of mobile professional clergy. The data also supported this second hypothesis.

These scientific findings carry practical implications for four main areas: for appreciating the distinctive strength of OLMs; for recognizing ways in which OLMs may be resourced to develop their ministry effectively; for understanding the dynamics that may develop between OLMs and the congregations from which they were called into ministry; and for anticipating some of the difficulties that may arise between resident OLMs and mobile professional clergy who move into the parish to work alongside them.

The three surveys conducted among OLMs demonstrate that between over one-half (54%) and nearly two-thirds (65%) of OLMs are shaped by the Epimethean Temperament (SJ). Oswald and Kroeger's (1988) characterization of the Epimethean Temperament as producing 'the conserving, serving pastor' provides helpful insights into the distinctive strengths of the majority of OLMs and into how such clergy may lead their congregations. Congregations managed by SJ pastors will not go through unnecessary change, and when changes are initiated, they will be implemented by evolution rather than by revolution. SJ clergy tend to work hard to foster a sense of loyalty and belonging in their congregations. They will prioritize a sense of social, moral and spiritual obligation throughout the congregation. They will want to develop sound plans, clear procedures and precise policies, and encourage others to adhere to them. SJ clergy tend to bring good skills to administrative functions, but find dealing with people somewhat more problematic. SJ clergy tend to take pastoral ministry very seriously and to want to approach pastoral ministry in a highly organized and practical way. They are realists who like a common-sense approach to pastoral counselling and to problem solving. For SJ clergy worship will be formal, generally dignified and always predictable. These are the strong cards that SJ clergy bring to ministry.

As well as bringing characteristic and distinctive strengths to ministry, each of the four psychological temperaments brings recognized dangers and weaknesses. It is in these areas of recognized dangers and weaknesses that ministerial continuing professional development may be fruitfully directed. In terms of resourcing and developing OLMs shaped by the Epimethean Temperament (SJ), clues are provided by the way in which Oswald and Kroeger (1988) discuss some of the difficulties faced by SJ pastors. Oswald and Kroeger speak of the tendency towards literalism and pessimism. For SJs, scripture may need to be interpreted with respect for the text, and they may find it difficult to accept more liberal and flexible approaches. For SJs, other people's visions and enthusiasms need to be subjected to stringent risk assessment, and they may be unaware of the damage that this could do to the commitment of those whose visions they sideline. SJs may become particularly vulnerable to burnout as a consequence of their commitment to rules, procedures and obligations. SJs may weary some members of their congregation by an apparent obsession with structure, order and discipline, and may be irritated by church members who fail to appreciate their importance. SJs may find individuals who reject conventional church teaching and conventional church discipline hard to accept. Dioceses working with OLMs may wish to offer psychological temperament awareness training to help SJ pastors to celebrate their strengths and to deal effectively with the potential weaknesses and dangers associated with their temperament.

In terms of understanding the dynamics that may develop between OLMs and the congregations from which they were called into ministry, clues are provided by identifying the strength of the SJ congregations, the difficulties that such congregations face and the potential for collusion between like-minded congregations and their SJ pastors. When things are going well, SJ congregations display many strengths. Because of the tendency for churches to attract introverts, women, and feeling types, there will be a high proportion of ISFJs in these congregations. Myers (1998: 7) provides an accurate profile of ISFJs at their best. They are:

> Quiet, friendly, responsible and conscientious. Work devotedly to meet their obligations. Lend stability to any project or group. Thorough, painstaking, accurate. Their interests are usually not technical. Can be patient with necessary details. Loyal, considerate, perceptive, concerned with how other people feel.

The problems, however, arise when congregations grow old and tired and are no longer able to provide the contexts in which ISFJs can flourish. When

ISFJs no longer find a place where they can use their gifts and be appreciated for their contributions, they may begin to feel frustrated and resentful. It is when ISFJ congregations become tired that they fail to draw on the intuitive function to see a way forward to build a new future. The danger with tired SJ congregations being led by SJ pastors is that these pastors may share the pessimism and collude with the downward spiral of decline. Dioceses may wish to offer some external consultancy to SJ congregations that are struggling to re-vision their future.

In terms of anticipating some of the difficulties that may arise between resident OLMs and mobile professional clergy who move into the parish to work alongside them, clues are provided by identifying the potential areas of conflict between the preferred approaches of the Epimethean Temperament (SJ) and the preferred approaches of the Apollonian Temperament (NF) or the Promethean Temperament (NT). As individuals who are more likely to share the predominant temperament of the congregation, the resident OLMs are more likely to appreciate the reluctance of Anglican congregations to seek change and innovation. When new mobile stipendiary clergy are appointed to parishes to work alongside well-established OLMs, there may be inevitable points of conflict between the more visionary and innovative approach of the Apollonian (NF) or Promethean (NT) incumbent and the more cautious and conserving approach of the Epimethean (SJ) resident OLM. Dioceses working with OLMs may wish to offer psychological temperament awareness training to help OLMs and newly appointed incumbents to appreciate each others' preferred styles of ministry and to negotiate effective ways of working together in the light of greater awareness of each others' psychological temperaments.

Conclusion

This chapter set out to explore the psychological profile of OLMs and to set this profile alongside what was already known about the psychological profile of Anglican Church congregations and the psychological profile of Anglican mobile professional clergy. By placing side by side three studies conducted among Anglican mobile professional clergy, two studies conducted among Anglican Church congregations and three new studies conducted among OLMs, three main conclusions emerged. Candidates recruited to serve as OLMs are significantly different in their psychological profile from candidates recruited to serve in mobile professional ministry. OLMs reflect quite closely the psychological profile of the congregations from which they are drawn. There is considerable scope for OLMs and for mobile professional clergy to conceptualize ministry in very different ways as a consequence of their psychological type preferences.

Drawing on psychological type theory and psychological temperament theory, these scientific findings have provided the basis for interpreting the strengths and potential weaknesses associated with Ordained Local Ministry, for understanding the distinctive dynamics between OLMs and their congregations, and for anticipating some of the tensions that may arise between resident OLMs and the mobile professional clergy with whom they work. These theories also offer helpful suggestions for the continuing professional development of OLMs and of the mobile professional clergy with whom they work.

Appendix

Table A.1 Psychological temperament profile for Church of England clergy and churchgoers

	N	NT (%)	NF (%)	SJ (%)	SP (%)
Mobile professional clergy					
Clergymen[1]	626	27	35	31	7
Clergymen[2]	622	28	39	27	6
Clergywomen[1]	237	15	50	29	6
Clergywomen[3]	83	11	49	33	7
Churchgoers					
Men[4]	116	13	19	56	12
Men[5]	1,169	13	10	71	7
Women[4]	211	4	21	55	20
Women[5]	2,135	6	13	73	9
OLMs					
Clergymen and clergywomen[6]	39	5	31	56	8
Clergywomen[7]	144	6	24	65	5
Clergywomen[8]	79	13	29	54	4
Clergymen[8]	56	9	27	57	7

Source: [1] From Francis et al. (2007); [2] from Francis et al. (2010); [3] from Francis et al. (2011); [4] from Francis et al. (2004); [5] from Francis et al. (in press); [6] from Francis and Holmes (in press); [7] from Francis et al. (2011); [8] from Francis and Village (in press).

Betty's story

Betty, ten years' experience as an OLM. Four and a half years ago, she took on a house for duty post, living in the vicarage in a rural village which, after pastoral reorganization, was attached to a large market town. Betty was one of the original members of the Local Ministry Team in the market town.

In the mid-1980s, I reclaimed this strong sense of God's purpose. I talked things through with my vicar who told me that he was thinking of starting a Local Ministry Team and that this would be an opportunity to explore and test my vocation as well as to grow in confidence.

At that time, I never considered ordination as an option; it just wasn't there even on the radar. The formation of the first Local Ministry Team (LMT) in our parish brought about tremendous growth and led to a number of people having a calling to licensed ministry; so at the end of the Local Ministry training, I offered for Reader ministry. (Looking back I should have offered for ordained ministry. Everyone in the church said so too . . . afterwards!) This is where I feel the church could have taken a more active, positive role in discernment. It was left entirely up to me and I was left floundering.

I now realize that part of my journey to being a Reader was because it was an easier route and there was less chance of being rejected. I did not feel worthy of ordination. In the end, after speaking to a wise minister, I was advised to apply and leave it to God's will.

I am left in no doubt that the calling to priesthood was right.

I have lived in this place all my life, and have the acceptance of people outside the church, they did not look upon the collar as a barrier; this gives me a tremendous licence. It has taken some adapting to being a priest (OLM) in a community where I am known, because of the different responsibilities this brings, and I have had to learn how to do this.

The LMT has been very special because of its acceptance of me. Once I was ordained, the chemistry of the team changed even though we had all trained together, and I needed to adjust to that. Having to learn to balance my leadership role without overpowering people, ministering as both leader and servant was important – the team helped me to do this.

House for Duty (HFD) carries more responsibility than an OLM would. I knew I was ready for more responsibility and offered for HFD in my Episcopal Review.

As a House for Duty Priest, I was uprooted from my home parish and from the LMT. So I did not have the support of the team members any more. I was on my own except for a stipendiary colleague based in the neighbouring town. To all intents and purposes, I was a parish priest.

My experience here of following on from a very autocratic incumbent is that it is very difficult to get people to understand what LM is. At the moment, they have nothing to compare it with; people lack confidence and think that it is all about leading worship. It has taken me four and a half years to set up a team here. Forming a 'real' team is not just about calling out those who are already doing things but also those on the periphery. There is potential for enormous growth and the opportunities for people to grow as a team and in confidence. Being a team, being collegiate is important for support, confidence and for a safe environment in which to say and do things. We need to have the courage to try and then learn through doing. It is important for there to be support, as a team, because the end product is that faith and commitment are even stronger.

OLM is an incredible ministry because it provides an opportunity to grow with the people who love and support you.

My experience of LM and then OLM has made me very much aware of certain people in the congregation who nurtured and supported me and has left me with a tremendous passion for the ministry of all Christians. I am convinced that God has called me here to do just that. It is wonderful yet dangerous because it changes your life

8

OLM: ministry in relationship

Elizabeth Jordan

Two features make Ordained Local Ministry distinctive. First, priests or deacons are called by, and from within, their local community, to hold the bishop's licence to serve specifically within and for that local community. Second, they work in the context of a Local Ministry Team and are an expression of the collaborative ministry of the whole local church. In short, they have a public sacramental ministry in the context of a collaborative leadership team. These features are essential, but controversial. This chapter demonstrates that, as the nature of ministry and of priesthood in particular, is reimagined in the twenty-first century, Ordained Local Ministry offers a model of public ministry that is essentially relational and is a distinctive contribution to the churches' life and mission.

While this chapter, and indeed this book, deals mainly with ordained local *priests*, it should be noted that a calling to an ordained local diaconate has been recognized by the church and experienced in at least one diocese. The nature of the diaconate is a matter for continuing debate, but the calling of the individual in question was clear – to be a representative of the diaconal calling of the church in service to those who were not otherwise connected with the church.

The ministerial formation of OLMs

There is much discussion about ministry in the Church of England at this time and a sense of anxiety felt by many church leaders over the future of public representative ministries. The cost of training, the confusing plethora of categories of authorized and ordained ministry and the needs of national and local neighbourhood are all debated. But there is some agreement: mission must be the foremost priority of the Church of England. Ordained Local Ministry 'will be judged on its contribution to the worship and mission of the Church in its parishes' (Torry and Heskins 2006: 9).

Ordained Local Ministry can appear (and has been described as) a bulwark against change. It does indeed sustain local church life in the face of all sorts of pressures to contract, and along with a team of lay leaders behind them, an Ordained Local Minister (OLM) can be a powerful conservative force. Many fears about OLMs are focused on the lack of change that may happen in their own lives, because they would not have had the experience of leaving their own Christian communities to train: Will it be possible for them to inhabit their new identity as priests representing the whole church? Researching this, I interviewed an illustrative sample of OLM ordinands, and those recently ordained, and I compared their responses with theological, psychological and sociological approaches to identity formation, questioning them about activities, relationships, dress and vocation (Jordan 2008). Listening to the tapes of the interviews, I was struck by the alteration in tone and language in which change was discussed. One interviewee recorded how members of the congregation had said they hoped he would not change after ordination, but feared he might become 'aloof'. Another expressed a strong desire to remain 'one of the people'. At this point in my research, the fears that Ordained Local Ministry represented resistance to change seemed well grounded! The OLMs were aware that wearing a collar could harm relationships with the local congregation; ordination may still be seen as 'going over to the other side'. Not that any of those I interviewed had particularly poor relationships with their incumbent, simply that he or she was seen as 'not one of us' by the congregation.

Being transformed?

Ministerial formation begins as humans understand and inhabit their identity before God. Two models predominate: Christological and Trinitarian. 'Christian identity is about Jesus, the primary reference point of what it means to be human in relation to God, to other people, and creation' affirms the Doctrine Commission of the Church of England (2003: 2), while McFayden (1990: 24) asserts 'the Trinitarian nature of God's being and self-communication is determinative for a Christian understanding of human being in God's image'. There is no inherent contradiction in a Trinitarian and Christological undergirding of identity: Jesus, whom 'we shall become like' (1 Jn 3.2) is a person of the Trinity in which there is a reciprocity of mutual self-giving and mutual interpenetration of love. But there are differences in emphasis.

Robin Greenwood (1994) has suggested that the church should move from a Christological model of formation to a Trinitarian one, encompassing mutuality, collaboration and interdependence. The imitation of Christ characteristically emphasizes *kenosis*, self-denial and being crucified with Christ. An emphasis on participation in the life of the Trinity will focus on the relational ontology of the priest: a priest by virtue of the relationship with others, not because of separation from them. John Zizioulas (1985), indeed, asserts that ordination should not be understood in terms of the ordained individual's function or the ontology of orders but in terms of the particular relationships which are a result of ordination. The priest needs the Christian community in order to be a priest, just as a person needs brothers and sisters in order to be a sibling.

How is the OLM related to the whole of the people of God? The submission of Lichfield Diocese's OLM Scheme to the House of Bishops (1995) contained these words:

> From time to time the Christian community is able to recognise in one of its members a charism of the Holy Spirit which enables that person to be a special focus of the representative task that is the calling of all. It has always seemed appropriate that those with this 'sacramental identity' should be set apart to preside at the church's Eucharist, when its own identity as the community of Christ is most sharply displayed.

But why shouldn't the stipendiary parish priest embody the sacramental, representative role? It has been the experience of those in the Local Ministry movement that, perhaps paradoxically, in order to give significance to lay ministry and leadership within a sacramental community, it is appropriate, even necessary, to ordain some local people.[1] Only in this way is the sacramental character of that community, as an expression of God's grace in that place recognized. This is especially true of communities which have painful histories of exclusion and powerlessness: it was, for example, the alienation of the working classes from the Church of England that persuaded the Diocese of Southwark to encourage new forms of selection and training for ministry in the early 1980s (Torry and Heskins 2006).

Rather than suggesting that the patterns of life adopted during training, or with other ordinands, are foundational for future ministry, training within the Lichfield Diocesan OLM Scheme encouraged reflection upon and attention to the relationships with the congregation. Just as a review of Ordained Local Ministry in 2006 (AC 2007a) found that it encouraged a view of vocation as coming primarily from the church rather than from an individual, their training discouraged an individualistic and subjective approach to ministry, and the OLM's transition to a representative role was negotiated within the fellowship of the church. But it is just this identification with the local congregation that appears to some to question the place of Ordained Local Ministry within a Catholic understanding of orders. It appears to claim that OLMs may be regarded as ordained in one place, but not in others. Having been called, however, by a particular

Christian community which has recognized their 'sacramental character', and been trained with that community in view as the place of ministry and mission, it is appropriate that the licence is to that place. This is less a limitation than a recognition of particular knowledge and relationship. The OLM may, in time, develop a wider ministry and then it might be right to negotiate a change of category that reflects a broader canvas, but the local licence represents an investment of the church for that time and that place.

The positive aspect of the OLM's identification with the congregation (identified in my research) was that several of those interviewed said that they were treated as a 'bridge person', as 'a go between', connecting the worlds of clergy and laity, church and society. Those interviewed were keenly aware of their calling *by* the congregation and recognized that their ministerial identity was rooted in their relationship with those people. The recognition of their 'sacramental character' had become expressive of the priesthood of the local congregation. The representative nature of their priesthood was less obscured by an apparent separation from the daily concerns of church members.[2] (*Apparent* because the research uncovered the perceptions of OLMs and members of their congregations, not necessarily the facts. But perceptions are significant. There is still a strong presumption among both church members and others that stipendiary clergy do not understand the stresses and strains of ordinary life.)

Living distinctively?

So that was the vision of Ordained Local Ministry in one diocese, Lichfield. But what is the distinctive nature of Ordained Local Ministry now? Having observed the work of many OLMs, I would describe them as a *local missionary-theologian*. The local theologian is one who can interpret the present in the light of God's revelation of past and future, understanding both the wisdom of the past and the hopes and fears of the local community. Throughout training, OLM ordinands were required to reflect on how their learning of the Christian traditions related to their present experience. They spent some time in another context than their own, so that their experience would be broadened and they could see their home territory with renewed eyes. A critical conversation took place between insights from the social sciences, study of the actual beliefs and practices of church members and biblical and theological teaching. OLMs are ideally suited to being local theologians, being theologically trained, with much knowledge of, for example, local customs and habits at birth and death, the activity of local authorities and voluntary groups and the lifestyles of different age groups.

They must also be missionary: at home in the local culture and vocabulary, they can proclaim afresh the Gospel for their locality. I remember talking to one OLM candidate who was concerned that his use of English was unconventional. But, as I said to him, as soon as I opened my mouth in his home town, I was immediately revealed as an outsider, whereas he spoke the local language and would be heard as one who knew about local hopes and fears.[3]

I have been struck by the OLMs' desire to engage in community-oriented work. This might include arranging an enquirer's group in the local community centre, befriending groups of youths on the street or being a member of a community regeneration partnership. Those in paid work, as a teacher, a check-out assistant, at the surgery or in the local farming community, for example, used their local networks to communicate with many who had little or no contact with church. They recognized the immense hurdle that entering a church building represented. I know from conversations with stipendiary clergy how many of them feel compelled to justify their work by reference to numbers in church. The pressure is on them to maintain Sunday attendance, to create new forms and contexts for worship and to ensure the flow of income. The search for a mission shaped church, rather than 'church shaped mission' requires the contribution of those whose perspective is the Kingdom of God in their community, not solely the growth or survival of the institutional church. Some stipendiary priests may envy OLMs' freedom to act without continual concern for the diocesan quota and attendance figures! There is an evident need for mutual appreciation among all who exercise public representative ministries and respect for each other's sphere of work.

OLMs complement, not replace, national ministry. There is, as proposed by the Faith and Order Advisory Group (AC 2007b), a great need to recover the balance of local and itinerant (apostolic) ministry that is evident in the New Testament. I have argued that priesthood is a relational state and a change in the role of laypeople and of self-supporting ministers must change the perception of the role and functions of the stipendiary. This is a role that has already changed many times. One recent and dramatic change is in the length of time that a stipendiary tends to stay in a benefice: seven to ten years is now far more common than several decades ago. Unlike a stipendiary priest, who will move house many times and learn the ways of a new community each time, the OLM will typically remain immersed in the same community. Both may act as reflective practitioners, but in distinct ways. The OLM is called out by the congregation and selected as one who is rooted in the locality. The stipendiary priest is one who has the perspective of a newcomer to the situation, offering resources and challenge from outside. Having, probably, received a longer and more complex theological education, they can offer the perspective of historical wisdom and close links with the wider church. Indeed, complemented by an OLM, he or she may be freer to offer a challenging, prophetic ministry. In many places, though, OLMs and nationally deployed stipendiary ministers have found it difficult to work together. A greater local knowledge on the one hand and a more sophisticated theological education on the other often appear to result in competition or suspicion. But without national, mobile ministry, the local congregation could quickly become inward looking, while without local leadership, the national church will appear increasingly alien to many sections of the population.

Ordained Local Ministry – priesthood in relationship

The survey of self-supporting ministers carried out by Teresa Morgan (2011) indicates their belief that difference within ministry is evaluated in a hierarchical way and self-supporting ministry was perceived as inferior by stipendiary ministers. There is a deep need to comprehend ideas of complementarity and relationality. The research that I carried out demonstrated an apparent failure of the Lichfield Training Scheme to form ordinands in the model of priesthood adopted in this country during the past century. But it disclosed the new identity that OLM and local church were together forming: an understanding of priesthood rooted in relationship.

In both psychological and sociological terms, it is well established that a sense of self is formed in relationship with others and that one cannot operate within a role without acceptance from others, a psychological contract. Research by Leslie Francis and Susan Jones (2003) suggests that the sociological marginalization of the clerical profession could be a cause of lower self-esteem among clergy than other members of the population. Without affirmation of their role from the surrounding community, the priest and the congregation must together maintain the plausibility structure of Christian discourse, in the face of considerable threat by those outside that reference group. So just as theologians such as Zizioulas (1985) and Greenwood (1994) have described priesthood as constituted by a relationship with the whole church, the present understandings of identity and leadership demonstrate how much each depends on relationships. In their formation as priests, OLMs are experiencing and expressing that interdependence which authenticates them as priestly representatives of their local Christian fellowship. Their own sense of belonging, to the congregation and to the local community, rather than being a threat to stipendiary clergy, may be viewed as a positive resolution of the tension of being a representative of God and the church in an alien world. Ordained Local Ministry, in this light, is an adaptation of ordained ministry to a new environment, a mutation that has the capacity to flourish (Percy 2006).

The development of lay discipleship – equipping the local church in mission

The previous section argued that OLMs are formed in relationship with the congregation and one might expect members of the congregation to be changed in this process. Ordained Local Ministry has arisen from the Local Ministry movement, which has championed the ministry of all the baptized, a common ownership of the life of the church and participation in the mission of God. Yet, since some voices, such as the *Reader Upbeat Report* (2009), express fears that Ordained Local Ministry undermines the value of lay ministry, it is right to ask what kind of lay training is necessary to prepare for a ministry complementary to that of Ordained Local Ministry, a ministry which is not threatened, but enhanced, by its existence?

This section will argue that the ordination of some who are called by the local congregation is the logical consequence of taking laypeople seriously, and that Ordained Local Ministry without effective lay development risks further clericalism. It demonstrates the effectiveness of collaborative training and ministry that will equip the local church in mission. Finally, the kind of preparation that will equip a congregation for an unknown future is considered.

The people of God, sharing in mission

Since ordained people represent only 3–5 per cent of the church, the idea of developing a theology of the laity separate from that of the church may seem a curious exercise. But, for the sake of clarity, one may still ask 'Who are the laity?' The name is often said to be derived from the *laos*, the people of God: the New Testament writers describe *all* Jesus' followers as the *laos*, while the Greek word *laikos* ('laity') denoted the common people, a term of disparagement. Laos was first used for believers by Clement of Rome in the late first century, apparently to refer to those not fit to lead worship. The word later translated as 'clergy', *kleros*, refers to an inheritance, or those picked out by lot, as in Acts 1.26 of Mathias, but also of Judas in Acts 1.17, and is used for all the people of God in, for example, Colossians 1.12.

By the third century, a distinction between clergy and laity had emerged that we would recognize today. But the monastic lifestyle was also developing at this time and a distinction between those who lived in the world and those whose primary vocation was monastic was more easily maintained than between clergy and lay. This may still be true: the situation of, say, lay academic theologians, salaried employees of the church or volunteers in ministry, may be very different from that of church members who spend the majority of their time outside the institutional church environment. So it can be said that the distinction among 'ordained,' 'lay' and 'laity' has varied in different times and circumstances, each with a different emphasis. Ordained Local Ministry draws attention to the life and mission of the local congregation, rather than the role of a separate order of those who are ordained. OLMs, being part of a team of ministers, are the sacramental expression of the work of all the people of God, without whom their individual calling lacks authenticity.

Indeed, although the focus of this book is Ordained Local Ministry, it is essential that attention is directed primarily to the ministry of the whole people of God. To concentrate first on Ordained Local Ministry is to risk falling into a well-populated trap: that of defining the role of the whole people of God by reference to the role and status of the ordained minority. Edward Schillebeeckx (1981) robustly asserted that priesthood must grow out of the Christian community and function within a community that itself possesses and sets forth other spiritual gifts. An engaged laity is, therefore, the necessary background for vocations to ordained life. The ordination of OLMs by the bishop confirms their place within a Catholic understanding of orders.

The representative task of all God's people is to act as priests to the world through the offering of intercession for the needs of the world, through the presentation of the fruits of work and the earth's produce at the altar and in acts of service and witness in the world. Passages such as Ephesians 4.1–16 indicate that publicly authorized ministers are intended to enable the people of God to discern and practise their own gifts of ministry, both in ecclesial and in secular spheres. This presbyteral ministry will involve both modelling for the church what its own ministry involves, and also exercising oversight of its implementation. The credibility of the Good News, in a society that has turned its back on meta-narratives, is found in testimony that is personal and expressed in the language of particular cultural networks. The way leadership is structured, the quality of life together and the activities of the Christian community in daily life are each as expressive of the beliefs which are held as the creed which is proclaimed. Fresh expressions of leadership need to replace the monarchical and patriarchal patterns of the past. As Frensdorff concludes, there is a great need to create 'ministering communities, rather than communities gathered around a minister' (cited in Palmer (nd): 3).

A biblical and theological rediscovery of the image of the church as a people and a body called and sent for mission and service has been encouraged by the marginalization of the institutional church in a post-Christendom world. Rather than the error of defining laypeople by reference to the role of clergy, all of God's people may now be shaped by their part in the divine mission. Some fulfil this calling by building up the Christian community, some by service and witness in the world. Both practically and theologically, there is a necessary interdependence between these callings, both of which are vital to the success of the church's mission. There should, ideally, be no conflict between participation and identification with the Christian community and being active as a Christian witness outside the institution, although in fact there is often friction, marked by suspicion between clergy and laypeople, with disparity of resources made available for each sphere. Funds for the training of ordinands are vastly greater than those available for other forms of ministry and even what is made available is concentrated on the growth of the gathered church. There are now few resources available for those who wish to equip themselves for discipleship in their daily lives. Morgan's (2011) survey of self-supporting ministers noted how few believed that much attention was paid to their activity outside of the institutional church, even when they were trained and licensed precisely for that work.

An enquiry about the nature of training for lay discipleship, then, must be in the context of equipping all parts of the local church for mission. Once the overall aim of resourcing all God's people for participation in mission is envisioned, particular roles will take their proper place. In the first section, the issue of stipendiaries' relationships with OLMs was discussed: here, it is necessary to note that other lay ministers, principally Readers, have expressed anxiety about Ordained Local Ministry. Readers who are also theologically trained and speak with a local voice can find themselves rarely used in a church that has, in recent decades, held more eucharistic services. The problem is exacerbated if the role of a Reader, or any other minister, for that matter, is defined in isolation both from other ministries and from the missionary calling of the church. The selection process for an OLM, even though carried out nationally, should take account of the needs of the local church. If it is decided that the church needs an OLM, the role of the Reader and other ministers may change – as will that of the stipendiary, since the arrival of a new member of the team will change the whole team. Being primarily a sacramental minister, the OLM does not replace the Reader, who are 'preachers, catechists and facilitators of learning with the skill to be examples to other laity as bearers and interpreters of the Word of God in daily working life' (AC 2009: 2). National guidelines and learning outcomes for Reader and ordination training have inhibited a clear understanding of the distinctive characteristics of each ministry, but training together and having an understanding of each other's roles have facilitated some collaboration and mutual respect.

So, in order to develop the gifts and abilities of all people, lay and ordained, the discovery of a local church's calling, the local church needs to be able to discern and articulate its vocation. A concentration on Local Ministry may itself result in putting the cart before the horse. Matters of ministry are secondary to the primary question: 'What is God calling us to?[4] It is necessary to begin with the missionary calling of the church before considering individual callings, to lay or ordained ministry. I have seen that the most effective parish development is taking place where skilled expertise in equipping people in ministry is allied with a clear focus on its use in God's mission. In the absence of such focus, the parish ministry team may lose its vision and rationale, becoming simply the group that draws up the rotas.

Once the local church has begun to address the primary question about mission, it can then ask, 'How will we meet the challenge?' Failing to pay attention to matters of ministry can lead to sterile, 'results-driven' churches. If one might generalize, it has seemed that diocesan and national mission departments have concentrated on goals and outcomes and ministry departments on processes and the internal dynamics of church life. Working together, both goals and the process of achieving them, both world-facing outreach and a rich internal life may be nourished. The work of mission and ministry is severely impoverished without cooperation and mutual respect, as each complements the other. There is a necessary link between Local Ministry and local mission; they can and should work together.

It is vital that attention is paid to the corporate and collaborative dimension of our life in Christ. In this way, the enrichment of being the Body of Christ becomes, increasingly, a reality for the people of God. Local Ministry Advisers in the Lichfield Diocese found that participation in such a body creates the motive for wanting to share that enriching life with others, overcoming previous inhibitions about mission.

Many dioceses are now using Mission Action Plans (MAPs) to help the local church shape its involvement in mission. The process by which MAPs are developed will be found to be as significant as their content. Experience of Local Ministry in working with congregations has much to contribute. Many churches are not good at making decisions and achieving consensus is even harder. But it is well known that collaborative decision-making increases ownership of the vision and its implementation. The aspiration of Local Ministry is that when leadership is shared, the omni(in)competent person becomes part of a collaborative team with complementary leadership gifts. The visionary and the pragmatic, the activist and the reflector learn to work together. Achieving this in practice requires patient and dedicated work. Churches may need help to identify individuals within their fellowship who can contribute to information gathering, assessment, prayerful reflection and strategic prioritizing. The experience of Local Ministry Advisers is that parish development needs to be accomplished by those who can give support, encouragement and long-term, personal befriending through times of change. This complements visits made by senior diocesan staff, who may give vision and challenge.

Local Ministry Advisers in the diocese of Lichfield found that the task of listening to God's call to each place, the particular vocation of that church, takes time. Listening and action may go together as part of the envisioning process. A strict timetable will discourage experimentation, further prayer and discernment as local context and local wisdom are taken seriously. Good participation in decision-making and healthy interpersonal relationships may hold up the MAP – but it will be less of a paper exercise and more of a part of the churches' identity. The goal, after all, is not the production of a MAP, but a church engaged in mission. There is the added benefit that the way that a church produces its MAP, through developing patterns of participation and team work, may act as a measure of its readiness to develop shared ministry and leadership and to call out an OLM.

Sharing in training and formation

As has been indicated above, the ministerial formation of OLMs is related to the congregations that they serve. They are representative of that Christian community both in their priestly service in worship and in their visible presence in the community. As I was told, they are seen as 'one of us'. Many dioceses require evidence of the shared ministry of church members before permitting an OLM to be ordained to a local church. This is both an expression of the collaborative nature of ministry, demonstrating that gifts are shared among several people rather than residing in one individual, and a guard against one local person, having acquired orders, becoming the sole focus of all leadership. It has also been a feature of many OLM training schemes that the local congregation has been involved in the training of OLMs, whether as local support groups, intentional congregational training groups or as the recipients of reflective ministry. It was the experience in Lichfield Diocese that team development workshops involving the ordinand's home church was the element that was most easily dropped from the curriculum: it was not a national requirement and took considerable effort to organize. But neglecting it emphasized distance between the ordinand and others in the local church, rather than linking the congregation to the diocesan structure, thus asserting the catholicity of Anglican life and opening up the possibility of other church members engaging in training.

Will ordaining local people undermine a lay vocation, by implying that only ordained ministries are 'valid', and that there is a hierarchy of importance? So much, of course, does give this impression, not least the ordination service, at which strenuous efforts need to be made to weaken the impression that ordained ministry is exclusive; a different species with whom no close relations are proper. The need for all God's people to be educated and well resourced for ministry has never been greater. But theological education has been absorbed by a clerical paradigm, encouraging laity to think that they do not know enough about their own experiences to be articulate about their own faith (Farley 1983). If the priest is 'father' (or 'mother'), church members are children who never reach sufficient adulthood in Christ to exercise ministry, while if the priest is 'pastor', members are always sheep intended to follow, not lead.

These criticisms are well known and, given the state of the church, hard to refute, but the question here is what effect OLM has had. The review of OLM carried out for Ministry Division in 2006 (AC 2007a) noted that in dioceses with OLMs, their presence was seen to help lay Christians rediscover their baptismal calling to discipleship. In Lichfield, OLMs were often called out through a congregation-wide exercise that aimed to identify a rich variety of callings, not just potential clergy. In some cases, an individual would hear a call to ordination accompanying the response of the whole church to the call to participate in God's mission; in others, the individual's call itself triggers consideration within the church about mission.

The purpose of this section has been to argue that OLMs, far from diverting attention and energy from lay ministry are, if called and trained in the context of a local team, affirming of the crucial significance of the whole people of God. A pattern of church life which encourages and sustains teamwork is essential. This should be nurtured and visible not only within a local congregation, but between the local church and the diocesan authorities. A covenant may be established between the local church and the diocese, clarifying expectations of mutual resources and service. The diocesan authorities can accept, indeed encourage and authorize, local initiatives that will vary from place to place while holding such experiments within the Catholic order. In many dioceses, official recognition is given to structural changes that establish shared leadership in churches through a Local Ministry 'mandate'. Incoming clergy are required to recognize the gifts and commitment of the church members. Without such diocesan authorization, the functioning teams may be disbanded as a new priest arrives, and much good work set aside. The new priest may also find it difficult to integrate into an established team; the situation requires clarification of expectations, a negotiation of roles and reaffirmation of the value of teamwork, work best done by an officer outside the existing parish structures. The diocese also needs to ensure that, whether OLMs are trained on a diocesan-based scheme or with other partners, the development of the parish-based team is not overlooked amidst other preparations for ordination.

The development of lay discipleship and the training of OLMs

Is it, then, possible to provide resources, training and structures for laypeople that will establish a complementary ministry to that of OLM? Experience shows that the training of OLMs within a local context offers an ideal route for the ministerial development of the entire congregation. What starts out as a support group for the ordinand may soon become a learning group. Parishes in which someone begins ordination training are likely to produce further vocations to a variety of ministries (AC 2007b). The formation of a learning community is a step towards the ministerial formation of a priestly community.

Asking 'What makes OLM training different from other forms of ordination training?' Godfrey (2006: 132–7) identifies three features. Collaborative ministry is taught and modelled, in the parish and with peer groups; the curriculum is delivered through experiential theological learning and a strenuous attempt is made to avoid 'market driven packages of discrete information' by seeking integration and wholeness across the curriculum. It is these three features which provide both an educational model for congregational participation in the learning process and a structure within which it may take place.

The OLM Scheme, which trained ordinands for Lichfield Diocese, recognized the diversity of ministries in the Church of England and the need for collaboration between them – Godfrey's first point. Diversity was expressed by naming categories of ministry: Evangelist, OLM, Pastoral Care ministers and Readers, for example. Collaboration was encouraged by shared training and by joint assessment. Thus, ordinands were trained alongside lay local ministers, with a common first year for all candidates, followed by training on specialist tracks. As well as modelling collaboration, there was considerable teaching and reflection on the nature of the Godhead as a collaborative Trinitarian community and on the practicalities of decision-making in church life, conflict resolution and in shared fellowship. It was found that the first element in the training to suffer, due to a shortage of personnel, was the development of the local team which ministered with the OLM.

Experiential learning, Godfrey's second point, opens up the learning process to everyone, as all have their own experience to contribute to an understanding of God's ways in the world. The use of the learning circle enables those with biblical or doctrinal wisdom to contribute, but only in dialogue with the lived experience of others (Green 2009). Whole congregation learning will always involve so-called mixed ability groups, but this is a great advantage when the learning is practical reflection on God's activity in that place. The OLM ordinand will have been asked to reflect on his or her own past experience of ministry and to encourage his or her fellow church members to think about ways in which they represent God in the world. There is growing academic interest in theology, which is expressed in practice, the 'operant theology' of the congregation (Cameron et al. 2010). The dynamic nature of revelation is clear when one observes how local churches are coming alive through active participation in the mission of God. This is theology at grass-roots level, finding out what God is doing now. Theology that arises from practice can itself give fresh insight on traditional beliefs; participants realize that they are contributing to the ongoing story of the people of God.

Third, following Godfrey, the entire curriculum must seek integration and wholeness. The purpose of the training is not to provide packages of biblical or doctrinal knowledge, but to form ministers of the Gospel. Packages of information will, in any case, be of little use in situations which are forever mutating; today's ministers must, as reflective practitioners, be able to envision the future because of their knowledge of the past and prayerful attention to the present. The future for the church seems somehow less predictable than it was in some other periods of history; so the challenge is to prepare ministers for the unknown. Is this possible? The three themes of identity, partnership and discernment are at the heart of this endeavour. God's people must know who they are; they must be sure of their identity as God's children, a status that does not depend on their own worthiness, their achievements in this world or any of the other variables that make life appear so unpredictable. It is an identity that is not fully disclosed, but enfolded in God's knowledge of us: 'we are God's children now, and what we will be has not yet appeared; but we know that when he appears we shall be like him, because we shall see him as he is' (1 Jn 3.12). They must know, secondly, how to form partnerships; to work collaboratively both with fellow believers and with others who have the interests of the common good at heart without a confessional basis to underpin it. Willingness to work with others is not simply a pragmatic step, but stems from a deep awareness of common membership of the Body of Christ and of the Spirit's activity in the world. With such a conviction, teamwork and collaboration become a theological necessity and acquiring the skills to facilitate it a matter of faithfulness and obedience. And thirdly, today's disciples must know how to read the signs of the times, to discern God's hand in the varied particularities of modern life, so that they are able to express the Gospel afresh in their own locality. Such discernment is helped by learning the skills of listening and of theological reflection.[5]

Thus, Ordained Local Ministry is distinctive, both in the ministerial formation of OLMs and in their relation with ordained and lay colleagues. It is not some watered down version of other forms of ministry, a cheaper alternative for those who are not otherwise suitable. Ordained Local Ministry demands considerable relational skills so that its potential is realized. It challenges many of the established norms of the Church of England but it is a development which has the capacity to refresh and renew public representative ministries.

Notes

1 Developed in the section 'The development of lay discipleship – equipping the local church in mission'.
2 As noted above, the ordained local deacon may also be one who represents the church at community and civic functions, overseeing ministry to those who do not attend church events, and so remind the congregation of their diaconal role.
3 This point also applies to Readers and to other lay ministers, authorized or not. Their situation is discussed in the next section.
4 Hence, the validation question as revised in 1999 is 'What is the training institution's understanding of the mission to which the Church of God is called and of the pattern of Church life and order through which the Church of England responds to that calling?' (AC 2010).
5 There is a host of literature on each subject. A stimulating perspective on reading the signs of the times is given by Veling (2005). Sedmak (2007) is an excellent survey of ways to re-appropriate scripture and tradition in the contemporary world.

Diane's story

Diane has about six years' experience as an OLM within a well-established Local Ministry Team in a large rural village that was amalgamated with neighbouring villages following pastoral re-organization a few years ago. After a short vacancy, a new priest has now been appointed and this OLM is about to be redeployed as an Associate Priest in another part of the deanery in a group of parishes that does not have a Local Ministry Team.

It all began with the church exploring team ministry within the Diocesan Local Ministry (LM) Scheme. We were aware of there being gifted people in the church. The Diocesan LM adviser spoke in a visionary way which struck chords with many people, not just me. He described the LM team as being like an engine room. The whole church was involved in this preparation process and eventually in the calling out of a LM team.

I was already a Reader and would have been automatically included in the team. However, to be called out by the congregation and to be seen as a person who would be vital to the team was tremendously affirming. As a team and individually, we wondered what all this might mean and we were both excited and unsure about what lay ahead. We found the two years' training challenging, stretching and key to us bonding together as a team. At the end of the training period, each team member had an individual review. This conversation coincided with the fact that I had been thinking about ordained ministry for some while. Then, with the help of the Associate Diocesan Director of Ordinands, I explored the call to ordination knowing that there was a call to something other than being an active Reader. Being a member of the LM team helped to push me along; having other people alongside who were also thinking more deeply about ministry, gave me the confidence to explore the next step. It was helpful to have other role models in the LM community so we were building as a team and building individually – journeying together if you like.

The fact that people I knew and trusted were involved in the calling out, and were willing to entrust me with the responsibility of OLM was vital. This was a sort of setting apart, and yet as a team we worked with each other and were fundamentally no different, other than that I was wearing 'the collar'. As a Reader, I saw myself as a bridge between the church and the people. As an OLM I didn't feel completely set apart, although I did have a role as an OLM that was very different from that of a Reader because of the sacramental bits.

Being an OLM is very special as it's not just about being a priest but also encompasses the things that you would do anyway as an active Christian in day-to-day life; and the fact that you do not do this alone, but with the rest of the team. You can't be an OLM without the community because you are part of that community. Yet, there are times when you have to stand on your own two feet, but you also have to model how to be more collaborative in ministry.

OLM is not widely understood, even by our diocesan bishop or the new archdeacons.

When our new incumbent was appointed, I was concerned about how and where I would fit in. When it was suggested I move on, I wondered what I had done wrong. It felt as if *they* were saying you have done well and now we can move you up to the next stage of Associate Priest.

So, thinking about the next stage in my journey from OLM to more of an associate priest role; yes, I am ready for more responsibility. It has been a journey of surprises gradually realizing that I could do what I thought I couldn't. What I would like to do is to take with me the key features of my ministry as an OLM, especially enabling others, being a bridge between church and community, being pastoral, being somebody who belongs in a community and is involved in making the church in a community. Also I'd like to take with me team working because it is such a privilege as each of us journey, individually and together, learning from each other.

I do feel that I cannot do much more here and that perhaps, although it is daunting leaving behind my team and the place in which I live and was called out from, there is sense of rediscovering through moving, who God has made me. God has got the whole thing in his hand.

9

What is the future of Ordained Local Ministry?

Elizabeth Jordan

Those who have contributed to this book are divided among themselves about the future for Ordained Local Ministry. The stories of parishes that have developed collaborative ministry and leadership are stories of excitement, persistence and long-term investment – as well as of disillusionment and stagnation. There are both high ideals and failure of nerve, both individual and corporate growth in faithfulness to God's calling and inward-looking absorption with the maintenance of the status quo. Twenty years after the first ordination, it is apparent that Ordained Local Ministry is far from full acceptance within the Church of England, yet cannot be dismissed as a departure from mainstream Anglican ecclesiology.

Many of the advocates of Ordained Local Ministry are frustrated that it is still a *stranger* in the wings (ABM 1998). They were optimistic that, following the experiments in south London in the 1960s and 70s, the Tiller report, and proposals of *Faith in the City* (ACUPA 1985), the benefits of indigenous, locally accountable ordained leadership working within a collaborative team, would be apparent to all. How could church leaders and congregations not see the obvious advantages and welcome the men and women who were prepared to volunteer and train for such a ministry? From the advocates' point of view, the story may be seen, as Tim Morris has suggested in Chapter 5, as a failure to take such resistance to change and associated theological objections seriously. Yet the story has as often been one of protecting clerical privileges as of inclusivity. From the advocates' point of view, the story may be seen, as Tim Morris has suggested in Chapter 5, as a failure to take such resistance and theological objections seriously, a result of which is that the baptismal theology of Local Ministry and hence of Ordained Local Ministry has not been received.

Yet, the church has been permeated by the ideals of Local Ministry in ways that are hard to quantify, but which may be noted. The ability to work 'collaboratively' is now a criterion for selection for ordination training; and anyone applying for a parish post will need to demonstrate that he or she can work within a team, whether formally or informally constituted. These teams may consist of the curate and associate priests, churchwardens, Readers and other lay ministers; they may be statutory as is the Parochial Church Council; they may embrace the benefice or deanery. Teamwork is a feature of present-day Anglican ministry. The period of time that the stipendiary minister will stay in one place has decreased markedly in recent decades and is now often less than a decade. As an incomer, he or she now, more than ever, needs to draw on the expertise and knowledge of local leadership if the time spent there is to be effective. No longer is lay responsibility confined to being guardians of buildings, pastoral care for children, young adults and the elderly; Local Ministry has articulated the notion that the whole people of God, ordained and lay, are responsible for enacting the mission of the church. These core values of Local Ministry have become common assumptions across the Church of England.

A renewed appreciation of the local context may have arrived through the influence of liberation and feminist theology as much as through 'Local Ministry', but the effect has been a revived interest in the local church and community as the place of God's action. Obeying Christ's command to seek the kingdom, the activity of God is seen in local action as well as the national and international stage. Many recent publications addressing the church's call to mission stress the role of the local congregation as it reaches out to a society which appears to be shedding its Christian identity. The health, growth and character of the local congregation are all matters of greatest concern to those who care for the church's future. The word 'mission' no longer refers to what happens overseas: those working in 'mission' and in 'ministry' are agreed on one thing: the local church is the place of God's activity.

But still, Local Ministry has not been widely adopted as a dominant discourse in diocesan ministry strategies, and Ordained Local Ministry Schemes have been ended in some dioceses. Although some might argue that the values of Local Ministry can be sustained without Ordained Local Ministry, I have argued (in Chapter 8) that ordaining those recognized as having a sacramental character in their locality is necessary to affirm lay leadership and the ministry of the People of God as a whole. This chapter will address the question of the future for Ordained Local Ministry, looking both at the challenges it faces and the gifts it brings to the church.

Can Ordained Local Ministry survive in today's church?

The research described in Chapter 8, 'Ministry in Relationship', has shown that the distinctive training and formation of Ordained Local Ministers (OLMs) creates local missioners and local theologians who interpret the Gospel in their own culture. They are reflective practitioners, whose local calling and formation in a local congregation equip them to minister in that context. I was privileged to meet OLMs who were at home in their particular networks and used their knowledge to build bridges with the church. They were part of the farming, banking or educational world, employed at the supermarket checkout or the YMCA hostel, knew the Health Service or the leisure industries as insiders. Yet, this section will explore whether changes in national policy, themselves a reaction to the contemporary situation, may now run counter to the distinctive contribution that they make. Since, however, ministry is a changing dynamic, always adaptive to the needs of the contemporary church, why should there be concern if Ordained Local Ministry does not survive or if a new mutation arises to replace it? Is there anything particular about Ordained Local Ministry which is worth retaining?

The present environment does not look favourable for Ordained Local Ministry. The history of Ordained Local Ministry in Chapter 3 shows that fears about selection and training to national criteria of academic standards which might restrict recruitment and prevent the calling of those who can best communicate in non-professional communities have long been present. In addition, the institutional church's desire for flexibility of deployment appears to conflict with the vision of indigenous ministers, speaking the language of the locality. The introduction of Common Tenure,[1] and consequent Ministerial Reviews (on the basis of individual competencies which all must attain), also poses a challenge to the locally embedded, collaborative nature of Local Ministry.

Theological training

The shape of theological education is (once again) in a state of flux. The Church of England has, for a number of years, relied heavily on HEFCE[2] funding for training through the accreditation of its courses by Institutes of Higher Education. The Ministry Division review of Ordained Local Ministry (AC 2007a) recommended that training be shared with regional courses, so as to deliver high-quality training and to reduce the cost. This appears to work well when a diocesan OLM officer remains to represent the interests of the OLM ordinands and to ensure that training continues to include the participation of the local church. Without this provision, there is a danger that training for Ordained Local Ministry will be distinguished only by the omission of some elements of the curriculum, not by the significant addition of the work done in the setting of the local church which places all other learning in context and forms the local church into a community of learning. Pressures on funding for theological education have arrived at the same time as demands for accreditation of training are increasing: it would, indeed, be hard to say which came first, HEFCE funding or a concern with standards. But the consequences of the expectations of accreditation in terms of recruitment and performance appear to pose severe risks for Ordained Local Ministry.[3] David Leslie has argued that the production of 'cultural capital' predominates in the existing educational system, transmitted through accredited courses with tightly controlled learning outcomes. His concern is that that the affective and behavioural domains of learning will be under-represented in both curriculum planning and assessment, because they are less easy to fit into measurable learning outcomes (Leslie 2004). But it is the formation of personality and behaviour with which preparation for public service in God's Kingdom should be most concerned.

These are fears expressed on behalf of all ordinands, but they are especially pertinent for OLMs. The standards of an institute of higher education, despite all its efforts at improving access to education, may well be an obstacle to the training of precisely the kind of person that a diocese wishes to attract to Ordained Local Ministry. Jeffrey Heskins reflected that, after accreditation, the Southwark course was too academic, leaving little time for mature reflection on faith. Though some of those who had completed training said they had valued the academic challenge, others said they would not have started training under the new scheme (Heskins 2006). It is not only the academic nature of the content, but the manner of teaching and assessment that can be alien. My own experience, whether in discipleship courses or ministerial training, suggests that collaborative working as part of a learning community has been a significant factor in enabling individuals with a poor experience of education at school to overcome their lack of confidence and engage in transformational learning. The report, *Shaping the Future: New Patterns of Learning for Lay and Ordained* (AC 2005), recognized that the proposed learning outcomes focused on the individual, but advocated work to 'develop clear rationale for how and why groups are gathered, and how they enable different kinds of learning, practice, reflection and formation'. Small groups have indeed become a feature of church life, both in the local church and in ministerial training groups, but the educational model used has not always changed from that of the pulpit and lecture room. Anglican theological training has adopted the individualistic, competitive, educational model of schools and universities in the past: it now has the opportunity to value corporate and mutual learning which the training and formation given to OLMs has piloted. Such a group is engaged in a process of participative learning, in which all present have much to teach and learn. The group leader is one who facilitates the learning cycle, not the only one who understands Christian tradition and ministry. A reluctance to let go of control of the learning outcomes of the group may mirror a reluctance to relinquish control in a parish, diocese or national training. Thus, a change in educational process, or resistance to such change, will reflect changes in leadership styles in the wider church.

The need to present a coherent apologetic within a diversity of cultures is sometimes given as the reason for requiring education to degree standard. Yet, the capacity to express the Gospel in the culture of the locality is precisely the reason why an OLM might be called out from within that community – sometimes a place and a people which is not easily accommodated into the middle-class, professional mindset which has dominated Anglican thinking about ministry formation. The OLMs may well need assistance in translating their theological learning into the idiom of his or her own place, but it is crucial that learning is not done in a way that exaggerates a sense of distance from that culture through being taught a different language altogether. Locally deployed ordinands need to retain a strong connection with the culture and community that has called them out, so as to speak with a locally authentic voice and to be an integral part of the local leadership. If potential OLMs are turned away, the church may find itself with a few more graduate ministers, but be even more restricted in its capacity to reach many parts of society. One OLM ordinand still told me that he felt he was 'breaking into the rich man's house' in becoming ordained: a mark of the perceived gulf that can exist between ordained ministry and congregation.

Local Ministry Officers fear that an increased emphasis on academic competence will result in the separation of ordinands from those training for other forms of ministry, accredited or otherwise. The training of Readers is under similar pressure to that of OLMs to meet academic standards, but training for pastoral care, evangelism and other lay ministries will not take place in institutes of higher education. The significance of an understanding of ministry as relational in a theological sense has already been argued, in Chapter 8, as has the benefit of licensed ministers training together. OLMs are not expected to be competent in all areas of ministry, but to take their part in a team, recognizing their weaknesses as well as their strengths. It might, for example, be expected that an OLM will be someone who is a spiritual guide in the church and, as a sacramental focus, one who prays and leads worship. But there is no inherent reason why that person should be a preacher and teacher: that may not be his or her gift, whereas it is expected that Readers will preach. Training alongside lay ministers, at least for some of the time, makes this expectation evident and contributes to the particular character of Ordained Local Ministry.

Team work/deployability

A review carried out in 2006 by the Bishop of Norwich as the chair of Ministry Division (AC 2007a) revealed that Ordained Local Ministry was gaining support in some dioceses at the same time that it was losing support in others. Using a very broad understanding of Ordained Local Ministry as locally grown ministry with an intention to deploy in the parish/benefice of origin, a third of the dioceses that responded were broadly in favour of this category of ministry. Four dioceses wanted to explore the introduction of such a ministry, while two wanted to reconsider their present scheme, but the fluidity of the debate was evident and there were strong cross-currents within dioceses on this matter. Dioceses with OLM Schemes saw one of the core values of Ordained Local Ministry as promoting a healthier view of vocation: the call coming from the church that then finds a proper response in the candidate. This was seen as a corrective to over-individualized understandings of vocation to ordained ministry. Ordained Local Ministry was embedded in a local community, expressing the contextual and relational nature of ministry, and collaborative learning during training had encouraged collaborative patterns of ministry.

Yet, the core values of Ordained Local Ministry, which were identified by the survey, do not include the essential ingredient of a team collaborating in shared ministry and leadership, out of which the vocation of an OLM emerges. Without this element, ordained locally based ministry can easily become another clerical solution to the church's needs. Some later mutations – non-stipendiary ministry with a local licence, for example – have not recognized that what Ordained Local Ministry has articulated is the foundational significance of a team, people who intentionally share ministry together. Such mutations are reactive; they return prominence to ordained ministry, as if the priority for the church's well-being was the number of sacramental ministers it has, rather than the active discipleship of the whole body in mission. And there may be practical problems when someone is licensed in a particular locality for long-term service without the support and corrective presence of a gifted and resourced team.

It appears very hard for the institutional church to conceive of ministry as shared, as corporate. So while diocesan bodies discuss the deployability of an ordained person, they are not likely to consider a parish team as deployable. Once, however, the nature of Ordained Local Ministry is understood, it makes as much sense to think as much about deploying the local church's team as deploying the OLM. To recognize the call of someone who is embedded in his or her local community, on the basis of which they represent that community and are able to communicate in that community's vocabulary – and then to complain that they cannot be sent somewhere else appears perverse! (The Church of England, indeed, does not 'deploy' any of its ministers, ordained or lay, without regard for their calling, their own preferences and their gifts and abilities.) An OLM may change his or her category of ministry; a local calling may be the first part of a journey to a wider national calling. But it cannot be assumed that this will be the case.

The history of Ordained Local Ministry in the Diocese of Truro demonstrates just how hard it is to effect change in the Church of England.

Right from the start, it was agreed that their scheme should be different because of their strong clerical tradition. It was felt that there was more chance of parishes accepting Local Ministry if the OLM came first and the lay team second. The idea was that OLM candidates should gather around them a local lay 'learning group' with whom they would share the ordination course. (The course itself was delivered by the South West Ministry Training Scheme.) In this way, OLMs would be trained locally and within the local context; and it was hoped that the laity would be 'set alight' by the experience of theological education, and would then move on to form a local ministry team for their parish. In a number of parishes, at first this seemed to work positively, but so strong was the tradition of clerical authority in local culture that, once the OLM had been ordained, the training teams faded away, and with 'our priest again', it was business as usual. As the bishop's staff saw it, the basic idea had been that the scheme would help to move a conservative diocese towards collaborative ministry, and this just was not happening – in fact, the reverse was happening.

The other problem facing the Truro Scheme was essentially financial. After the initial surge of ordinands, the number recommended for training fell and the cost of training them escalated. This was compounded when funding rules were changed and the training of an OLM became a charge of the diocese. The bishop's staff discovered that the best way out of this situation was to recommend only good 'local' candidates but to send them to national rather than to local selection conferences. This meant that, if they were accepted for 'local' non-stipendiary ministry, their training was no longer a charge of the diocese.

For these two reasons, the OLM scheme in the Diocese of Truro was wound up in 2001. From then on, local candidates have been sent forward to national conferences with a 'local' tag. At the same time, the diocese has launched a series of courses to train local laypeople for ministry in their parishes; and so far, 500 lay people have been commissioned as local worship leaders or pastoral assistants. So, though with hindsight, it is probably fair to say that the way in which the Truro Scheme was set up was doomed from the start; ironically, its demise has led to an initiative that has moved the local church a little further towards collaborative ministry. Unintended consequences may be beneficial as well as detrimental, even while it remains true that intentional change is problematic.

Dioceses continue in their desire to work in a more strategically mission-focused way. Working flexibly across parish boundaries should be encouraged in a church that recognizes the network nature of relationships in contemporary society. A 'local' licence does not have to be defined geographically. The bishop's licence could be given to a team of ministers of a particular community, such as those who work on the land, or the employees who commute to a particular workplace. They might require special skills and training, such as sign language or youth work qualifications. The experience of chaplaincy and of pioneer ministry indicates the value of such ministry, but it is only in recent years that new ventures, such as street pastors, have been consciously undertaken as a corporate venture. The provision of Bishop's Mission Orders recognizes this and encourages such local initiatives.[4] The authorization of the local licence is not then a restriction, but a protective boundary which focuses the particular gifts of group members, enabling them to be local theologians and missioners. It provides a protection against the inevitable pressure to spend time and energy sustaining existing Christian communities that remain dependent on help from without. The local licence enables the distinctive contribution of Ordained Local Ministry to be made.

The one serious area of weakness in a system in which OLMs always returned to their sending parish that I noted was in the unknowable quality of supervision that they would receive. As the preparation and review of other training incumbents improved, it became ever more apparent that some OLMs were receiving very little supervision and support in the first years after ordination. The significance of these early years is well known and a diocese has a responsibility to ensure consistent oversight of ministry. It takes particular skill to pastor and supervise someone who knows the area and has wider contacts than oneself and, since the incumbents of OLMs are, by their very nature, not chosen for this role, they need resources and support.

Common Tenure

The introduction of Common Tenure for clergy has significantly redefined the roles and expectations of clergy and dioceses. Its influence on the development of ministry, not least Ordained Local Ministry, is not yet apparent. The Ministerial Development Review Schemes which have been developed by dioceses alongside Common Tenure provide an opportunity for regular, often annual, reflection for all clergy. It will be tempting to apply a one-size-fits-all template to the review process, one which reinforces a clerical paradigm. It has already been noted that the learning outcomes, outlined in *Shaping the Future* (AC 2005), expected at each stage of ministry are individualistic, requiring identical competencies regardless of whether the ordained person is working within a team or not. If dioceses wish to encourage collaborative ministry, they will need to ensure that review schemes include enquiry about ministers' competency as team players and involve feedback from colleagues. In some dioceses, the licence of an OLM was directly linked to the licence given to a team, often for five years. This had the effect, in Lichfield for example, of placing OLMs in an awkward position when the five years came to an end when, for whatever reason, the licence had not yet been renewed. Common Tenure, which will not allow for fixed-term licences in such circumstances, has had the benefit of removing this anomaly and has also made enquiry about team-work skills possible.

Since Common Tenure applies to all ordained ministers, stipendiary or not, OLMs have been affirmed in their orders but at the same time distinguished from their lay ministry colleagues. The resources which must be made available for ministerial review and for continuing ministerial development for clergy are not so likely to be available for lay ministers, even those holding the bishop's licence. This fact alone may tend to disconnect the OLM from the local team of which he or she is a part.

Should Ordained Local Ministry have a future?

Ordained Local Ministry has not emerged primarily from a desire to change the nature of priesthood, but as an outcome of developing the potential of local churches and their congregations. It must always be exercised within the context of a team and that team is far more than a support group, or even a training group, but a genuine partnership of leadership and ministry within the church. Ordained Local Ministry is not likely to work effectively unless the church adopts a more consistently collaborative approach to all forms of ministry. Both dioceses and local churches have welcomed ordinands called from their own congregations to serve in the local area. 'Locally deployed SSMs' have been ordained even where there is no formal OLM Scheme. But it has been argued that this is an extension of institutional clericalism, not a new vision of ministry. The story of Ordained Local Ministry may be the story of a church that is willing to experiment with shared leadership and clergy and laity working together, but which easily reverts to inherited models of ministry.

Ordained Local Ministry does present many challenges to these inherited assumptions about clerical authority and leadership. This is apparent at the point of ordination: the ordinal does not truly reflect the situation of a priest whose vocation was local, whose ministry will be local and whose ministry will be exercised collaboratively with a team of local laypeople (Weston 1999). OLMs have, in their training and formation, contributed to a fresh understanding of ministry as relational and reminded the church that it needs local theologians and missioners as much as it needs academic theologians. The pattern of OLM training has re-enforced the need to pay serious attention to the contextual nature of theology and has encouraged the inclusion of a participative, collaborative model of education. But the pressure of finance and attendant moves towards accreditation of all training, together with well-defined, individualistic learning outcomes at later stages of ministry, threaten the distinctive nature of Ordained Local Ministry. I have described OLMs as having a public sacramental ministry in the context of a collaborative leadership team (Chapter 8). Without the essential ingredient of a collaborative team, the foundational insight of

Local Ministry, the theological and education radicalism of Ordained Local Ministry is lost.

Notes

1 See www.commontenure.org for a full explanation of the new terms of service for clergy in the Church of England.
2 HEFCE is the acronym for Higher Education Funding Council for England.
3 The report on the Structure and Funding of Ordination Training (the 'Hind' Report 2003) advised that a degree in theology should be the norm for clergy. It noted that this was now the case for other practitioners such as teachers and nurses but did not enter into discussion about whether the clerical 'profession' was analogous to these, or whether the practice of nursing and teaching skills had been improved as a result.
4 See http://www.sharetheguide.org/section5/bmo for further details of Bishop's Mission Orders.

Alice's story

Alice, priested in 2011 in an inner city parish

It was the encouragement of a conversation I had with my incumbent in which he asked 'had I thought about ordination?' We already had a Local Ministry team and I was involved in helping to lead worship.

I have always had this heart for the community. I was already involved in many things; I approached everything from a Christian viewpoint. So this did not necessarily come as a surprise. I was concerned, 'will they dismiss me?' but this disappeared as I became more confident.

In my own case, the process to training and selection was quite hurried. I was conscious of my age and how old I would be once I'd finished training. I would not encourage anyone to be rushed. The preparation towards it for both team, congregation and OLM is important.

I felt so strongly that if I had been called, God would not let me down.

I thought that an OLM was a priest in a local community bringing the strengths of local knowledge and a heart for the local community, someone who would head up the Local Ministry Team helping them to grow and work in the leadership role together.

The reality has proved different because of the personality/leadership style of the incumbent. It became obvious that a shared leadership role was not going to happen and some of this was to do with his self-esteem and lack of security.

The team was not prepared for an OLM. I suspect that they were not part of the selection process despite the diocesan recommendations.

I was pleasantly surprised during the whole time of training that we were treated no differently to any ordinand on the course (with the exception of diocesan book grants!). I did not feel any lesser than any one else. I think if anything where you do feel lesser is as part of the whole NSM/stipendiary thing. You can see the priority given to stipendiary curates and the opportunities they are given. This can make you feel less valued even if it is unintentional.

I am pretty certain that not all the stipendiary curates, if any, understand OLM or LM.

I think this is because they think it (OLM) is a lesser thing to do. Or that it is not ambitious enough or that an OLM has not got what it takes. Many do not understand it, nor do they want to, because it impacts on their status. On the whole, among those who have no knowledge of LM–OLM, it seems they are just not interested in finding out or are unwilling to see the vision for how it might work.

The most important characteristic of an OLM is the ability to be collaborative.

I am aware of the danger of giving a new incumbent the impression that you know everything there is to know about the local community. You need to be able to stand back to let them establish themselves.

As an OLM, I do not want to end up as the person who does all the odd jobs that the incumbent does not want to do or cannot see him- or herself doing. You are very vulnerable as an OLM because so much depends on your incumbent.

I am not convinced that the other clergy in my deanery understand OLM or the fact that I am happy to be part of a wider team. I am getting the feeling that my role is being affirmed more, not that it was not accepted, since I have been presiding at the Eucharist. It has given me a physical, a visual authority. People are feeling safe with me in this role.

I would hope as I grow in experience that I will always take with me a strong sense of community and use the skills I have to foster community. I would also hope to have a role in encouraging and nurturing others as they develop their own special gifts and ministries.

10

The Gloucester story

Andrew Bowden

One of the most interesting characteristics of Ordained Local Ministry Schemes is their diversity. They really are local, tailored to the geographical needs and the ecclesiological views of the staff of that particular diocese. As enthusiasm for Local Ministry developed, it spawned a national network with an annual conference which led to a healthy exchange of ideas among the schemes; but at root, every diocese did it differently, and every diocese had its own spin on what it meant by 'local', by 'ministry' and by 'OLM' – a diversity that is strongly affirmed in the Advisory Board for Ministry's[1] Policy Paper No. I in 1991.

However, this chapter is not concerned with the minutiae of how different dioceses do Local Ministry, let alone with what works best. That has been well covered in a number of excellent books by Robin Greenwood and by a number of papers circulated within the Local Ministry Network.[2] We are concerned to see how the 'vision' as reflected in diocesan reports has developed over the twenty years since 1991.

These reports have been produced by dioceses, usually for internal consumption, with the intention of monitoring progress; and they are supplemented by the regular Ministry Division (MinDiv) inspection reports of schemes. It has not been possible to read or assemble all these documents, but in those studied, a pattern begins to emerge. The development of the scheme in the Diocese of Gloucester is examined in detail, and the chapter concludes with a brief discussion in the light of the reports about the present state of play.

The Gloucester story – the foundations laid

In the 1980s, Bishop John Yates of Gloucester took a number of initiatives to encourage 'all-member-ministry' in the diocese. He set up two residential conferences at Swanwick to which 200 laity were invited by their parishes, and 250 clergy were invited. For those who had attended clergy-only conferences, these events were a glimpse of a church renewed – exciting and positively revolutionary.

The bishop had appointed Canon Robin Greenwood as Diocesan Missioner, who then launched a Lent initiative with the declared object of encouraging the parishes to think about collaborative ministry. The bishop also appointed a Rural Group and a Rural Officer with the aim of raising the profile of rural ministry, and of highlighting the dilemma faced by clergy ministering in ever larger multi-parish benefices. A visit to Lincoln Diocese to see how their Local Ministry Scheme worked led to the Rural Group bringing a paper to the 1992 Diocesan Synod entitled 'A Vision for the Rural Future', which recommended the setting up of a diocesan Local Ministry Scheme on the Lincoln model. With the backing of the Synod, the idea was taken to the parishes in the form of a diocesan road show and, to the amazement of the organizers, the meetings were oversubscribed: 200–300 people signed up to act as 'change-agents' in their parishes. Within 6 months, Local Ministry officers were appointed, the Gloucester Scheme was approved by MinDiv and the first tranche of LM teams had begun a three-year course of training.

The early years

To a large extent, the Local Ministry officers were sailing in uncharted waters. They had to develop a scheme that fitted the local context by simple trial and error. A glance at the records of the early national Local Ministry Network meetings show how each diocese wanted to learn from the others because in those days there was no agreed solution.

A reading of the policy documents at Gloucester show a number of key concerns. The officers recognized that any move towards all-member-ministry was going to involve a major cultural shift in the way the parish was perceived by clergy, by members of the congregation, and by nominal Christian parishioners. They realized it was not going to be easy and they set up a series of professionally run training days in order to clarify their message to the parishes. They also used a professional 'change consultant' (who happened to be ordained) to work out innovative ways of meeting the challenge and persuading people to change their model of 'being church'. They recognized that the parish priest – the chief change agent – had to lead from the front, and that the parish had to be behind the move if there was any hope of serious movement.

The establishment of a team could only usefully emerge after a lengthy period of preparation for the whole parish. And even then, the way in which the team was chosen was fraught with difficulty. If the congregation and parishioners were to recognize team members as authentic 'ministers', they had to be seen to have an official part in the selection of the team; but the clergy had to be happy that those nominated were 'fit for purpose'. Further, laypeople needed to have some 'authority' from the bishop (as churchwardens do) if they were to 'minister' in the parish. In Gloucester, the bishop agreed that, after three years' training, he would grant the team his 'mandate'.

A number of the Local Ministry officers had trained as teachers, and they were persuaded that the scheme would best be served by using a 'transformative training method' that valued and drew out the gifts and wisdom of those with few educational qualifications, as well as those with higher degrees. It was a method that had been developed and used with success in the inner-city schemes of Liverpool and Manchester (Leslie 2004), and was flexible enough to be adapted to the local context. As the minutes of the diocese's Local Ministry Management Committee show, this led to the writing of new modules specially designed for the Gloucester Scheme and to phasing out the use of material which had been 'borrowed' from the diocese of Lincoln.

The first OLMs

The development of these new modules overlapped with the emergence of the first Ordained Local Ministers (OLMs) within the diocese's Local Ministry Scheme, and was, in part, a response to the difficulties that had arisen. The Lincoln Scheme had been prepared on the assumption that the course for the team would qualify as the first year of the course for OLMs. In practice, it satisfied no one. Many lay members felt they were being put through a course in theology when what they needed was a course in practical team-centred ministry: and MinDiv, whose mandate is to ensure the theological quality of ordination training, reckoned that it was frequently inadequate. Even at this early stage, there was a real tension seen in the minutes of the Gloucester Local Ministry Scheme Governing Body between the 'vision' of Local Ministry, that the appropriate setting for training local priests was the local place and the belief of MinDiv and the principal of West of England Ministerial Training Course (WEMTC), that the training of priests has to be theologically challenging and rigorous. It is a tension that has never been satisfactorily resolved. Ultimately, MinDiv withdrew their authorization of the Gloucester Scheme, and the responsibility for training OLMs was transferred to WEMTC with a diocesan Local Ministry officer sitting as an adviser on their boards and committees.

The Bracegirdle review

In 1999, Dr Pat Bracegirdle, a former University Lecturer and Chief Inspector of Schools, was asked to review the Scheme. The inspection was rigorous and highly professional, and it revealed a real success story. Within five years, 27 teams involving 240 laypeople were either mandated or in training, and they and their parishes came over as bubbling with enthusiasm. 'The atmosphere in Church has changed.' One of her interviewees reported, 'The whole place feels right – joyful, caring, happier, more relaxed' (Bracegirdle 1999: 18).

Of course, there are a number of recommendations – 18 of them – about how things could be done better, but the final conclusion of this experienced inspector was this.

> It is very clear from this exercise that almost everywhere Local Ministry . . . is working well, and from this point of view the scheme is very successful . . . The atmosphere of joy and excitement is almost tangible in some parishes, not only in team members but in the church as a whole. (Bracegirdle 1999: 39)

Over the next few years, Local Ministry continued to enjoy the full support of both the bishop's staff and the Synod. By 2004, there were the equivalent of four full-time diocesan staff with secretarial back-up, supporting 45 teams covering nearly 40 per cent of the parishes in the diocese. In 2000, the bishop told Synod that it was his personal hope that there should be a Local Ministry Team in each parish in the diocese by the time he retired, and that he regarded the annual Local Ministry mandating service as one of the three great ministerial occasions of the year alongside the Petertide ordination and the annual commissioning service for Readers. In 2001, a report to the finance committee of the diocese showed that, even if there were the stipendiary priests available to fill all vacancies, the diocese would not be able to support them financially in the long term, and that the continued support of Local Ministry was the best economic option to prepare for the future.

Emerging problems

However, 2004 was in fact to prove the high watermark of Local Ministry in the diocese. The problems inherent in the scheme were emerging, the financial climate was changing and the personnel at Church House in Gloucester were changing too.

Local Ministry cost a lot of money. Not only could it take three to four years of officer time to bring a parish to the point of choosing a team but also, once trained, teams needed to be 'serviced'. Because they were 'mandated' – effectively licensed by the bishop – teams needed to be inspected and their licence renewed every five years (originally it was every three years, but this was found to be too demanding of officer time). While an evident strength of the scheme was to create a Local Ministry 'family of parishes' who drew strength from each other – a mega-deanery that actually worked – this 'koinonia' could only flourish on the back of diocesan training days and other opportunities to meet socially. These get-togethers mopped up hours of officer time, and the records are full of examples of their detailed planning. Most of them were successful – even memorable – but they all cost a lot of money to stage. The fact that so many busy people were prepared to give up weekends to join such events speaks volumes for their quality and for the effectiveness of the scheme; but to those who were 'outside', it seemed increasingly that Local Ministry parishes were enjoying a gold-standard training denied to others. So, when cuts in diocesan staff had to be made for financial reasons, Local Ministry was inevitably a prime target.

It was also becoming apparent that there was a fundamental difference of theological emphasis between the Local Ministry staff and many of the clergy. The officers believed they were on a mission to change the ecclesiological culture so that 'the priesthood of all believers' could become a practical reality of parish life. Their jackdaw file of teaching material reveals that for them 'collaboration' meant a priest working as an equal alongside laypeople, exercising a priestly facilitator role, but not necessarily a management role unless that happened to be their particular gifting. Whereas for many parishes 'collaboration' simply meant the vicar working with a few vicar-chosen 'vicar's helpers', while in other, largely urban parishes, the ecclesiological premise was that the leadership role was 'by nature' the spiritual gifting of the incumbent.

This largely unarticulated confusion about the meaning of 'collaboration' led to growing resentment and irritation. Parishes who imagined themselves to be collaborative resented being regarded as second-class citizens by Local Ministry purists, nor did they see why they needed a major course designed to change the clerical-dependency culture before they could progress into the premier league. The difficulties are particularly well chronicled in the notes of the regular meetings between the Local Ministry officers and the archdeacons, with the latter pressing for certain parishes to be taken into the fold, and the officers demurring because they believed this would mean abandoning core standards.

Perhaps the most traumatic issue was the appointment of new incumbents to Local Ministry parishes. The Bracegirdle Report records how the flagship team of the north Cotswolds was dismantled by a new incumbent who did not accept the ecclesiological premises of local ministry, even though he had accepted the offer of the living. As a result of this debacle, team members were deeply hurt spiritually, and no other parishes in the deanery were prepared seriously to consider the Local Ministry option for a decade.

At least the bishop's staff appreciated the seriousness of what had happened; and as a result, from then on Local Ministry officers were invited to take part in appointment panels for Local Ministry parishes. Further, new incumbents to Local Ministry parishes were instructed to have an induction interview with one of the officers. Nevertheless, once inducted, incumbents often proved extremely reluctant to accept anything like an effective Local Ministry induction course, and over the years, another four teams have been deliberately disbanded by new incumbents.

Even if they did not actually disband their teams, new incumbents with no previous experience of Local Ministry often found the going hard. A particular gripe was that the team they had inherited did not seem to be clear about what their role was. It was a difficulty that was frequently aired at the clergy/officer meetings for incumbents of Local Ministry parishes that were held twice a year (and proved an invaluable opportunity for puzzled incumbents to let off steam). When unpacked – and there are copious references in the minutes to the time and care taken by officers to try to unpack perceptions – what this usually amounted to was that the incumbent had come with an understanding of what a team was for which did not match with the team's idea of their own role. The truth was that no two teams had the same role. Over a period of years, each team had painstakingly hammered out a role for themselves that was felt to fit their local context. It meant that a new incumbent needed to submit to a 'joining process' that would inevitably take months rather than hours if they were to integrate fruitfully with their team. That required great commitment to 'the cause' – and great humility. Local Ministry officers for their part had become aware that the role of a team tended to vary widely depending on the gifts of the team members, and they honoured this because it took the local context seriously: but it was difficult to explain to someone with no Local Ministry experience.

All of this contributed to a growing perception among the bishop's staff that Local Ministry parishes – though good in so many ways – were hard work. The emergence of OLMs within the teams also raised difficult issues. We have seen how the need to train OLMs 'in house' led to problems about how this should be done: and this was later compounded when funding rules were changed and the training of OLMs became a charge on the local diocese. The issue then arose about how and where they could be deployed. No one except the Local Ministry officers and the OLMs themselves could really understand why OLMs, once ordained, could only be used to take services within their own home parish: and this was of course a particularly urgent concern in ever expanding multi-parish benefices. It was also difficult for incumbents to continue to treat – and to be seen to treat – OLMs as 'just one of the Local Ministry clergy-lay team'. They clearly needed to be one of the liturgical/pastoral subcommittee, and this was where the core work of the parish was usually discussed in-depth. These were concerns that were regularly discussed in the clergy/officer meetings and in the meetings with the archdeacons. A great deal clearly depended on the spiritual maturity of the OLM and the incumbent, and on their commitment to the ethos of local ministry. They needed to be very strong to resist the insidious temptation to drift into a cosy clerical in-group.

Apart from these difficulties with the day-to-day running of the scheme, the diocese naturally developed in other directions. New issues emerged that wanted their place in the sun – and their desk in Church House Gloucester. We all had to recover our sense of MISSION, but Mission Action Plans needed an officer to drive them. The Synod felt there should be a desk for Ecology and Climate Change – though this was achieved by a merger with the Rural Affairs Officer. The running of Church Schools became more and more complicated, and a new Secondary School meant that there could be no cuts in the Education Department. And then there was the Communications Explosion, as a result of which the diocese now boasts two Communications Officers, a Head of IT Systems and a Data-base Assistant. Local Ministry is no longer the only pebble on the beach – nor is it at the top of the diocesan agenda.

The new bishop

Some of the understandable defensiveness that was beginning to creep into Local Ministry is echoed in the letter sent by the LM officers to the Vacancy in See Committee in 2004. It makes a powerfully argued case for the appointment of a new bishop committed to the ethos of Local Ministry – because it was clearly felt that such a case now needed to be powerfully made; support for Local Ministry could no longer be assumed.

When he arrived, the new bishop visited a number of Local Ministry parishes, but he also listened carefully to the concerns of those clergy who were outside the Local Ministry family. In 2007, when he had got a measure of the local situation, he held a residential conference for clergy and lay workers. This in itself was a departure from the pattern of clergy/lay diocesan conferences referred to above, and marked a clear distinction between those under the authority of the bishop and the person in the pew. In his opening address, he underlined the significance of the 'college of clergy' – a new term for Gloucester – and shared with them the need he felt for the diocese to have an agreed strategy for ministry and the details of pastoral care, which was to be – in the mildest possible way of course! – enforceable across the board. The conference was, he said, to be supplemented by two day-long meetings a year for the same group, when the bishop would share issues with them and agree key strategies and regulations. In effect, this means that a group of clergy and diocesan employees who are all licensed to the bishop, rather than the Synods which are shared by clergy and laity and elected by local congregations, now take a very significant role in the preparation of diocesan strategy. One other significant change was that the Maundy Thursday Service for the blessing of oils was greatly enhanced and took on the nature of an annual affirmation of the ordained ministry. It became clear that it was regarded by the bishop's staff as of greater significance than the annual service for the renewal of licences by Local Ministry Team a significant shift in focus from the position taken by his predecessor in 2000.

In these circumstances, it is not perhaps surprising that the Department of Discipleship and Ministry has been reorganized, with Local Ministry now firmly part of the Ministry team rather than being an independent unit. Broadly speaking, the new department covers all aspects of ordained and Reader ministry, and also has a brief for 'parish development' and the encouragement of all-member-ministry. It remains to be seen whether such a re-arrangement will allow a truly collaborative culture to flourish in the parishes. The hope that it may do so is expressed in a very interesting way in a recent paper that we need finally to consider.

A new pattern for ministry

In January 2008, the bishop circulated a paper titled 'The Pressure on Our Ministry' (Perham 2008a). With great sensitivity, it highlights the overwhelming pressures now placed on the clergy – 'spinning like a top, whirling away into invisibility. . . . kitten limbed and crucified by centrifugal force' as Iris Murdoch eloquently puts it. As the bishop sees it, the situation, especially for stipendiaries and their families, is becoming intolerable. Our expectations of 'the Vicar' have got to change; and the vicars' expectations of themselves have got to change too. He outlines a number of ways in which the bishop's staff and the departments of the diocese are determined to support the clergy and their families up to the hilt.

In an extended section on the nature of the priestly ministry, the bishop quotes Monica Furlong and Gregory Nazianzus – an interesting combination! – to make the point that priests are first and foremost called to be holy and for that they need 'space'. Nevertheless, he continues to assume that the incumbent is also called to 'leadership', and he particularly commends a Leadership Course for Clergy being offered by the diocese.

As he sees it, there is a major problem and there has to be radical change: but not apparently a change that involves abandoning the Anglican tradition of clerical incumbency. Priests are to remain the leaders and are not to be released from the ultimate burden of responsibility for management. It is not envisaged that they should be transformed from managers into 'holy facilitators'.

In parallel with this document, the bishop was also preparing another paper, 'A Parson in Every Parish' (Perham 2008b), and was consulting widely with groups in the diocese with the hope of getting it right. It is perhaps best seen as a follow on from the first paper and explores how the parishes and parish-based clergy can do their bit to help to share the burden of ministry. What is especially interesting is that it revolves around a number of insights – even core values – of Local Ministry. The local place is still recognized as the basic unit for ministry. Local people would be expected to cooperate across boundaries, but ultimately local people are to be supported in running their own show.

Although the stipendiary clergy (as incumbents) are still seen as being 'in charge', they are here described as 'having a ministry of oversight – an Episcopal role – perhaps to be a teacher and trainer, and to develop the skills to hold together in collaborative ministry the clergy and the teams'. But they cannot **and should not try** to be the 'persona' for every settlement.

Yet, every settlement is reckoned to need a 'persona' – someone for local people to look up to, both as representing the church and as mirroring the life of holiness to which we are all called. Though the persona may be a layperson, the concept is clearly modelled on the OLM, and in the paper, the place and ministry of OLMs is given extended, largely positive consideration. There are also frequent references to teams of laypeople and to the 'vocation' of laypeople to a variety of ministries – another core Local Ministry idea.

So, in a whole variety of ways, it can be seen that many of the core values of Local Ministry are now regarded as being mainstream, and indeed as essential if the pressure on the stipendiary clergy is to be eased.

However, in the original draft of the paper, the 'persona' remains obstinately singular. Nor is there any serious exploration of the theological premises that undergird Local Ministry – the Holy Trinity as the touchstone of what the church is called to be, and therefore as the normative model for ministry; baptism as a sacrament of ordination to all-member-ministry; the priesthood of all believers and the perception that the threefold clerical ministry emerges from within the general priesthood of all, and is not separate from it. In this way, as one of the responses to the bishop put it, the paper missed an opportunity to carry forward that serious commitment to collaborative all-member-ministry that Local Ministry had pioneered in the diocese.

Effective ministry in every parish

The bishop listened to the suggestions of others, and the paper was eventually presented to the Synod, not as 'A Parson in every Parish', but as 'Effective Ministry in Every Parish'. The 'persona' has become plural – or at least surrounded by a group or team of laypeople, and the paper now begins and ends with a resounding affirmation of the principles of Local Ministry.

> This paper relies heavily on the work of Local Ministry Teams. With all the talk about a more flexible style to Local Ministry it is time to reiterate the core principle . . . The vision of Local Ministry is the ministry of all God's people; it is radically inclusive. It is a vision that will take different shapes in different places. . . . All our strategy is directed at sustaining the Christian community as it celebrates the grace of God by using the gifts He has given in the service of His world. (Gloucester Diocesan Synod 2008: 7.4)

The national story

The value of following the detailed story of Local Ministry in one diocese is that it mirrors what has happened elsewhere. A similar historical exercise could be done in Lichfield, Hereford, Lincoln, Guildford, Oxford, Newcastle and probably many other dioceses. In all of them, similar patterns would be seen: an explosion of enthusiasm and a release of all-member-ministry within congregations; difficulties about the training and formation of OLMs, and the near impossible task of keeping them local and un-clerical; a growing resentment against Local Ministry by those who felt it was not for them; the emergence of new causes that claimed their own diocesan officer and their place in the sun; a major financial crisis that led to a cutback in the numbers of Local Ministry staff, and often to the LM Department losing its autonomy.

Most Local Ministry Departments have shown great resilience in the face of challenges. Some like Guildford have kept their training standards high and have ensured that the training for OLMs and Readers remains firmly anchored to local issues. Others like Lichfield and Lincoln have developed specialist training for laypeople to help them minister in their local parishes. Some like Hereford now welcome parishes on their own terms, not imposing a set scheme but working with local people to implement a collaborative ministry that local people think is best for their context. Even those dioceses like Truro that have wound up their official OLM schemes have gone on to stimulate genuine lay ministry in different ways.[3]

What certainly emerges on the positive side is that a number of the core insights of Local Ministry have been taken into the diocesan bloodstream, even when the resources for schemes have been severely curtailed. It is now 'normal' to expect that a vocation to ordained ministry will have its roots in the encouragement of a local congregation. The role of the congregation in recognizing and testing a vocation to priesthood is now accepted as essential. Training for the ordained ministry is now 'normally' related to a series of local projects. Collaborative ministry is recognized as 'a good thing', and it is assumed, even if this is not always achieved, that all ordinands will be trained to work collaboratively, not just with other clergy but also with lay teams. Indeed, the latest national guidelines for ministry selectors suggest that candidates should show evidence of being 'team players'. It is assumed that ministerial teams, even in large parishes, will include laypeople as well as clergy. It is assumed that all of God's people are commissioned by their baptism to His ministry in His world.

What has not yet changed, in most dioceses and most parishes, is the culture of dependence on the clergy. Diocesan staff, most of whom have never worked in a Local Ministry Team themselves, still put their faith in the stipendiary as 'incumbent'. As seen in a previous chapter, the diocese of Northern Michigan regards stipendiaries as essentially 'companions along the way' – advisers and facilitators. Except in a few places, English dioceses and English clergy and English congregations do not see it that way – yet.

But perhaps, the time will come. Over the last year (2010–11), the diocese of Lichfield has radically reorganized their Local Ministry Scheme for a variety of local reasons, but in the same sort of direction as the Diocese of Gloucester. And yet, the Bishop of Shrewsbury (a suffragan of Lichfield) could write with passion and great good humour in the autumn 2010 issue of *Country Way* about his own 'conversion' to collaborative ministry. He describes how as a parish priest he had to change all his ecclesiological presuppositions about 'vicaring'.

'The effective role of a vicar is more talent spotter than performer and more trellis-builder than planter.' The doctrine of the Holy Trinity gives us the model. 'If the Trinity speaks of unity in diversity, then rural teams that cherish the local and individual whilst gaining strength from belonging together will be showing the way forward for the Church in the twenty-first century.' (Rylands 2010: 21)

What Local Ministry officer could put it more succinctly?

Notes

1 The name of the national church's department for ministry has changed over the years. 'Ministry Division', familiarly termed 'MinDiv', is the current title and is used throughout this chapter.
2 www.localministry.net/home
3 Copies of diocesan reports are usually available from diocesan offices or from Diocesan Ministry Departments.

Reflection on the stories

The opportunity to listen to and reflect on the stories of OLMs in the Diocese of Gloucester has been humbling and inspiring. I am struck by the fragility of their vocation to priesthood within a diocesan context which is now shaped by a very different ecclesiological discourse to that ten to fifteen years ago.

We are reminded of the importance of vocational identity and for this to be nourished and affirmed however it might be expressed. We are able to sense the humility, the faithfulness and the obedience in each OLM's response to being called, their determination to get on with it in the face of partiality, discrimination and sheer ignorance. These are stories of the struggle to integrate their vocational journey with that of stipendiary and other self-supporting clergy, rooted in an ecclesiology of the local church as the priestly people of God. These are stories of hope and commitment. Commitment to the local community and the determination to nourish spiritually and pastor faithfully; commitment to the ministry of the whole of the baptized, encouraging and affirming the ministry of others; commitment to wanting to work collegially with others, nourished by the affirmation of being called and affirmed themselves in their vocation by their local community, if not all of their clerical colleagues. These are stories of growth in depth of faith, of the emerging sense of vocational identity ratified and authenticated locally as well as through national selection processes. These are stories of growth in the confidence and capacity of folk who would never have had sufficient self-belief to offer themselves outright for ordination. There are important insights into appropriate leadership and to the tendency to benchmark all ministries by the characteristics of stipendiary priesthood. These are encouraging stories of the strength, resilience and wisdom of OLMs, their care for the nurture of the leadership and ministries of others, together with a belief in the potential for people to grow into vocational maturity individually as well as collectively.

These stories demonstrate that Ordained Local Ministry is a challenge both theologically and ecclesiologically to the wider church in its pressing reminder of the importance of

- The rootedness, provenance and authenticity of ministry within the local;
- The affirmation and encouragement of the corporate priesthood, the giftings and vocations of the local congregation and the role of the ordained in validating and releasing this;
- The role of local congregations, as the Body of Christ, in vocational discernment;

- The role of the local congregation in sharing with the ordained the responsibility of learning how to be church collaboratively;
- The need to pay serious attention to local-contextual as well as institutional professionalized responses to issues of ministry and mission;
- The role of eucharistic presidency as being only fully authentic in the context of meaningful pastoral relationships within the community, at a time when there is an ever pressing need for deployable priests for Sunday duty;
- The need for the church to respond to context, time and place in its ongoing evolution and development.

All in all, the four OLM voices, those of Alice, Betty, Colin and Diane, represent a powerfully prophetic voice that begs for an evidence-based deconstruction of the attitudes and pitfalls cited so vociferously by the opponents of OLM–LM.

Canon Kathy Lawrence

11

Ordained Local Ministry: a personal reflection

Graham James

Localness: assessing its significance

In 1981, I became very cross with the Advisory Council for the Church's Ministry (ACCM). A young ordinand in my parish, whose vocation I had nurtured, was conditionally recommended for training at his selection conference. He was required to undertake two years of study under the Aston Training Scheme. He had no degree though he was widely read and had one of the most curious and speculative minds of anyone I had then met. It was true that he had only lived in one place so his experience of the world was grounded in a single locality. He was only in his twenties. I don't think the selectors understood him. Putting him through a five-year process seemed excessive. I wonder how angry I would have been if he had not been recommended at all.

Parish clergy are often especially protective of ordinands in their congregations. It is understandable. A sense of vocation to the ordained ministry cannot be a disembodied experience within an incarnational religion. Role models are important. Many priests would testify that it was one particular priest who inspired them to consider ordination in the first place. Hence, many clergy identify very closely with those in their parishes exploring the possibility of ordination. They invest much of themselves in the nurture of their ordinands. That can make them less than objective in the assessment of an ordinand's vocation. They may even feel their own ministry is on trial in the selection process. I did.

Back in 1981, I was both right and wrong to be cross with ACCM. Right in the sense that context and culture played too little part in the selection procedures at that time. The local was subordinated to the national since it was assumed that deployment anywhere was necessary in every priest. Yet, all of us fit some localities better than others. All of us are shaped by the localities in which we have been nurtured and by the cultural networks we have inhabited. It seemed to me thirty years ago that what was unusual and specific about this candidate was to be ironed out of him in a two-year process making him more like other candidates for ordination. As it turned out, the Aston Training Scheme was infinitely better than I expected. I came to appreciate its significant contribution to the life of the church and regret its passing. I think, however, I was right to be suspicious about what the selectors themselves expected of it – something very different from what it delivered.

I was also wrong to be cross with ACCM at the time since local judgements about vocation are not sufficient in themselves. The ordained have a role representing the whole body of Christ to those within and outside local congregations. A wider perspective is needed. The strength of our system of selection in the Church of England is the relative disinterestedness of Bishops' Advisors (called selectors all those years ago) in anything but the well-being of the whole Church. The most unhappy Christians I have ever met are those who are ordained and should never have been ordained. They replicate their unhappiness in local churches. That is why selection procedures which lack rigour contribute to church decline. When I attended a Bishops' Selection Conference myself as long ago as 1971, I was fascinated by the process. Ten years later, it was getting cross with the system in my parish which reactivated my interest. Within a few months, I found myself applying to become a Selection Secretary. To my surprise, I was appointed.

Poacher to gamekeeper

In the mysterious ways of God, I was soon dealing with one of the initial local non-stipendiary ministry (LNSM) candidates to come to a selection conference. We (by now ACCM was 'we' rather than 'they') were far from sure how to deal with 'localness'. LNSM candidates came to a selection conference at a venue as near to them geographically as we could manage. In those days, there were far more conference venues spread across the country. This enabled a diocesan representative (often the director of ordinands or an archdeacon) to come and talk about the local context in which the particular candidate's vocation had been nurtured and in which they would minister in future. This took place at the end of the selection conference, prior to the selectors' meeting when decisions about recommendations would be made. Looking back on it, it was an odd time for this encounter, since by then the candidate had left. Any questions which might have arisen and could have been addressed by the selectors were no longer capable of being asked.

It was not at all satisfactory. Many of the selectors puzzled about how to evaluate 'localness' and were equally puzzled that any priest should only exercise ordained ministry within a single locality. This often led to discussions about a priest's licence and the way in which the licence of an LNSM was barely distinguishable from that of a stipendiary priest. Discussions in selectors' meetings frequently focused on the balance between the catholic and the local rather than on the qualities of LNSM candidates themselves.

It was only in 1983 that the House of Bishops first approved the criteria for selection for ordination in the Church of England. Previously, there had been some notes for selectors but nothing very extensive. This was because it was assumed that everyone knew what was required in being a Church of England clergyman. It was not such a ludicrous notion as it may now seem. In the 1950s and for much of the 1960s, all selection conferences received only males for stipendiary ministry. The vast majority were going to be incumbents in parishes. There was a coherence about it all. Gradually, things changed. Very high figures of ordination candidates at the beginning of the 1960s turned into very low numbers at the beginning of the 1970s. In 1971, I was one of only 254 candidates recommended for training. It was the lowest number recorded in any year in the twentieth century. We now expect double that number every year. In 1971, however, most of us were young and the total number of years we would dedicate to ordained ministry in the Church of England was probably as high, if not higher, than the aggregate number of years from much greater numbers of candidates now. What we were not to know was that over the coming two decades, the variety of forms of the ordained ministry in the Church of England was to grow considerably. Arguably, the most interesting development was that of Ordained Local Ministry.

Local and national: getting the process of selection right

Location has a high profile in the New Testament. Jesus of Nazareth is firmly located in an undistinguished Galilean village as his home. Mentions of Capernaum (Mk 2.1), 'the country of the Gerasenes' (Mk 5.1), the villages of Caesarea Philippi (Mk 8.27), 'the region of Judea beyond the Jordan' (Mk 10.1) and Bethphage and Bethany (Mk 11.1) are simple indicators of the determination of Mark, the first of the Gospel writers, to earth the teaching and ministry of Jesus in particular places. The birth narratives are equally insistent on place. It might have been possible for the primitive church to preserve the teaching of Paul as general instructions, but they remain in the New Testament as letters written to distinct communities in particular places at a particular time. None of this is to deny universal significance across space and time. But the groundedness of the Christian revelation in history finds local expression first. God did not send us a theory. He sent us Jesus of Nazareth.

Extensive theologies can be developed from these simple New Testament principles, though the nature of churches as institutions is that national and international structures can find the particularity of the local a challenge. The introduction of national selection procedures in the Church of England after the Second World War did prevent the inconsistency whereby an ordination candidate turned down by one bishop would go to another diocese and find a kinder or more desperate bishop willing to ordain him. This had been undermining the credibility of the Church's discernment of vocation itself. National selection procedures became dominant in the 1950s and 1960s when the work done by Diocesan Directors of Ordinands and Vocations Advisors was relatively vestigial. Much of the process of discernment was focused upon the selection conference itself in a way which is not at all characteristic of our procedures now. The Bishops' Advisory Panel (the current name for a selection conference) is simply part of a much longer and more thorough process of discernment, a great deal of which takes place at diocesan and local level.

In the early 1980s, it was the Diocese of Lincoln which saw the development of LNSM as a key strategy in providing ordained ministry in its many scattered rural parishes as well as in its urban settlements where stipendiary clergy were unwilling to serve. The theoretical deployability of stipendiary clergy has never been matched by their willingness to go anywhere in England.

During my tenure at ACCM, Lincoln's candidates for LNSM had special local selection conferences, often taking place over a weekend in Lincoln itself. They were based on the pattern of the normal bishops' selection conference, but comprising only local candidates, selectors from elsewhere, and, at that stage, the Principal and architect of the local LNSM scheme deeply involved with all aspects of it.

Often, there were too few candidates to replicate the dynamics of group work at a selection conference, made more difficult by the fact that candidates knew each other already and so also knew each others' opinions. They had already formed bonds with each other in their preparation. It felt as if we were national inspectors coming to question the validity of already determined local decisions; so the sense of corporate discernment was largely missing. Worse, a different and special selection procedure gave the impression that different and less demanding criteria were being applied to Local Ministry than to all other forms of ordained ministry.

Later, when I became Bishop of St Germans in the Diocese of Truro in 1993, I inherited the chairmanship of a relatively newly established LNSM scheme. Truro initially had its own local selection conferences, but I determined that all our local candidates should go in future to a national conference. The selectors were provided with details of the Truro scheme, and an assessment of the benefice in which the candidate would serve and its potential for collaborative ministry as well as details of the candidate concerned. We trusted that selectors would have enough imagination and perception to come to an appropriate recommendation. By then, the number of LNSM candidates had grown considerably; so selectors were more familiar with this category of ministry. They were also better prepared in their own training by the staff of the Advisory Board of Ministry (as ACCM had then become prior to its later transformation into the Ministry Division – the capacity of the Church of England to rename this body has been industrious if not particularly imaginative).

What was noticeable in the Diocese of Truro in the early 1990s was that this decision that all LNSM candidates should attend the usual Bishops' Selection Conferences gave LNSM ordinands greater confidence. They knew they had not been selected by a procedure which other ordinands and clergy thought to be less demanding. Indeed, many of the LNSM candidates might well have been NSM or stipendiary candidates. It was often the local context which had shaped their sense of vocation and they had no desire or call to minister beyond it – at least as far as they understood God's leading of them into ordained ministry.

On my appointment as Bishop of Norwich in 1999, I moved to a diocese which also had an OLM Scheme in place (by now LNSMs had become OLMs). Much the same procedures were followed in Norwich as in Truro. They have largely continued unchanged to the present time, save for a much closer identification, though not complete absorption, of our OLM scheme with the regional non-residential course.

An unexpected high watermark for OLM in the Church of England

A report on the development of LNSM in the Church of England, *Stranger in the Wings*, was published in 1998. Its 28 recommendations now read like refinements of a still expanding form of ministry. The authors of the report seemed to anticipate it would expand still further. 'We recommend that all training for stipendiary and non-stipendiary clergy should include an understanding of LNSM' – seems one example of an assumption that Local Ministry would grow. The report also recommended the use of a new title – Ordained Local Minister (OLM) – one which was quickly adopted. What *Stranger in the Wings* did not anticipate was that within a few years, some of the key dioceses which had developed Local Ministry (Truro, Carlisle, Southwark and Blackburn) would close their schemes. Each would argue that a local pathway in training would still be available though it is hard to see how the distinctive charism of Ordained Local Ministry has not been adversely impacted. The 1998 Report now seems like a high watermark following which the tide has ebbed gently. In 2006, a Ministry Division survey revealed that only 12 dioceses were committed to a continuing development of OLM in its classic form, that is, a locally grown ordained ministry intended to be deployed in its locality.

Yet, I believe it would be mistaken to imagine Ordained Local Ministry was a bold experiment which has failed. It has taught the Church of England important lessons about vocation and ministry, some of which have been learned while others remain to be fully appreciated.

1. *OLM has provided a necessary corrective to highly individualized understandings of vocation to ordained ministry.*

I still cherish the look of surprise on the face of a Cornish farmer whose congregation had identified him as the person they believed should be a priest for the local community in which he had lived all his life. They knew he had the gifts and graces for ordained ministry. He was only too painfully aware of his lack of any academic achievement or experience of life beyond his home village. There was no chance that he would have ever responded to general vocational initiatives. But he did respond in slightly bewildered but delighted obedience to his own community. To see him grow in his training and then observe the crowd at his ordination to the priesthood in his parish church was to observe the missionary potential of such a ministry. This was vocation properly expressed as the will of the church (tested at a Bishops' Selection Conference as well as within the diocese itself) to which an individual had responded. This was vocation as a claim upon someone's life. It was not simply a personal response to a personal call then tested by the wider church. It was one in which vocation was primarily understood as a charism of the church herself. Too often in recent years, vocation has been understood personally. This has led to a great deal of talk by clergy, Readers and others about 'my ministry', 'my vocation' and 'my calling'. The words me and my do not appear in the Lord's Prayer. Restoring a corporate dimension to the nurturing of vocation is to recall the church to its own vocation as the people of God.

This cheering vocational story of the Cornish farmer raises a difficult issue, however, which has bedevilled the development of Ordained Local Ministry. It is one which may account for the high watermark being reached sooner than the authors of the 1998 Report anticipated. What becomes of the role of the incumbent of a parish where such a local priest has been identified, selected, trained, ordained and will minister for a good many years? The OLM may well become the local parson. It takes a good deal of grace and generosity as well as understanding of collaborative ministry for such a priest and his or her incumbent to work creatively together. Does the genuinely local priest leave an incumbent-shaped hole, and what might the gap look like?

I cannot now recall where I came across the term 'resident alien' for an incumbent of a benefice. There is a need for a voice from outside, even if some incumbents quickly go native. A balance between the two can be achieved and often has been where the OLM's vocation has been nurtured not just by the benefice but by the incumbent as well. The difficulties often arise where a well-established OLM has become the parson and a new incumbent is not given space or resents the territory held by his or her colleague. The well-loved OLM priest has considerable power and, when misused, it can diminish a new incumbent's capacity to develop an appropriate authority. What we have failed to do sufficiently as a church is to manage these transitions creatively, not helped by the way in which the Patronage (Benefices) Measure 1986 took no account of the development of Ordained Local Ministry since it was in such a formative stage at the time.

2. *OLM has endorsed a theology of place in an increasingly networked world.*

We still ask 'where do you come from?' but an increasing number of people find that question hard to answer. Yet, our identity is often related to a sense of 'home' somewhere. What is evident is that OLM has most often been successful in cherishing places and locations which are not always honoured in our society, for example, the outer housing estate or the very rural settlement. Marginalized places are given dignity. Sometimes, these are places with a weak identity. The local priest can become a focus for community as well as church renewal. I can think of OLM clergy deeply embedded not simply in local church life but also in a local drama group or horticultural society, Women's Institute or local agricultural show. The drama group which then puts on a Passion play on the streets of a council estate or the local agricultural show which makes the local priest its president for a year begins to break down some of the boundaries between the sacred and the secular too easily erected in recent decades. OLM as a counter-cultural protest against the privatization of religion seems to have been too little celebrated.

The least successful experience of Ordained Local Ministry has often come about where OLMs have been ordained after living in a place for only a few years, perhaps in retirement. Their ministry reveals that they are not as genuinely local as might be imagined. The local foundations do not go very deep (in Norfolk and Cornwall, it can take a generation or more to be accepted as genuinely local). The skills and capabilities of the individuals themselves have been quickly recognized by local congregations but there is no wider ownership by the community. Such OLMs are not fully linked into local networks. Their vocational path may be wholly authentic but as in the parable of the sower, the seed is planted in rather shallow soil, which springs up quickly but cannot be sustained. Local means more than the church congregation for Ordained Local Ministry to flourish.

3. *Ordained Local Ministry made theological learning a corporate enterprise including the laity within the local church.*

This has been a positive corrective to patterns of ordination training which have invariably withdrawn ordinands from their local church to a residential seminary. Even non-residential courses have generally advised ordinands to reduce the level of their commitments within the local worshipping community given the demands of their training.

While OLM Schemes have varied across the country, the majority have included some local learning with a group of laypeople from the benefice studying together and with the ordinand often leading the group aided by a tutor. In some cases, this group has been the ministry team, whereas in others, the ministry team was clearly differentiated from the local training group. Either way, in most benefices, eight to ten people (sometimes more) would take part in some serious adult theological learning. They did so to support their ordinand. The ordinand grew in a leadership role as a teacher within the local community. The group grew together in knowledge, resourced often by a local tutor as well as the incumbent and by the OLM Scheme staff as well. This was significant adult Christian education by stealth. There are many people (it must run into thousands) who have undertaken such courses but would never have normally responded to an invitation to do theological learning at such depth for any other reason. In some parishes, it led to a second generation of OLMs, or nurtured vocations to Reader ministry and to other forms of lay work. It has certainly produced a better informed laity and made serious theological study part of the life of some benefices where there was little such tradition beforehand.

In one case, I recall an OLM ordinand making it her business to find one or two people outside the church community who were willing to participate. That was a sign of wider community ownership of a local vocation beyond simply the church congregation. It also sharpened the need for an adequate apologetic to be developed within the group. Theological colleges and courses often speak of the importance of engaging in the academy with those beyond a confessional tradition (though very often most of the teaching is within the seminary or course itself), whereas in training for Local Ministry, the possibilities for encounter with those beyond the community of faith can be very considerable. They haven't always been fully exploited.

This local dimension of training has often been acknowledged by theological educators as one which may well enrich their own patterns of training. As things stand, I am far from convinced that it is at all well developed and seems to be one of the gifts of Ordained Local Ministry which is already fading in the church at large.

4. *Ordained Local Ministry was genuinely driven by the dioceses (and parishes) and not directed from the 'centre'.*

OLM was a response to a keenly felt need. Numbers of stipendiary clergy were declining. Non-stipendiary clergy numbers were increasing but seemed to emerge most often in places already well provided for in ministry. How could places where the Church of England was weak numerically or lacked self-confidence become nurseries of Local Ministry?

The impact of LNSM Schemes and emphatic episcopal endorsement within a diocese generated vocational response in unexpected places. One Cornish priest sent a letter to every person on his electoral roll asking them to nominate anyone in the congregation whom they thought should be ordained. Twelve people received nominations, two of them much more emphatically than the rest. Those two people have now been ordained for some years. This was never the way the Church of England did these things.

But it has not changed the culture. Ordained Local Ministry has been on the ebb tide partly because of the ability of the wider church to normalize new developments into pre-existing patterns. Too often, highly personalized understandings of vocation re-emerged as candidates suggested themselves for Ordained Local Ministry in parishes. Clergy and Parochial Church Councils became nervous of saying no to people with powerful personalities who were unsuitable. This meant that diocesan and national systems of selection were sometimes used inappropriately. If the local parish or benefice could not take responsibility in this area, how would Local Ministry flourish?

5. *A growing proportion of OLMs are no longer ministering in their local parishes a decade on from ordination but have moved elsewhere, a sign of vocational development.*

There are no reliable statistics on this issue. But my own examination of nearly nineteen years of episcopal ministry in two dioceses with OLMs is that ten years after ordination, over half are no longer ministering locally. This follows the pattern of NSMs in an earlier generation, many of whom found their way into stipendiary ministry. (Mark Hodge's report in 1983 traces this clearly and the evidence is that the pattern has continued.)

Is this a failure? Not necessarily. Sadly, in some cases, OLMs have moved unwillingly elsewhere because of a breakdown in relationship with a new incumbent. There are frequently faults on both sides and this refers back to the issue I raised earlier about the attention which needs to be given to such transitions. In a significant number of cases, however, the local priest has matured in ministry and sometimes the needs of the church have turned out to be greater elsewhere than the home benefice. The gifts of the OLM concerned can be offered gladly by the benefice where his or her vocation has been nurtured. I think of a former OLM ministering now on a house for duty basis in a small group of rural villages where the need for ministry is enormous, whereas in his original benefice, the Ministry Team is large. I think of a younger OLM, surprised by her call to ministry while still in her thirties, who is now, twenty years later, a stipendiary parish priest. Her vocation has continued to grow and develop. Being local is not the same as being static. Another OLM remains in the parish from which she came but is now also a stipendiary hospital chaplain, defying easy categorization. She has changed secular employment for full-time ministry though still not directly employed by the church. This is scarcely a failure in Local Ministry but a sign of development within it. The local context should not be a prison from which the priest is unable to break free.

Somehow the rhetoric of Local Ministry has meant that these vocational developments have not always been celebrated. It has been assumed by some observers that OLM is an experiment which has not quite worked, especially by those with objections to Ordained Local Ministry in the first place.

The church's calling: helping the church to be what God calls her to be

This brief reflection simply serves as one bishop's personal account of spending the best part of thirty years helping to nurture vocations to Local Ministry, discerning where God has seemed to be at work, supporting and shaping training patterns as well as ordaining deacons and priests for Local Ministry and being willing, often gladly, to see the sort of vocational development which has led to a move beyond the immediate locality where someone's vocation was formed. This book is a welcome exploration of the significance of the development of Local Ministry. For me, the most important contribution of Ordained Local Ministry to the life of our church lies in the way in which it has reshaped our understanding of vocation. It is not simply related to vocation to ordained ministry itself but to the church's own vocation to be the body of Christ, brought into being by God's mission to the world.

A vocation is realized when someone recognizes that the person they are and the work to be done come together so completely that they feel more integrated and authentic as human beings. This is not confined to religious vocations. An engineer or a soldier may experience this just as much as a teacher or a nurse. Some people cannot help being priests. It is what they are made for, just as others may be made to be surgeons or funeral directors or bus drivers.

The vocation of the local priest will undoubtedly have various dimensions to it. Intriguingly, the use of forms of vocational language is more prevalent in our vocabulary than we sometimes realize. But such language is often too little employed within the church. For example, invocation is involved in every minister's call. Prayer must lie at the heart of vocation, not just the prayers of the candidate but the prayers of the whole local church community. It is from that corporate life of prayer that so many vocations have emerged. There is a word for that sort of corporate life, which is already used within our church – convocation. Perhaps, instead of limiting its use to bodies comprising solely of clergy, we should remember that convocation is to do with the calling of the church corporately to be whom God wants her to be.

A calling (whether to be a teacher, a waitress or a priest) also involves revocation. We always have to lay aside other options. Life is narrowed down as it opens up. There are choices to be made, especially in the life of the local priest. Some patterns of behaviour are no longer suitable. Finally, there is provocation. Many are the OLMs who have been provoked, prodded, pushed into a calling which they had not recognized to be theirs. For all clergy, there is a need for continuing provocation of the people of God so that they may be witnesses and disciples in the apostolic mission Christ has given to his church. And clergy need provocation too if their sense of vocation is to remain fresh.

All these things apply to the church herself and not simply to a small number who have a cherished 'vocation'. As a bishop, Ordained Local Ministry has helped me see all this more clearly. That is why I think its greatest contribution to the life of our church may prove to be in reshaping our theology of vocation itself.

12

Strangers and partners – reimagining ministry

Andrew Bowden, Elizabeth Jordan
and Oliver Simon

At the Local Ministry Network Conference in November 2010, participants shared their experiences of LM schemes that were helping to 'keep alive the rumour of God in a godless generation' – both maintaining church life and reaching out into their communities. There was encouraging input about the development of a theology of collaborative ministry that sought to bridge the gap between clergy and laity. They considered the Church of England Ministry Division's latest stark predictions about future numbers of stipendiary clergy and they heard about a recent rural conference when participants expressed their grave concern for the future of ministry in small villages – a ministry that seems tailor-made for LM. And yet, the overall impression was that participants felt deserted by their dioceses and demoralized. There was a real fear that the efforts and achievements of the last twenty years were going to be shelved, or even binned, by the Church of England.

On the last morning of the conference, Bishop Gavin Reid put it this way. If the numbers of stipendiary clergy are falling rapidly; if everyone agrees that all-member-ministry is God's will for His Church at this time; if a respectable theology to underpin collaborative ministry has been worked out – what is the problem? Why doesn't every diocese take it up? That, he challenged the participants, is the question you have got to answer; and if you truly believe in your 'vision', that is the issue you have to tackle.

This book has investigated the theological thinking that inspired the pioneers of Ordained Local Ministry and Local Ministry. It has surveyed significant pieces of research which seek to test whether the experiment is working. It has looked at some of the ways in which OLM and LM insights have been recognized and incorporated into the 'normal' practice of the church. What challenges and prospects does OLM offer to the church?

A cairn

In systematic terms, ministry is a subset of ecclesiology. The account of Ordained Local Ministry in this book sheds light on their interrelationship. Careless misuse of the word 'ministry' to mean simply 'ordained ministry' leads to clericalism, the 'clerical default', which claims a privileged position within the ecclesiology of the Church of England. This is demonstrated by the sizeable budget which the national church attaches to clergy training[1] and the similar scale for clergy stipends and pensions within diocesan budgets, budgets which are translated into levies (quotas) on the parish with the added emotional pressure of supporting one's parish priest. The task of the church has become inverted. The people of God, supporting their minister end up by transferring responsibilities which are properly theirs onto their public representative, becoming dependent rather than interdependent.

OLMs challenge traditional assumptions about ordained ministry. Their vocation derives primarily from a local congregation. Their training values local knowledge, previous experience and local placement in a way traditional clergy training tended not to. Their licence covers one local area – as does that of every clergyperson in the Church of England and in other traditions, such as Orthodoxy, as well – although, for OLMs, this has been applied in a particularly prescriptive way. They are not expected to have all the gifts of the Spirit that are perhaps needed for an incumbent; rather their calling is to collaborate with 'Spirit gifted' laypeople in mutual ministry. They were intended to be, and they remain, 'strangers in the wings', and many traditional clergy find this uncomfortable to live with.

Ordained Local Ministry is a challenge to the church because it offers an approach to ministry which redresses the dominance of the clergy. It does this by recognizing the priority of the ministry to which *all* are called. Some are called to a particular, sacramental and representative ministry but this is exercised in collaboration with other expressions of ministry in the church. Ordained Local Ministry has never sought to displace stipendiary ministry within Anglican ecclesiology, but rather to complement it in ways that are suggested in Chapter 2 and outlined in Chapter 8. As has been suggested, stipendiaries have a vital 'new' role as 'bishops-in-little', as companions and facilitators to local congregations. Apostolic and local ministries have always been and will continue to be necessary to each other.

Ordained Local Ministry draws inspiration from the ecclesial margins of the Church of England, from the Bethnal Green experiment in East London and from writing which comes out of experience of church planting overseas.

The experience of local ministry development in Northern Michigan and elsewhere has also been formative at least for those in the Church of England who have observed or reported on it. There are differences, particularly accentuated in urban Britain, but the time has surely come for the church intentionally to promote a mission-focused culture of local ministry rather than one which focuses on retrenchment as a result of the retirement and non-replacement of stipendiary clergy. Ordained Local Ministry can then be a strategy which refreshes the Church of England through the introduction of a strain hitherto under-represented, people held by those closest to them on the ground to have the charisms required for public representative ministry. The quality, the aptness, of those who are called out, judged holistically rather than in narrow academic terms, will be the significant criterion.

Far, then, from being peripheral, Ordained Local Ministry is at the centre of a web of related issues that touch the essence of the church at the heart of her ministry and mission. This can be symbolized by imagining Ordained Local Ministry as a cairn, a visible waymarking of the changing path in the life of the church.

Local Ministry

'Local Ministry', the term which has come to express a rebalancing of the focus of ministry within the life of the church, is also a waymark, a way of transitioning the nineteenth-century clerical–professional model of ministry into a more inclusive articulation of what belongs to the people of God as a whole. Local Ministry is not a diminutive term: it lies behind all the strategies to 'mobilize' or 'develop' the local church. Within an ecclesiology which takes seriously the capacity of the people of God in any one place or context to be the universal church, Local Ministry speaks of the missiological mandate (Mt. 28.19) to bear witness to God's love 'where we are'.

During the last twenty years, advocates of Local Ministry have come to believe in the core values of LM as vitally important to the health of our church.

- Local Ministry recognizes that by baptism, all are 'ordained' to share in the ministry of the church, and that, of its nature, ministry is 'relational'.
- Local Ministry is about valuing the locality and empowering the local congregation.
- LM is about recognizing the need for every local Christian assembly to be able to celebrate the Eucharist weekly.
- LM is about recognizing the authenticity of vocation to an ordained ministry that is local.

- LM is about a team called out by the whole congregation, not just by the incumbent.
- LM is about 'vocation', not about filling gaps.
- LM is about 'recognized ministry', not simply about discipleship.
- LM believes that a major part of the training for ministry should be locally based.
- LM recognizes the need for training and ongoing support for OLMs and teams.
- LM is about stipendiary clergy being ready to take a companion–leadership role.
- LM is there to facilitate a 'healthy church'; it is there to create the 'energy for growth'.
- LM is about encouraging mission to and within society.

While it is true that some of these values have been recognized and adopted by the wider church, others have not. They are values that are too important to lose. They remain the cornerstone of a vision for the future that is theologically and practically valid. The section which follows outlines the objections to some of these values and the way in which the church is, wittingly or otherwise, moving towards accommodating others.

Obstacles that lie in the way

As this book indicates, there is resistance to this mutation in ministry particularly on the part of those leaders who represent the mind of the church as a whole. We have described how decisions can be made on the basis of an inadequate understanding of the theology of Ordained Local Ministry, inadequate empirical evidence or reluctance to be radical in the face of limited resources. Even a new vision, as in the renewal of the role of the Province in the Scottish Episcopal Church, can have what might have been the unintended consequence of reducing resources for Local Ministry. We are glad to have episcopal contributions in this book. There is more to learn and understand about the processes of decision-making and about the role of those who influence ecclesial policy. More empirical research may well help to clarify the mechanisms of retrenchment which are a cause of sadness to advocates of Local Ministry; such research should aim to identify structural impediments to that freedom of spirit to which the church is called to give voice and which, precisely because of such a vocation, need to be addressed.

The Church of England is not alone in neglecting to resource empirical research – although the Research and Statistics Department has co-sponsored an annual Faith in Research Day since 2006. In theological training, the phrase 'reflective practitioner' is frequently urged but, institutionally, it is not applied, at least in an empirical sense. One reason may be that empirical research costs money. Fortunately, however, there is a rich if uncoordinated vein of independent research material emerging from academic programmes and individual initiatives and we have identified at least some of this in the bibliography. The research outlined in Chapters 6–8 is an example of what is being done to study Ordained Local Ministry. Stories from Scotland and Gloucester and the experience of the authors argue the case for more attention to what is taking place rather than to inherited presumptions or perceptions, as the basis of policy.

Local Ministry and mission

We also note the centrality of mission in the church's life at this time. Is the Church of England assisted in its task of bearing witness by those whose journey to public representative ministry is but one part of the journey of the Christian community in that place? Undoubtedly, yes! Not only do such clergy reflect more closely the personality of the people of God than their stipendiary colleagues, their own ministry development is intrinsically and fruitfully the development of the ministry of others. Furthermore, they amplify the foundational understanding of the local church as the instrument of the *missio dei* by asserting that ours is a God who resources the church to fulfil that vocation. It is a misconception that Local Ministry and mission are pursuing different ends. Here, as elsewhere, we need to value the relationship between different approaches. We make no stand for the replacement of stipendiary clergy by OLMs. Rather, we appeal for the recovery of the complementarity of apostolic and local ministries, ordained and lay, for the vision and the courage to test the proposals of pioneers from Henry Venn to John Tiller.

Collaboration is hard work

It will take vision and courage, for Local Ministry is demanding. Where there is Local Ministry, there is a danger of misunderstanding and personality conflict – especially when a new clerical member joins the team as incumbent. Like all teams, clergy–lay teams are subject to the fundamental laws of fallen humanity. The problem from the diocesan point of view is that to sort out a non-functional team or relationship is extremely time consuming. To adapt a dictum of Mark Twain, it is not that collaborative ministry has been tried and found wanting; it has been found to be difficult and therefore is being abandoned.

Purists need allies

During the last twenty years, LM 'purists' have come to believe passionately in their 'gospel'. As Chapter 9 outlines, the essential nature and distinctive contribution of Ordained Local Ministry may sometimes be lost in adapting to new developments in training and deployment. As the purists see it, the core values of Local Ministry must be established if parishes are to avoid trouble later on. Local Ministry requires committed advocates as well as well-intended bystanders. In their understandable desire to keep standards high (and to guard their backs against the criticisms of an ever watchful MinDiv), LM officers have developed 'systems of good practise' that can withstand the vicissitudes of parish life. However, they have also proved to be expensive. Edged off the top of the church's agenda by other concerns (like mission), LM departments have become a natural target for diocesan cuts in a time of financial austerity.

And yet, despite cutbacks in the numbers of LM officers and the absorption of LM into other diocesan departments, the desire and enthusiasm for some form of collaborative ministry is, if anything, greater than it was in 1991. It is just that not everyone wants 'the full English Breakfast'. Clearly many now find the language of LM a put-off. Many parishes do not want to have, as they see it, something overcomplicated imposed on them. In what is after all good LM practice, they want to work out for themselves what they feel they need, what they can reasonably take on and what is right for them NOW. There are many who want to practise some form of collaborative ministry and are naturally irritated if LM purists seem to belittle their achievements. LM purists must accept that any move in the direction of serious lay–clergy collaborative ministry is good and is to be applauded. And if that means adapting the language – so be it. *Stranger in the Wings* included diagrams picturing LM as a journey, a pilgrimage from 'vicar-does-it-all' to 'mutual ministry' (ABM 1998: 46–7). As we have always known, Local Ministry is a journey from one culture to another, and that takes time and cannot be hurried. We are all on the journey and those who are not against us have to be recognized as for us – welcomed as our allies.

The times they are a'changing. While the core values of LM remain the cornerstone of our vision for the future of the Church of England, if they are to continue to refresh a weary institution, LM purists will need to regard them as something to be aimed at over time, rather than mandatory from the start. We need to celebrate the way in which the thinking which LM embodies is being absorbed into the bloodstream of the church.

Conclusion

In this book, we have set out to tell a story, describe a process and evidence research which deepens and elaborates its meaning. Local Ministry speaks prophetically of the need for reflexivity, continuing awareness of the limitations in Anglican thinking and practice about ministry. Ordained Local Ministry speaks of competencies and capacities which have lacked affirmation or have been diverted into less fulfilling directions (both for the church and for the individual). The 'strangers in the wings' are in reality vital partners for the well-being of the people of God and the coming of the kingdom. Local Ministry, and Ordained Local Ministry, understood in this sense is a form of emancipation for the church as a whole.

Note

1   About 43.5% of the total national church budget in 2011.

Bibliography

Web Resources

Church of England: shared ministry at: http://www.churchofengland.org/
education/adult-education-lay-discipleship-and-shared-ministry/developing-and-
supporting/lay-and-collaborative-ministry.aspx – includes links to websites on
shared ministry elsewhere in the Anglican Communion.
Episcopal Diocese of Northern Michigan at: http://www.dioup.org/
Local Ministry Network at: http://www.localministry.net/home.
Scottish Episcopal Church at: www.scotland.anglican.org

Advisory Board of Ministry of the General Synod of the Church of England [ABM]
(1991) *Local Non-Stipendiary Ministry: The Report of a Church of England
Working Party*. London ABM Policy Paper No. 1.
—. (1992) *A Review of LNSM Schemes*. ABM Ministry Paper No. 4.
—. (1993) *Order in Diversity*. ABM Ministry Paper No. 5.
—. (1998) *Stranger in the Wings. A Report on Local Non-Stipendiary Ministry*.
London: Church House Publishing ABM Policy Paper No. 8 (GS Misc 532).
Advisory Council for the Church's Ministry [ACCM] (1968) A Supporting
Ministry. Being the Report of a Working Party of the Ministry Committee of the
Advisory Council for the Church's Ministry on Priests in Auxiliary Parochial
Ministries in the Church of England. London: Church Information Office.
— (1973) *The Place of Auxiliary Ministry Ordained and Lay*. London: The Church
information Office.
— (1974) *Local Ministry* (Occasional Paper No. 1). London: ACCM.
— (1980) Local Ordained Ministry (GS 442).
— (1987a). *Education for the Church's Ministry* (Occasional Paper No. 22).
London: Church House Publishing ('ACCM 22').
— (1987b) *Guidelines for Local Non-Stipendiary Ministry* (Occasional Paper No.
24). London: Church House Publishing.
— (1991) *Good Practice in Group and Team Ministry* (Occasional Paper No. 39).
London: ACCM.
Allen, R. (1962a) *Missionary Methods: St. Paul's or Ours?* Michigan, Grand
Rapids: William B. Eerdmans.
— (1962b) *The Spontaneous Expansion of the Church: And the Causes which
Hinder It*. Michigan, Grand Rapids: William B. Eerdmans.
Anglican Consultative Council [ACC] (1976) *ACC-3. Anglican Consultative
Council: Third Meeting, Trinidad*. London: ACC.

— (1985) *Bonds of Affection*. Proceedings of ACC-6 Badagry, Nigeria, 1984. London: Anglican Consultative Council.

Anglican – Orthodox Dialogue [A-OD] – The 'Cyprus Agreement' (2006) *The Church of the Triune God*. London: Anglican Communion Office.

Anglican Roman Catholic International Commission [ARCIC] (1994) *Clarifications of Certain Aspects of the Agreed Statements on Eucharist and Ministry of the First Anglican-Roman Catholic International Commission*. London: Church House and Catholic Truth Society.

Archbishops' Council of the Church of England [AC] (2000) Council for Christian Unity/House of Bishops. *Bishops in Communion. Collegiality in the Service of the* Koinonia *of the Church*. London: Church House Publishing.

— (2004) *Mission-Shaped Church: Church Planting and Fresh Expressions of Church in a Changing Context. Report of a Working Group of the Church of England's Mission and Public Affairs Council*. London: Church House Publishing.

— (2005) Faith and Order Advisory Group. *Shaping the Future. New Patterns of Learning for Lay and Ordained*. London: Church House Publishing.

— (2007a) Ministry Division, OLM Survey. *OLM – A Ministry in Flux*. London: Church House Publishing.

— (2007b) Faith and Order Advisory Group. *The Mission and Ministry of the Whole Church. Biblical, Theological and Contemporary Perspectives (GS Misc 854)*. London: Church House Publishing.

— (2007c) *Common Worship Ordination Services*. London: Church House Publishing.

— (2009) *Reader Upbeat*, available at: http://www.readers.cofe.anglican.org/crc_doc_one.php?112

— (2010) Ministry Division. *Quality Assurance and Enhancement in Ministerial Education. Inspection, Curriculum Approval, Moderation. Handbook August 2010*. London: Church House Publishing.

The Archbishop of Canterbury's Commission on Urban Priority Areas [ACUPA] (1985) *Faith in the City. A Call for Action by Church and Nation*. London: Church House Publishing.

Arndt, W. F. and Gingrich, F. W. (1957) *A Greek-English Lexicon of the New Testament and Other Early Christian Literature*. Chicago: The University of Chicago Press.

Ashton, P. (1983) 'Authority and Oversight in the Local Church', in Graham Dow, Peter Ashton, David Gillett, David Prior, *Whose Hand on the Tiller? The Future of the Church's Ministry as a Response to the Tiller Report*. Bramcote: Grove Books (Pastoral Series No. 16), pp. 8–13.

Augustine of Hippo *Sermon 272*, available at: http://www.earlychurchtexts.com/public/augustine_sermon_272_eucharist.htm.

Avis, P. (2005) *A Ministry Shaped by Mission*. London: T & T Clark.

Baab, L. M. (2000) *Personality Types in Congregations*. New York: Alban Institute.

Barry, F. R. (1930) 'Who are Fit Persons?' Comment in *The Guardian*, April 11, p. 309. Reprinted in James M. M. Francis, and Leslie J. Francis (1998) *Tentmaking. Perspectives on Self-Supporting Ministry*. Leominster: Gracewing, pp. 77–80.

— (1960) 'The Case for Part-Time Priests', in Robin Denniston (ed.), *Part Time Priests? A Discussion*. London: Skeffington, pp. 10–15.

Beach, M. H. F. (2010) 'The Ecclesiology of John Tiller: Ideal Blueprint or Concrete Reality?' (unpublished DMin thesis). London: Kings College.

Borgeson, J. and White, L. (eds) (1990) *Reshaping Ministry.* Colorado: Jethro Press.

Bosch, D. J. (1991) *Transforming Mission. Paradigm Shifts in Theology of Mission.* Maryknoll, New York: Orbis Books.

Bowden, J. (1983) *Edward Schillebeeckx. Portrait of the Theologian.* London: SCM Press Ltd.

Bracegirdle, C. A. (2005) 'Curriculum design, practice and evaluation in ordained local ministry in the Diocese of Manchester', *Research in Post-Compulsory Education, 10,* 211–25.

Bracegirdle, P. H. (1999) *Local Ministry in the Diocese of Gloucester 1994–1999.* Gloucester: Church House.

Brueggemann, W. and Miller, E. D. (eds) (1994) *A Social Reading of the Old Testament.* Minneapolis: Fortress Press.

Bulley, C. (2000) *The Priesthood of Some Believers.* Carlisle: Paternoster.

Burton, L., Francis, L. J. and Robbins, M. (2010) 'Psychological type profile of Methodist circuit ministers in Britain: similarities with and differences from Anglican clergy', *Journal of Empirical Theology, 23,* 64–81.

Cameron, E. & Gavine, M. (eds) (2008) *Local Collaborative Ministry – The Story So Far.* Edinburgh: Scottish Episcopal Church.

Cameron, H., Bhatti, D., Duce, C. et al. (2010) *Talking About God in Practice: Theological Action, Research and Practical Theology.* London: SCM Press.

Carr, J. H. (1851) *The Local Ministry: Its Character, Vocation and Position Considered, With Suggestions for Promoting Its More Extended Usefulness.* London: J. Kaye & Co.

Cattell, R. B., Cattell, A. K. S. and Cattell, H. E. P. (1993) *Sixteen Personality Factor Questionnaire: Fifth Edition (16PF5).* Windsor: NFER-Nelson.

Cavanaugh, W. T. (1998) *Torture and Eucharist: Theology, Politics, and the Body of Christ.* Oxford: Blackwell Publishers.

The Church Times (1916) 'An Unprofessional Priesthood' – editorial, 27 October.

Clark, S. J. W. (1923) *The Indigenous Church.* London: World Dominion Press.

Collins, J. N. (1992) *Are All Christians Ministers?* Newtown NSW Australia: E. J. Dwyer.

— (2006) 'Ordained and other ministries: making a difference', *Ecclesiology, 3:1,* 11–32.

Costa, P. T. and McCrae, R. R. (1985) *The NEO Personality Inventory.* Odessa, Florida: Psychological Assessment Resources.

Countryman, L. W. (1999) *Living on the Border of the Holy: Renewing the Priesthood of All.* Harrisburg: Morehouse.

Craig, C. L., Francis, L. J., Bailey, J. and Robbins, M. (2003). Psychological types in Church in Wales congregations. *The Psychologist in Wales, 15,* 18–21.

Croft, S. (ed.) (1999) *Ministry in Three Dimensions.* London: Darton, Longman & Todd.

— (2006) *The Future of the Parish System. Shaping the Church of England for the 21st Century.* London: Church House Publishing.

Cundy, I. (2006) 'Reconfiguring a Diocese Towards Mission', in S. Croft (ed.), *The Future of the Parish System. Shaping the Church of England for the 21st Century.* London: Church House Publishing, pp.152–69.

Davies, D. J., Watkins, C. and Winter, M. (1991) *Church and Religion in Rural England*. Edinburgh: T & T Clark.

Davison, A. and Milbank, A. (2010) *For the Parish. A Critique of Fresh Expressions*. London: SCM Press.

Delis-Bulhoes, V. (1990) 'Jungian psychological types and Christian belief in active church members', *Journal of Psychological Type*, 20, 25–33.

Doctrine Commission of the Church of England (2003) *Being Human – A Christian Understanding of Personhood Illustrated with Reference to Power, Money, Sex and Time*. London: Church House Publishing.

Donaldson, C. (1992) *The New Springtime of the Church*. Norwich: Canturbury Press.

Donovan, D. (1992) *What are They Saying About the Ministerial Priesthood?* New Jersey: Paulist Press.

Doyle, D. M. (2000) *Communion Ecclesiology. Visions and Versions*. Maryknoll, New York: Orbis Books.

Duncan, B. (1993) *Pray Your Way*. London: Darton, Longman and Todd.

Dwyer, M. T. (1995) *No Light Without Shadow*. Thornbury, Australia: Desbooks.

Eysenck, H. J. and Eysenck, S. B. G. (1991) *Manual of the Eysenck Personality Scales*. London: Hodder and Stoughton.

Faivre, A. (1990) *The Emergence of the Laity in the Early Church* – trans. David Smith. New York: Paulist Press.

Farley, E. (1983) *Theologia: The Fragmentation and Unity of Theological Education*. Philadelphia: Fortress.

Forrester, D. (2000) *Truthful Action: Explorations in Practical Theology*. Edinburgh: T & T Clark.

France, W. F. (1929) 'Unpaid clergy – the proposal criticised', *The Review of the Churches*, New Series 6, 333–9.

Francis, L. J. (2005). *Faith and Psychology: Personality, Religion and the Individual*. London: Darton, Longman and Todd.

Francis, L. J., Craig, C. L., Whinney, M., Tilley, D. and Slater, P. (2007) 'Psychological profiling of Anglican clergy in England: employing Jungian typology to interpret diversity, strengths, and potential weaknesses in ministry', *International Journal of Practical Theology*, 11, 266–84.

Francis, L. J., Duncan, B., Craig, C. L. and Luffman, G. (2004) 'Type patterns among Anglican congregations in England', *Journal of Adult Theological Education*, 1, 66–77.

Francis, L. J. and Holmes, P. (2011) 'Ordained local ministers: the same Anglican orders, but different psychological temperaments?' *Rural Theology*, 9, 151–60.

Francis, L. J. and Jones, S. H. (2003). 'The pastoral care of the Anglican clergy today: a matter of low self-esteem?' *Journal of Empirical Theology*, 16:1, 20–30.

Francis, L. J., Robbins, M. and Craig, C. L. (in press) 'The psychological type profile of Anglican churchgoers in England: compatible or incompatible with their clergy?' *International Journal of Practical Theology*.

Francis, L. J., Robbins, M., Duncan, B. and Whinney, M. (2010) 'Confirming the psychological type profile of Anglican clergymen in England: a ministry for intuitives', in B. Ruelas and V. Brisero (eds), *Psychology of Intuition*. New York: Nova Science, pp. 211–19.

Francis, L. J., Robbins, M. and Whinney, M. (2011) 'Women priests in the Church of England: psychological type profile', *Religions*.

Francis, L. J., Robbins, M. and Jones, S. H. (in press) 'The psychological type profile of clergywomen in ordained local ministry in the Church of England: pioneers or custodians?'

Francis, L. J., Robbins, M., Williams, A. and Williams, R. (2007). 'All types are called, but some are more likely to respond: the psychological profile of rural Anglican churchgoers in Wales', *Rural Theology*, 5, 23–30.

Francis, L. J. and Village, A. (in press) 'The psychological temperament of Anglican clergy in ordained local ministry (OLMs): the conserving, serving pastor? A matter of low self-esteem?' *Journal of Empirical Theology*, 16:1, 20–30.

Frensdorff, W. (1992) 'The Captivity of the Sacraments', in *The Witness*, Massachusetts, Cambridge: Episcopal Divinity School, April 1992, pp. 5–6.

General Synod Board of Education (GSBE) (1985) *All Are Called. Towards a Theology of the Laity*. London: Church House Publishing.

General Synod of the Church of England (GS) (1974) *General Synod November Group of Sessions. Reports of Proceedings*, Vol. 5 No. 3. London: Church Information Office.

— (1980) Local Ordained Ministry *Advisory Council for the Church's Ministry*. London: Church Information Office (GS 442).

— (1981) *To a Rebellious House? Report of the Church of England's Partners in Mission Consultation 1981*. London: CIO Publishing.

— (1985) *Teams and Group Ministries*. London: Church House (GS 660).

General Synod of the Scottish Episcopal Church (SEC GS) (2003) 'The next steps in the home mission of the Scottish Episcopal Church – the journey of the baptised'.

— (2011) *Mission & Ministry Board Report – Whole Church Mission and Ministry Policy.*

Gerhardt, R. (1983) 'Liberal religion and personality type', *Research in Psychological Type*, 6, 47–53.

Gloucester Diocesan Synod (2008) 'Effective Ministry in Every Parish' – Synod Paper, available from the diocesan office – see www.gloucester.anglican.org.

Godfrey, N. (2006) 'Training Ordained Local Ministers', in Malcolm Torry and Jeffrey Heskins (eds), *Ordained Local Ministry*. Norwich: Canterbury Press, pp. 129–48.

Green, L. (2009) *Let's Do Theology: Resources for Contextual Theology*. London: Mowbray.

Greenwood, R. (1988) *Reclaiming the Church*. London: Collins.

— (1994, 1999) *Transforming Priesthood. A New Theology of Mission and Ministry*. London: SPCK.

— (2000) *The Ministry Team Handbook*. London: SPCK.

— (2002) *Transforming Church – Liberating Structures for Ministry*. London: SPCK.

Greenwood, R. and Pascoe, C. (eds) (2006) *Local Ministry. Story, Process and Meaning*. London: SPCK.

Gunton, C. E. (1997) 'The Community. The Trinity and the Being of the Church', in *The Promise of Trinitarian Theology* (2nd edn). Edinburgh: T & T Clark.

— (2003) 'The Church and the Lord's Supper: "Until He Comes". Towards an Eschatology of Church Membership', in *Father, Son and Holy Spirit. Essays Towards a Fully Trinitarian Theology*. London: T & T Clark.

Hardy, D. W. (2006) 'Afterword: Evaluating Local Ministry for the future of the Church', in Robin Greenwood and Caroline Pascoe (eds), *Local Ministry, Story, Process and Meaning*. London: SPCK, pp. 131–50.

Heskins, J. (2006) 'In Training', in Malcolm Torry and Jeffrey Heskins (eds),
    Ordained Local Ministry. Norwich: Canterbury Press, pp. 85–102.
— (2006) 'Being Ordained Local Ministers', in Malcolm Torry and Jeffrey Heskins
    (eds), *Ordained Local Ministry*. Norwich: Canterbury Press, pp. 103–19.
Heywood, D. (2011) *Reimagining Ministry*. London: SCM Press.
Hodge, M. (1983) *Non-Stipendiary Ministry in the Church of England*. London
    (GS583A).
Holeton, D. R. (1996) *Renewing the Anglican Eucharist: Findings of the Fifth
    International Anglican Liturgical Consultation, Dublin 1995*. London: Grove
    Books.
House of Bishops of the General Synod [HoB] (1997) *Eucharistic Presidency*.
    London: Church House Publishing (GS 1248).
Huddleston, T. and Sheppard, D. (1972) *Local Ministry in Urban and Industrial
    Areas – Report of a Working Party*. London: Mowbrays.
Ind, W. (2001). *Towards a Theology of the People of God*. Diocese of Truro
    publication.
Jenkins T. (1999) *Religion in Everyday Life. An Ethnographic Approach*. New
    York: Berghahn.
Jones, S. H., Village, A. and Francis, L. J. (2011) 'Assessing the impact of Ordained
    Local Ministry on the performance of Church of England dioceses, 1991–2003',
    Journal of Practical Theology, 4, 213–25.
Jordan, E. A. (2008) 'The place of Ordained Local Ministry in the Church of
    England', *Practical Theology, 1:2*, 219–32.
Jung, C. G. (1971) *Psychological Types: The Collected Works*, Vol. 6. London:
    Routledge and Kegan Paul.
Käsemann, E. (1964) 'Ministry and Community in the New Testament', in *Essays
    on New Testament Themes*. London: SCM Press Ltd, pp. 63–94.
Kay, W. K. and Francis, L. J. (2008) 'Psychological type preferences of female Bible
    College students in England', *Journal of Beliefs and Values, 29*, 101–5.
Kay, W. K., Francis, L. J. and Craig, C. L. (2008) 'Psychological type preferences of
    male British Assemblies of God Bible College students: tough minded or tender
    hearted?' *Journal of the European Pentecostal Theological Association, 28*, 6–20.
Keirsey, D. and Bates, M. (1978) *Please Understand Me*. Del Mar, California:
    Prometheus Nemesis.
Kelly, H., SSM (1916) 'The Pattern of a Missionary Church' and 'The Pattern of the
    Early Church in the Formation of the Ministry', *The East and the West*, London:
    Society for the Propagation of the Gospel, XIV, pp. 182–92 and 429–39.
Kelsey, J. (2003) 'Can God Set a Table in the Wilderness?', address given to the
    New York Church Club, Feb. 9, 2003.
Kujawa-Holbrook, S. A. and Thompsett, F. H. (2010) *Born of Water, Born of Spirit*.
    Herndon, Virginia: The Alban Institute.
Lambeth Conference (1968) *The Lambeth Conference 1968. Resolutions and
    Reports*. London: SPCK.
Lavriotes, M. (2010) 'The Thanksgiving of Eastern Christendom', in *Eucharist –
    The Liturgy of St. Basil* Cambridge: Kouphisma, 10 Warkworth St.
Lederach, J. P. (2005) *The Moral Imagination. The Art and Soul of Building Peace*.
    Oxford: Oxford University Press.
Leech, K. (ed.) (1996) *Myers-Briggs: Some Critical Reflections*. Croydon: The
    Jubilee Group.

Leslie, D. (2004) 'Transformative learning and ministerial education in the Church of England – some examples of appropriate ways of engaging the public realm in the context of late modernity.' *British Journal of Theological Education*, 14:2, 168–86.

Lewis-Anthony, J. (2009) *If You Meet George Herbert on the Road, Kill Him: Radically Re-thinking Priestly Ministry*. London: Continuum.

Lichfield Diocese (1995) *The Submission to the House of Bishops*.

Lloyd, J. B. (2007) 'Opposition from Christians to Myers-Briggs personality typing: an analysis and evaluation', *Journal of Beliefs and Values*, 28, 111–23.

Long, C. H. and Rowthorn, A. (1998) 'The Legacy of Roland Allen', in James M. M. Francis and Leslie J. Francis, *Tentmaking. Perspectives on Self-Supporting Ministry*. Leominster: Gracewing, pp. 355–63.

Lyon, S. (2006) 'A working party is formed', in Malcolm Torry and Jeffrey Heskins (eds), *Ordained Local Ministry: A New Shape for Ministry in the Church of England*. Norwich: Canterbury Press, pp. 40–54.

Mason, K. (1992) *Priesthood and Society*. Norwich: Canterbury Press.

Maybee, M. (ed.) (2001) *All Who Minister*. Toronto: ABC Publishing.

Mcfayden, A. I. (1990) *The Call to Personhood: A Christian Theory of the Individual in Social Relationships*. Cambridge: Cambridge University Press.

Melinsky, M. A. H. (1992) *The Shape of the Ministry*. Norwich: The Canterbury Press.

Morgan, T. (2011) *Survey of Self-Supporting Ministers*, available at: www.1pf.co.uk/SSM.html.

Morris, T. (2006) 'Local Ministry Development in Scotland', in Robin Greenwood and Caroline Pascoe (eds), *Local Ministry. Story, Process and Meaning*. London: SPCK, pp. 36–44.

Myers, I. B. (1998) *Introduction to Type: A Guide to Understanding Your Results on the Myers-Briggs Type Indicator* (5th edn, European English version). Oxford: Oxford Psychologists Press.

Myers, I. B. and McCaulley, M. H. (1985) *Manual: A Guide to the Development and Use of the Myers-Briggs Type Indicator*. Palo Alto, California: Consulting Psychologists Press.

Obiora, A. (2006). 'Pioneers together', in Malcolm Torry and Jeffrey Heskins (eds), *Ordained Local Ministry: A New Shape for Ministry in the Church of England*. Norwich: Canterbury Press, pp. 54–60.

O'Meara, T. F. (1983/1999) *Theology of Ministry*. New York: Paulist Press.

Oppenheimer, H. (1979) 'Ministry and Priesthood', in Eric James (ed.), *Stewards of the Mysteries of God*. London: Darton: Longman & Todd, pp. 11–19.

Oswald, R. M. and Kroeger, O. (1988) *Personality Type and Religious Leadership*. Washington, DC: The Alban Institute.

Ott, E. S. (2004) *Transform Your Church with Ministry Teams*. Michigan, Grand Rapids: W. B. Eerdmans.

Oxley, M. and Tomlinson, A. (2006) 'Congregational Learning in Shetland, Scotland', in Robin Greenwood and Caroline Pascoe (eds), *Local Ministry. Story, Process and Meaning*. London: SPCK, pp. 18–35.

Palmer, A. (nd) 'Rethinking the Church on the Estates: The Challenge of Total Ministry', available at: http://www.culf.org.uk/files/Rethinking.pdf

Paton, D. M. (1960) *The Ministry of the Spirit. Selected Writings of Roland Allen*. London: World Dominion Press.

— (1968) *Reform of the Ministry. A Study in the Work of Roland Allen.* Cambridge: The Lutterworth Press.

Patzia, A. G. (2001) *The Emergence of the Church.* Downers Grove: InterVarsity Press.

Peberdy, A. (2006) 'The Incumbent's View', in Malcolm Torry and Jeffrey Heskins (eds), *Ordained Local Ministry: A New Shape for Ministry in the Church of England.* Norwich: Canterbury Press, pp.72–84.

Percy, M. (2006) *Clergy: The Origin of Species.* London: Continuum.

Perham, M. (2008a) *The Pressure on Our Ministry.* Gloucester: Diocesan Church House.

— (2008b) *A Parson in Every Parish.* Gloucester: Diocesan Church House.

Pickard, S. (2009) *Theological Foundations for Collaborative Ministry.* Farnham, Surrey: Ashgate Publishing Company.

— (2010) 'The Collaborative Character of Christian Ministry', *Expository Times,* June 2010, 429–34.

Pounds, N. J. G. (1999) *A History of the English Parish: The Culture of Religion from Augustine to Victoria.* Cambridge: Cambridge University Press.

Ray, T. and Kelsey, J. (2006) 'Creating a Hospitable Environment for Mutual Ministry', in Robin Greenwood and Caroline Pascoe (eds). *Local Ministry: Story, Process and Meaning.* London: SPCK, pp.45–56.

Rehak, M. C. (1998) 'Identifying the congregation's corporate personality', *Journal of Psychological Type,* 44, 39–44.

Robbins, M. and Francis, L. J. (2011) 'All are called, but some psychological types are more likely to respond: profiling churchgoers in Australia', *Research in the Social Scientific Study of Religion,* 22, 213–29.

Roberts, T. (1972) *Partners and Ministers.* London: Falcon Books.

— (2006) 'A Novelty or Back to Basics? The Bethnal Green and Bermondsey Experiments', in Malcolm Torry and Jeffrey Heskins (eds), *Ordained Local Ministry.* Norwich: Canterbury Press, pp.11–17.

Roman Catholic Bishop's Conference of England and Wales (1995) *The Sign We Give.* Chelmsford: Matthew James publishing.

Rosato, P. (1987) 'Priesthood of the Baptised and Priesthood of the Ordained', *Gregorianum,* 68/1–2: 215–66.

Ross, C. F. J. (1993) 'Type patterns among active members of the Anglican church: comparisons with Catholics, Evangelicals and clergy', *Journal of Psychological Type,* 26, 28–35.

— (1995) 'Type patterns among Catholics: four Anglophone congregations compared with Protestants, Francophone Catholics and priests', *Journal of Psychological Type,* 33, 33–41.

Rylands, M. (2010) 'Multi Church Ministry: Pioneering Leadership for Today', *Country Way – Life and Faith in Rural Britain.* Stoneleigh Park, Warwickshire: Arthur Rank Centre (55, October 2010), pp.20–1.

Sanneh, L. O. (2008) *Disciples of All Nations.* London: Oxford University Press.

Schillebeeckx, E. (1980) 'A Creative Retrospect as Inspiration for the Ministry in the Future', in Lucas Grollenberg (ed.), *Minister? Pastor? Prophet? Grass-roots Leadership in the Churches.* London: SCM Press Ltd, pp.57–84.

— (1981/2006) *Ministry, A Case for Change.* London: SCM-Canterbury Press.

— (1990) *Church. The Human Story of God.* London: SCM Press Ltd.

Scottish Episcopal Church (SEC) Local Collaborative Ministry Task Group (nd). 'A Local Habitation? The Importance of Place Within Today's Scottish Episcopal

Church', available at: http://www.scotland.anglican.org/media/organisation/
    boards_committees/lcm/files/a_local_habitation.pdf
— (1984) *Ordination Services.*
— (1985) *Ministry and Worship in Rural Areas.*
— (1998) *Christian Initiation.*
Sedmak, C. (2007) *Doing Local Theology: A Guide for Artisans of a New
    Humanity.* New York: Orbis Books.
Serbutt, E. (2006) 'Journeying Together in the Parish', in Malcolm Torry and Jeffrey
    Heskins (eds), *Ordained Local Ministry.* Norwich: Canterbury Press, pp.61–71.
Stockton, I. G. (1992) 'What is local?', *Theology*, XCV:767, 353–60.
Strudwick, V. (1981) 'Local Ordained Ministry: Yesterday's Case for Tomorrow's
    Church', reprinted in James M. M. Francis and Leslie J. Francis (eds),
    Tentmaking. Perspectives on Self-Supporting Ministry. Leominster: Gracewing
    1998, pp.364–71.
Sykes, S. (1995) *Unashamed Anglicanism.* London: Darton, Longman & Todd Ltd.
Thew Forrester, K. L. (2003) *I have Called You Friends.* New York: Church
    Publishing Incorporated.
Thompsett, F. H. (1988) 'The Laity', in Stephen Sykes and John Booty (eds), *The
    Study of Anglicanism.* London: SPCK, pp.245–60.
Tiller, J. (1983) *A Strategy for the Church's Ministry.* London: Church Information
    Office.
— (1990) 'Towards a theology of local ordained ministry', *Anvil*, 7:3, 241–6.
— (1993) *Tiller Ten Years On. Changing Prospects for the Church's Ministry.*
    Bramcote: Grove Books Ltd (Pastoral Series 55).
Torry, M. and Heskins, J. (eds) (2006) *Ordained Local Ministry: A Theological
    Exploration and Practical Handbook.* Norwich: Canterbury Press.
Turnbull, M. (2001) 'The Parish System', in Gordon W. Kuhrt, *Ministry Issues –
    Mapping the Trends for the Church of England.* London: Church House
    Publishing, pp.213–15.
Vaughan, P. H. (1983) 'Historical Background', in Mark Hodge, *Non-Stipendiary
    Ministry in the Church of England.* London: Advisory Council for the Church's
    Ministry (GS583A), pp.9–24.
— (1990) *Non-Stipendiary Ministry in the Church of England: A History of the
    Development of an Idea.* San Francisco: Mellen Research University Press.
Veling, T. (2005) *Practical Theology: On Earth as it is in Heaven.* Maryknoll,
    New York: Orbis Books.
Warren, M. (1971) *To Apply the Gospel. Selections from the Writings of Henry
    Venn.* Grand Rapids, Michigan: William B. Eerdmanns Publishing Co.
Watkin, G. (2006) A Survey of Ordained Local Ministry in the Diocese of Lichfield.
    Unpublished.
Weingarten, D. (1995) 'A Century of Faith and Ministry', in *The Church in
    Hiawathaland, Journal of the Episcopal Diocese of Northern Michigan,
    Michigan, Marquette*, October 1995.
West, M. (1995) ' "Second Class Priests with Second Class Training"? A Study
    of Local Non-Stipendiary Ministry in the Church of England diocese of St
    Edmundsbury and Ipswich' (unpublished PhD thesis, University of East Anglia).
— (1999) 'Developing Identity as a Local Non-Stipendiary Priest', in Leslie J.
    Francis (ed.), *Sociology, Theology and the Curriculum.* London: Cassell,
    pp.197–206.

Weston, S. (1999) *Ordained Local Ministers in Collaborative Ministry – Towards a Revision of the Ordinal.* Dissertation for Mid-Service Clergy Course XLVIII Windsor: St. George's House.

Williams [C] P. (2000) ' "Not Transplanting": Henry Venn's Strategic Vision', in Kevin Ward and Brian Stanley (eds), *The Church Mission Society and World Christianity, 1799–1999.* Grand Rapids, Michigan: William B. Eerdmans Publishing Company, pp. 147–72.

Williams, P. (1984) 'The Tiller Strategy: Local and Diocesan Priests', *Anvil,* 1:1, 55–60.

Williams, R. (2009) Address to the Alcuin Club 20 May, available at: http://www.archbishopofcanterbury.org/2449.

World Council of Churches (WCC) (1964) *The Fourth World Conference on Faith and Order.* Faith and Order Paper 42. London: SCM Press Ltd.

— (1982) *Baptism, Eucharist and Ministry.* Faith and Order Paper 111. Geneva: WCC.

— (1990) *Baptism, Eucharist & Ministry 1982–1990. Report on the Process and Responses.* Faith and Order Paper No. 149. Geneva: WCC.

— (2005) *The Nature and Mission of the Church. A Stage on the Way to a Common Statement.* Faith and Order Paper No. 198. Geneva: WCC.

Zabriskie, S. C. (1995) *Total Ministry.* New York: Alban Institute.

Zizioulas, J. (1985) *Being as Communion: Studies in Personhood and the Church.* London: Darton, Longman and Todd.

— (1993) *Ministry and Communion.* New York: St Vladimir's Seminary Press.

INDEX

Ordained Local Ministry in the Church of England

To our good memories on the Holy Hill —

Andrew B.